Charles D

Hard Times/1

CW00350471

ANALYSING TEXTS

General Editor: Nicholas Marsh

Published

Jane Austen: The Novels   *Nicholas Marsh*
Aphra Behn: The Comedies   *Kate Aughterson*
William Blake: The Poems   *Nicholas Marsh*
Charlotte Brontë: The Novels   *Mike Edwards*
Emily Brontë: *Wuthering Heights   Nicholas Marsh*
Chaucer: *The Canterbury Tales   Gail Ashton*
Daniel Defoe: The Novels   *Nicholas Marsh*
Charles Dickens: *David Copperfield/Great Expectations   Nicolas Tredell*
Charles Dickens: *Hard Times/Bleak House   Nicholas Marsh*
John Donne: The Poems   *Joe Nutt*
George Eliot: The Novels   *Mike Edwards*
F. Scott Fitzgerald: *The Great Gatsby/Tender is the Night   Nicolas Tredell*
E. M. Forster: The Novels   *Mike Edwards*
Thomas Hardy: The Novels   *Norman Page*
Thomas Hardy: The Poems   *Gillian Steinberg*
John Keats   *John Blades*
Philip Larkin: The Poems   *Nicholas Marsh*
D. H. Lawrence: The Novels   *Nicholas Marsh*
Marlowe: The Plays   *Stevie Simkin*
John Milton: *Paradise Lost   Mike Edwards*
Shakespeare: The Comedies   *R. P. Draper*
Shakespeare: The Histories   *John Blades*
Shakespeare: The Late Plays   *Kate Aughterson*
Shakespeare: The Sonnets   *John Blades*
Shakespeare: The Tragedies   *Nicholas Marsh*
Shakespeare: Three Problem Plays   *Nicholas Marsh*
Mary Shelley: *Frankenstein   Nicholas Marsh*
Webster: The Tragedies   *Kate Aughterson*
Virginia Woolf: The Novels   *Nicholas Marsh*
Wordsworth and Coleridge: Lyrical Ballads   *John Blades*

Further titles are in preparation

Analysing Texts
Series Standing Order ISBN 978–0–333–73260–1
(outside North America only)

You can receive future titles in this series as they are published by placing a standing order. Please contact your bookseller or, in the case of difficulty, write to us at the address below with your name and address, the title of the series and the ISBN quoted above. Customer Services Department, Macmillan Distribution Ltd, Houndmills, Basingstoke, Hampshire. RG21 6XS, UK

BY THE SAME AUTHOR

Charles Dickens:
Hard Times/
Bleak House

NICHOLAS MARSH

 macmillan education   palgrave

First published 2015 by
PALGRAVE

Palgrave in the UK is an imprint of Macmillan Publishers Limited, registered in England, company number 785998, of 4 Crinan Street, London, N1 9XW.

Palgrave Macmillan in the US is a division of St Martin's Press LLC, 175 Fifth Avenue, New York, NY 10010.

Palgrave is a global imprint of the above companies and is represented throughout the world.

Palgrave® and Macmillan® are registered trademarks in the United States, the United Kingdom, Europe and other countries.

ISBN: 978–1–137–37957–3 hardback
ISBN: 978–1–137–37956–6 paperback

This book is printed on paper suitable for recycling and made from fully managed and sustained forest sources. Logging, pulping and manufacturing processes are expected to conform to the environmental regulations of the country of origin.

A catalogue record for this book is available from the British Library.

A catalog record for this book is available from the Library of Congress.

Library of Congress Cataloging-in-Publication Data
Marsh, Nicholas, 1948–
    Charles Dickens : Hard Times/Bleak House / Nicholas Marsh.
       pages cm. — (Analysing texts)
    Includes bibliographical references and index.
    ISBN 978–1–137–37956–6 (paperback) — ISBN 978–1–137–37957–3 (paperback)
    1. Dickens, Charles, 1812–1870. Hard times.   2. Dickens, Charles, 1812–1870.
Bleak House.   3. Literature and society—Great Britain—History—19th century.   I. Title.
    PR4561.M37 2015
    823'.8—dc23   2015023920

Printed in China

For Ella

Contents

General Editor's Preface

This series is dedicated to one clear belief: that we can all enjoy, understand and analyse literature for ourselves, provided we know how to do so. How can we build on close understanding of a short passage and develop our insight into the whole work? What features do we expect to find in a text? Why do we study style in so much detail? In demystifying the study of literature, these are only some of the questions the *Analysing Texts* series addresses and answers.

The books in this series will not do all the work for you, but will provide you with the tools, and show you how to use them. Here, you will find samples of close, detailed analysis, with an explanation of the analytical techniques utilised. At the end of each chapter there are useful suggestions for further work you can do to practise, develop and hone the skills demonstrated and build confidence in your own analytical ability.

An author's individuality shows in the way they write: every work they produce bears the hallmark of that writer's personal 'style'. In the main part of each book we concentrate therefore on analysing the particular flavour and concerns of one author's work, and explain the features of their writing in connection with major themes. In Part II there are chapters about the author's life and work, assessing their contribution to developments in literature, and a selection of critics' views are summarised and discussed in comparison with each other. Some suggestions for further reading provide a bridge towards further critical research.

Analysing Texts is designed to stimulate and encourage your critical and analytical faculty, to develop your personal insight into the author's work and individual style, and to provide you with the skills and techniques to enjoy at first hand the excitement of discovering the richness of the text.

NICHOLAS MARSH

A Note on Editions

References to *Bleak House* and *Hard Times*, in this book, are to the Oxford World's Classics editions of both novels, for no other reason than that they are easily available. As Oxford World's Classics are sometimes re-edited, this note gives the specific editions used: *Bleak House*, edited with an introduction and notes by Stephen Gill (Oxford University Press, 1996); *Hard Times*, edited with an introduction by Paul Schlicke (Oxford University Press, 1989).

Page references to these editions appear in the text in brackets and preceded by '*BH*' for *Bleak House,* and '*HT*' for *Hard Times*, as for example (*BH*, 21–22) for *Bleak House*, pp. 21–22.

PART 1

ANALYSING *BLEAK HOUSE* AND *HARD TIMES*

Introduction

The aim of this book is to take a fresh and critical look at two of Dickens's most studied novels, developing our insights from the close analysis of extracts from the text. *Bleak House* and *Hard Times* were written between 1852 and 1854, and they share some qualities. Both novels open with a powerful critique, announcing that the text will campaign against Chancery (*Bleak House*) and Utilitarianism (*Hard Times*) respectively.

When we study these texts, it is important to remember the circumstances in which they were produced, which were different from publishing practice today. Dickens wrote his novels in episodes, for serial publication in magazines. *Bleak House* came out in 20 monthly instalments between March 1852 and September 1853, and *Hard Times* in 20 weekly parts, between 1 April and 12 August 1854. This form of publication influenced the organisation of the story. Dickens frequently provided suspense at the end of an issue to encourage his readers to buy the next instalment, or wrote a descriptive 'set piece' at the start of an episode.

Hard Times is the shortest novel Dickens wrote, and *Bleak House* the longest. *Hard Times* is written in a less expansive style, with less elaboration of setting, plot and characters. We start with passages from *Hard Times*, then move on to the more complex, elaborate *Bleak House* because this enables us to meet features of the Dickensian narrative in a comparatively plain context before coming across them again in the longer and more complex text.

One last point before we turn to the analysis of our first extracts. We are about to plunge into the analysis of two Dickens texts. One of them (*Hard Times*) is told by the author, while the other (*Bleak House*) has two narrators: Esther Summerson, and the third-person omniscient narrator who accounts for about half of the novel. In both of these texts we must be prepared for the unremitting the-atricality of Dickens's own voice and the many other distinct and lively voices that constantly keep us company as we read. This aspect of the writing makes for vivid dialogue. However, Dickens's voice has an additional quality. As one critic puts it, the 'first impression, and a continuing one, in Dickens's prose is of a voice manipulating language with pleasure and pride in its own skill'.[1] We might say that Dickens manipulates us as well as the language. When reading Dickens, we are in the constant companionship of the author, have the sense that he is with us, moment by moment, and most of all, that he expects us to share his emotions and agree with his opinions. Dickens may cajole us, and he may browbeat us, but we will have to become used to his company and its pressures, for he is always there, telling us how we should think and feel.

---

[1] Robert, Garis, *The Dickens Theatre*, Oxford: (Clarendon Press, 1965).

1

Facts and Fog: Opening Salvos

Both *Hard Times* and *Bleak House* open with passages that are justly famous: frequently anthologised as examples of fine writing, and much used in the classroom to teach critical analysis. Each opening is a Dickensian tour de force, and each declares war upon a target that is anathema to the author. We begin our study with a detailed look at these opening statements, in part because it is the obvious, almost unavoidable first approach to these two novels, and in part for two other reasons: first, as an introduction to the rhetorical features of Dickens's style, and second, to use these passages as a benchmark against which we can measure the novels as wholes. How successfully, having declared war, does Dickens fight and win his battles in the rest of the book?

The opening of *Hard Times* is set in a schoolroom, and targets the philosophy called Utilitarianism, which is presented as only valuing 'fact', and which was a sub-form of materialism.[1] Dickens's anger is kindled against the use of such a 'fact'-based outlook as a guiding principle in education, and the consequent abuse of children by suppressing imagination and natural emotion:

---

[1] Utilitarianism developed from the ideas of Jeremy Bentham (1748–1832). John Stuart Mill's enormously influential *Principles of Political Economy* (1848) came out just six years before Dickens was writing *Hard Times*.

CHAPTER I
THE ONE THING NEEDFUL

'NOW, what I want is, Facts. Teach these boys and girls nothing but Facts. Facts alone are wanted in life. Plant nothing else, and root out everything else. You can only form the minds of reasoning animals upon Facts: nothing else will ever be of any service to them. This is the principle on which I bring up my own children, and this is the principle on which I bring up these children. Stick to Facts, sir!'

The scene was a plain, bare, monotonous vault of a schoolroom, and the speaker's square forefinger emphasized his observations by underscoring every sentence with a line on the schoolmaster's sleeve. The emphasis was helped by the speaker's square wall of a forehead, which had his eyebrows for its base, while his eyes found commodious cellarage in two dark caves, overshadowed by the wall. The emphasis was helped by the speaker's mouth, which was wide, thin, and hard set. The emphasis was helped by the speaker's voice, which was inflexible, dry, and dictatorial. The emphasis was helped by the speaker's hair, which bristled on the skirts of his bald head, a plantation of firs to keep the wind from its shining surface, all covered with knobs, like the crust of a plum pie, as if the head had scarcely warehouse-room for the hard facts stored inside. The speaker's obstinate carriage, square coat, square legs, square shoulders, – nay, his very neckcloth, trained to take him by the throat with an unaccommodating grasp, like a stubborn fact, as it was, – all helped the emphasis.

'In this life, we want nothing but Facts, sir; nothing but Facts!'

The speaker, and the schoolmaster, and the third grown person present, all backed a little, and swept with their eyes the inclined plane of little vessels then and there arranged in order, ready to have imperial gallons of facts poured into them until they were full to the brim.

CHAPTER II
MURDERING THE INNOCENTS

THOMAS GRADGRIND, sir. A man of realities. A man of facts and calculations. A man who proceeds upon the principle that two and two are four, and nothing over, and who is not to be talked into allowing for anything over. Thomas Gradgrind, sir – peremptorily Thomas – Thomas Gradgrind. With a rule and a pair of scales, and the multiplication table always in his pocket, Sir, ready to weigh and measure any parcel of human nature, and tell you exactly what it comes to. It is a mere question of figures, a case of simple arithmetic. You might hope to get some other nonsensical belief into the head of George Gradgrind, or Augustus Gradgrind, or John Gradgrind, or Joseph Gradgrind (all supposititious, non-existent persons), but into the head of Thomas Gradgrind – no, Sir!

In such terms Mr Gradgrind always mentally introduced himself, whether to his private circle of acquaintance, or to the public in general. In such terms, no doubt, substituting the words 'boys and girls,' for 'Sir,' Thomas Gradgrind now presented Thomas Gradgrind to the little pitchers before him, who were to be filled so full of facts.

Indeed, as he eagerly sparkled at them from the cellarage before mentioned, he seemed a kind of cannon loaded to the muzzle with facts, and prepared to blow them clean out of the regions of childhood at one discharge. He seemed a galvanizing apparatus, too, charged with a grim mechanical substitute for the tender young imaginations that were to be stormed away.

'Girl number twenty,' said Mr Gradgrind, squarely pointing with his square forefinger, 'I don't know that girl. Who is that girl?'

'Sissy Jupe, sir,' explained number twenty, blushing, standing up, and curtseying.

'Sissy is not a name,' said Mr Gradgrind. 'Don't call yourself Sissy. Call yourself Cecilia.'

'It's father as calls me Sissy, sir,' returned the young girl in a trembling voice, and with another curtsey.

'Then he has no business to do it,' said Mr Gradgrind. 'Tell him he mustn't. Cecilia Jupe. Let me see. What is your father?'

'He belongs to the horse-riding, if you please, sir.'

Mr Gradgrind frowned, and waved off the objectionable calling with his hand.

'We don't want to know anything about that, here. You mustn't tell us about that, here. Your father breaks horses, don't he?'

'If you please, sir, when they can get any to break, they do break horses in the ring, sir.'

'You mustn't tell us about the ring, here. Very well, then. Describe your father as a horsebreaker. He doctors sick horses, I dare say?'

'Oh yes, sir.'

'Very well, then. He is a veterinary surgeon, a farrier, and horse-breaker. Give me your definition of a horse.'

(Sissy Jupe thrown into the greatest alarm by this demand.)

'Girl number twenty unable to define a horse!' said Mr Gradgrind, for the general behoof of all the little pitchers. 'Girl number twenty possessed of no facts, in reference to one of the commonest of animals! Some boy's definition of a horse. Bitzer, yours.'

The square finger, moving here and there, lighted suddenly on Bitzer, perhaps because he chanced to sit in the same ray of sunlight which, darting in at one of the bare windows of the intensely white-washed room, irradiated Sissy. For, the boys and girls sat on the face of the inclined plane in two compact bodies, divided up the centre by a narrow interval; and Sissy, being at the corner of a row on the sunny side, came in for the beginning of a sunbeam, of which Bitzer, being at the corner of a row on the other side, a few rows in advance, caught the end. But, whereas the girl was so dark-eyed and dark-haired, that she seemed to receive a deeper and more lustrous colour from the sun, when it shone upon her, the boy was so light-eyed and light-haired that the self-same rays appeared to draw out of him what little colour he ever possessed. His cold eyes would hardly have been eyes, but for the short ends of lashes which, by bringing them into immediate contrast with something paler than themselves, expressed their form. His short-cropped hair might have been a mere continuation of the sandy freckles on his forehead and face. His skin was so unwholesomely deficient in the natural tinge, that he looked as though, if he were cut, he would bleed white.

(d. Paul Schlicke, *Hard Times* [Oxford University Press, 2006, pp. 7–9]). Future references to this edition will give the page numbers in brackets, preceded by the abbreviation *HT*, thus: (*HT*, 7–9).

This passage hits hard, straight away. The word 'Facts', a short word ending in hard consonants with a suggestion of spitting, could be compared to a shot or the crack of something hitting a table, and it hits five times in the short first paragraph. Also in the first paragraph, there is a flurry of absolutes: 'nothing … alone … nothing … everything … only … nothing … ever'. This is an over-emphatic, exaggerated form of speech. The sentences are short and declamatory, seven in the first paragraph. Looking at sentence structure, we see that the first three sentences are single and simple, the next three are double but only repeat the simple view already expressed, and the final sentence is single and very short, again.

The reader may have a moment's uncertainty about the voice, but by the time we have read 'Teach these boys and girls nothing but Facts', we know that we have been plunged into the middle of a dramatic situation. There are 'boys and girls', probably in a schoolroom ('teach'), and we are listening to the voice of an emphatic and distinctive character. So, the reader undergoes some intensive, but obvious, detective work and deductive reasoning. Our brains are activated: this is a novel with strong elements of theatre and the first paragraph of the book stimulates and excites us. Dickens's decision to expose us to Gradgrind's voice without mediation, as our first experience of *Hard Times*, ensures that we are immediately gripped and mentally busy.

We have remarked upon the single sentences, which indicate the crude simplicity of Gradgrind's ideas. The double sentences make a further suggestion about the way his mind works. The first two are balanced between opposites: 'nothing ... everything'; 'Facts ... nothing else'; then the third triumphantly states the approved gospel twice, once for 'my own children' and again for 'these children'. The effect is that all opposition has been dismissed. All that is not 'fact', that was referred to as 'everything else' and 'nothing else', has now disappeared, and the world – whether in Gradgrind's family at home, or in his school outside – is now governed entirely according to the one 'principle'. Even here, Dickens manipulates our expectations in a dramatic manner. Listening to the voice, we hear two sets of patterned opposition. The third double sentence is clearly constructed on the same pattern: but what does it give us? Instead of the opposition we anticipate, we are given only repetition. Our bemused disappointment is a powerful foretaste of the Gradgrind philosophy, with its simple-minded and rigid mental poverty.

We do not need to spend a great deal of time teasing out the meaning of this passage, or the author's attitude: these are obvious. Gradgrind's philosophy is clearly anathema to the author, so the characterisation of Gradgrind is like a sustained sarcasm, and the passage is a powerful attack on Utilitarianism. How does Dickens achieve this effect?

So far we have noticed some features of the first paragraph: repetition of 'facts'; a large number of absolutes; and the use of single and double sentences. Now we can go further and notice some of the more technical rhetorical features Dickens employs. Remember, however, that technical terms are only useful as a shortcut to describe a feature of style, and the feature is only interesting if it has an effect. Some examples help to make this clear.

Anaphora is the repetition of a sequence of words at the beginnings of neighbouring clauses. There is an example in the first paragraph, where Gradgrind says 'this is the principle on which' twice, once for his own children and once for those in the classroom. We remarked that this sentence is effective in dismissing the opposition that balanced the two preceding sentences. The fact that both halves of the sentence begin with the same sequence of words (in other words, the *anaphora*) emphasises the singleness and narrowness of Gradgrind's philosophy. Thus the *anaphora* highlights how Gradgrind dismisses 'everything else' in the world, and how impoverished his outlook is therefore.

We have noticed Gradgrind's repetitions of 'fact', and using specialist terms for this feature[2] would add nothing to our understanding. With *anaphora*, on the other hand, the technical term helps. We either say, 'The *fact that both halves of the sentence begin with the same sequence of words* emphasises the narrowness of Gradgrind's philosophy', or we can say 'the *anaphora* emphasises the narrowness of Gradgrind's philosophy'. The technical term renders our comment clear, and much shorter.

In the second paragraph, notice the fourfold *anaphora* of 'The emphasis was helped by ... ', which heightens our sense that listening to Gradgrind is like being bludgeoned with repeated blows. Further, see how this is enhanced by the final sentence, where 'helped the emphasis' is transposed to the end, and an increasingly comical list of Gradgrind's characteristics, culminating in his 'very neckcloth' as a 'stubborn fact', builds to that climax. We can see from these examples that the term *anaphora* has been useful, but others of the technical terms may not help us. If the feature of style can be identified and described concisely and naturally, it is best not to have recourse to the technical language.

Another problem is that technical terms, although precise, can narrow your perception. For example, we have noticed *anaphora*, *anadiplosis* and *epistrophe* in the first paragraph of *Hard Times* (footnote 2). Picking out these features is, however, only a very small part of the job we undertake when analysing the passage. Look more widely, virtually every word and every phrase in that paragraph stands in a synonymous or opposed relation to every other word or

---

[2] In this case *epistrophe* and *anadiplosis*.

phrase in the paragraph. The entire edifice is constructed from identity and opposition, so that the whole strikes us as an unnaturally limited and repetitive piece of language. So, we must try to notice and respond to the whole style, not just the two or three features to which we can give a technical name.

Notice also how the whole style and the small features work together. For example, when Gradgrind is compared to 'a kind of cannon loaded to the muzzle with facts', he is said to be ready to blow the children out of 'the regions of childhood'. This phrase has an unexpectedly potent effect, as 'regions of childhood' comes to represent emotion, affection, sensitivity, imagination, pleasure, entertainment and so on, and consequently carries a disproportionate weight of meaning. How has this effect been achieved? The cannon simile is vivid, of course, but in the context of the passage the implication of mechanic aggression is not new. The 'regions of childhood' is quite natural, also: the classroom is full of children, so the phrase is not even really figurative. What, then, is extraordinary about this phrase, that makes it echo so resoundingly?

The answer is: nothing in itself, but everything about its context within the whole passage. Up to this point we have been immersed in Gradgrind and his 'facts'. We have been bludgeoned by his 'emphasis' and assaulted by images of wall, cellar, caves; dryness, squareness (many times repeated), knobs; and we have existed in a 'plain, bare, monotonous vault'. There have been references to 'nothing else', and 'everything else' has been dismissed. Just as Gradgrind will never allow any other 'nonsensical belief' into his head, so we, as readers, have spent two long pages deprived of anything other than 'facts'. 'Regions of childhood' therefore comes to the reader as a welcome relief, a sudden revelation of the 'everything else' banished by the Gradgrind formula. We can say that Dickens has starved us of natural life, thereby creating a greater effect when he finally mentions 'regions of childhood'.

There has been one previous hint at what these other things, that are not facts, might be; but that hint came in the form of the sarcastic *oxymoron*, 'parcel of human nature',[3] leaving a bitter

---

[3] An *oxymoron* is a phrase in which words of opposite meaning or implication are placed next to each other. In this case, 'parcel' (artificial, trivial, commercial object) is placed next to 'human nature'.

satirical taste quite unlike the expanding significance and vulnerability of 'regions of childhood'. So, the reader has been hammered
into a bleak wasteland of dry fact, and deprived of nature, fertil-
ity and humanity for two pages. Then, the cracks in Gradgrind's
gospel begin to appear, and they become more apparent as the passage proceeds. First 'parcel of human nature' and then, much more
powerfully, 'regions of childhood' begin that process: life fighting back against the threat of destruction by 'facts'. Gradgrind's
wrongness, and inevitable ultimate failure, begins to be exposed
as he finds himself defending his factual universe from Sissy Jupe's
innocent naturalness. He is driven to the laughable absurdity, and
more importantly the distortion of truth, when he calls Sissy's
father, a circus rider, a 'veterinary surgeon'. What kind of a 'fact'
is that? Later in the passage, the irony of the sunbeam, which is
the real reason for the 'square finger' to light on Bitzer, reveals that
Gradgrind's actions are just as randomly determined as those of
any other person.

Now, we will look at the imagery in this extract, of which there is a
great deal. In cases where there are numerous images it can be helpful
to make a list:

Chapter I:

1. 'Plant nothing else, and root out everything else': teaching facts
   compared to gardening;
2. 'vault': suggestion that the room is like a tomb;
3. 'underscoring': the speech compared to writing that can be
   underlined for emphasis;
4. 'square wall of a forehead';
5. 'commodious cellarage', 'two dark caves, overshadowed by the
   wall', for Gradgrind's eye-sockets;
6. 'a plantation of firs' for Gradgrind's hair;
7. Gradgrind's bald head likened to the knobby crust of a plum pie;
8. 'warehouse-room ... stored inside': Gradgrind's head compared
   to a warehouse;
9. his neckcloth compared to an animal or person taking Gradgrind
   by the throat;
10. the pupils compared to 'little vessels' waiting for 'imperial gal-
    lons of facts' to be 'poured' into them.

Chapter II:

1. The 'rule', 'scales' and multiplication table in Gradgrind's pocket may literally be there; or they may be imaginary extensions of his character: *as if* he always had measuring equipment with him;
2. 'parcel of human nature': people compared to parcels;
3. 'pitchers' to be 'filled so full of facts' are the children compared to cups or bowls;
4. 'sparkled': Gradgrind's eyes compared to a firework or a lit artillery fuse; Their sockets the 'cellarage' again;
5. Gradgrind a 'cannon' loaded with 'facts' aimed to blow the children out of childhood (by implication a place of imagination);
6. Gradgrind a 'galvanising apparatus' loaded with a 'grim mechanical substitute' (presumably a new factual surface) to take the place of the children's 'imaginations';
7. 'stormed away': the imaginations are to be charged or attacked (military) or blown, rained, thundered (nature) away;
8. Gradgrind 'waved off' an idea with his hand;
9. 'little pitchers', the children again compared to bowls or cups;
10. Bitzer so pale that he looks as if he would 'bleed white', i.e., as if his blood is white.

Now think about this list of images: does anything strike you about the list as a whole? Are there groups of images, or is there any one dominant idea? The answer is, yes, there are a number of images that treat the living world as if it were made of dead objects or materials. So, for example, the children are 'vessels' and 'pitchers' (twice) waiting to be 'filled to the brim'. Gradgrind is a 'wall' with 'cellarage' or 'caves', then 'a kind of cannon', and a 'galvanising apparatus' like a charging army, and with eyes like a lit fuse. Gradgrind's head is a 'warehouse', and he is equipped with scales and ruler.

There are some images that refer to nature, such as the comparison of Gradgrind's hair to a 'plantation of firs', and the invocation to 'plant' facts and 'root out' all else; and there is the unexpected reference to a plum pie. However, these are overwhelmed by the persistence of anti-natural imagery, which highlights how opposite and incompatible are the 'fact' philosophy and nature. The de-naturalising images, in their turn, are further strengthened by the diction. So, for example, Gradgrind has a 'square' forefinger, with which he points 'squarely': he also has a 'square' forehead, a 'square coat, square legs, square shoulders'. This creates an unnatural, mathematical effect that is supported by clusters of adjectives with negative connotations, such as 'thin', 'set', 'inflexible, dry, and dictatorial', 'hard', 'obstinate' and 'stubborn'.

There are two further observations to make before we attempt to sum up what we have learned from this first analysis of Dickens's writing. First, we should remark on the obvious fact that Dickens has named his character in order to suit and reveal his personality: 'Gradgrind' combines 'Grad' (associated with 'graduate' and 'grade', in education, and perhaps 'graduated' to suggest measurement and scales) with 'grind', a mechanical process as well as a word expressing unnatural, slow and unsuccessful learning. On page 12 the schoolteacher is named M'Choakumchild, and we meet Mr. Bounderby soon after that. As we will see in the next chapter, these caricatural names, satirical of the grotesque people depicted, are a common initial stage of Dickens's characterisations.

Our second observation is that Dickens develops some of his metaphorical ideas, treating them more and more literally as the reader becomes used to them. In our passage there are two examples. We are introduced to the 'speaker's square forefinger', and on the next page he is 'squarely' pointing with it. By this time, the reader knows to whom the finger belongs. So, on the following page, Dickens can write, 'The square finger, moving here and there, lighted suddenly': we now know that this is Gradgrind's finger, but it is described as if it has a life of its own. In this way, Dickens achieves a slightly disgusting, disturbing effect: the disembodied finger is, if anything, even more unnatural than the cannon, galvaniser, wall, cellars and so forth we have also met. Next, follow the development of the 'inclined plane of little vessels', Dickens's metaphor for the children. This is introduced on page 7; then, on page 8, Thomas Gradgrind presented himself to 'the little pitchers before him', having called them 'boys and girls' so the reader is clear that 'pitchers' are really children. Finally, on page 9, Gradgrind talks for 'the general behoof of all the little pitchers'. Dickens no longer needs to mention or indicate children: he writes as if the figurative side of his metaphor (pitchers) were literal. The children disappear from the language, and the metaphor for them, 'little pitchers', takes their place. We will find this to be an habitual technique Dickens uses as he elaborates upon his scenes, characters and themes.

We have looked at several aspects of style while analysing this passage, and in the course of our analysis we have taken as understood that Mr. Gradgrind's philosophy is adequately presented in the text: it glorifies facts, mathematics, weights and measures, and is the enemy of imagination, fancy, and emotional or sensitive human values. Gradgrind therefore approves of uniformity, and dismisses variety. This is why he thinks of the children as an 'inclined plane of little vessels', and fails to notice that each child is a unique individual. Gradgrind does not notice the contrast between Sissy Jupe and Bitzer, although this is forcefully visualised in the final paragraph of our extract, where Sissy received 'a deeper and more lustrous colour' from the same sunbeam which seemed to 'draw out of' Bitzer 'what little colour he ever possessed'.

These opening pages of *Hard Times*, then, present a grotesque and angry caricature of the 'fact' philosophy and its misuse in education, and enlist the reader in the author's campaign against it. It is a devastating attack. As we have remarked, it stands like a declaration of war at the opening of the book. We have also noticed that this attack does more than simply present a stupid or grotesque man: it goes further, for Gradgrind's mistake is already seen to be a weakness that has the potential to lead Gradgrind himself into terrible errors of judgement. We have mentioned two elements from this extract that prefigure the mistakes he makes with his own children. First, the gross distortion of 'fact' when he calls Sissy's father a 'veterinary surgeon', and second, the unconsciously random way in which not reason, but a natural chance – the sunbeam – leads Gradgrind's 'square forefinger' to Bitzer. The further irony is that Bitzer is exactly that favourite pupil most likely to give the right answer: so the sunbeam leads Gradgrind's finger the way his finger wants to go, because Bitzer has the answer he wants.

We shall return to the Gradgrind philosophy several times in later chapters, in order to measure Dickens's success in following up this exceptional opening salvo. For now, however, we will turn to *Bleak House*, which opens with an equally angry and powerful attack, this time upon the Court of Chancery:

CHAPTER ONE
In Chancery

London. Michaelmas term lately over, and the Lord Chancellor sitting in Lincoln's Inn Hall. Implacable November weather. As much mud in the streets as if the waters had but newly retired from the face of the earth, and it would not be wonderful to meet a Megalosaurus, forty feet long or so, waddling like an elephantine lizard up Holborn Hill. Smoke lowering down from chimney-pots, making a soft black drizzle, with flakes of soot in it as big as full-grown snowflakes – gone into mourning, one might imagine, for the death of the sun. Dogs, undistinguishable in mire. Horses, scarcely better; splashed to their very blinkers. Foot passengers, jostling one another's umbrellas in a general infection of ill temper, and losing their foothold at street-corners, where tens of thousands of other foot passengers have been slipping and sliding since the day broke (if this day ever broke), adding new deposits to the crust upon crust of mud, sticking at those points tenaciously to the pavement, and accumulating at compound interest.

Fog everywhere. Fog up the river, where it flows among green aits and meadows; fog down the river, where it rolls defiled among the tiers of shipping and the waterside pollutions of a great (and dirty) city. Fog on the Essex marshes, fog on the Kentish heights. Fog creeping into the cabooses of collier-brigs; fog lying out on the yards and hovering in the rigging of great ships; fog drooping on the gunwales of barges and small boats. Fog in the eyes and throats of ancient Greenwich pensioners, wheezing by the firesides of their wards; fog in the stem and bowl of the afternoon pipe of the wrathful skipper, down in his close cabin; fog cruelly pinching the toes and fingers of his shivering little 'prentice boy on deck. Chance people on the bridges peeping over the parapets into a nether sky of fog, with fog all round them, as if they were up in a balloon and hanging in the misty clouds.

Gas looming through the fog in divers places in the streets, much as the sun may, from the spongey fields, be seen to loom by husbandman and ploughboy. Most of the shops lighted two hours before their time – as the gas seems to know, for it has a haggard and unwilling look.

The raw afternoon is rawest, and the dense fog is densest, and the muddy streets are muddiest near that leaden-headed old obstruction, appropriate ornament for the threshold of a leaden-headed old corporation, Temple Bar. And hard by Temple Bar, in Lincoln's Inn Hall, at the very heart of the fog, sits the Lord High Chancellor in his High Court of Chancery.

Never can there come fog too thick, never can there come mud and mire too deep, to assort with the groping and floundering condition which this High Court of Chancery, most pestilent of hoary sinners, holds this day in the sight of heaven and earth.

On such an afternoon, if ever, the Lord High Chancellor ought to be sitting here – as here he is – with a foggy glory round his head, softly fenced in with crimson cloth and curtains, addressed by a large advocate with great whiskers, a little voice, and an interminable brief, and outwardly directing his contemplation to the lantern in the roof, where he can see nothing but fog. On such an afternoon some score of members of the High Court of Chancery bar ought to be – as here they are – mistily engaged in one of the ten thousand stages of an endless cause, tripping one another up on slippery precedents, groping knee-deep in technicalities, running their goat-hair and horsehair warded heads against walls of words and making a pretence of equity with serious faces, as players might. On such an afternoon the various solicitors in the cause, some two or three of whom have inherited it from their fathers, who made a fortune by it, ought to be – as are they not? – ranged in a line, in a long matted well (but you might look in vain for truth at the bottom of it) between the registrar's red table and the silk gowns, with bills, cross-bills, answers, rejoinders, injunctions, affidavits, issues, references to masters, masters' reports, mountains of costly nonsense, piled before them. Well may the court be dim, with wasting candles here and there; well may the fog hang heavy in it, as if it would never get out; well may the stained-glass windows lose their colour and admit no light of day into the place; well may the uninitiated from the streets, who peep in through the glass panes in the door, be deterred from entrance by its owlish aspect and by the drawl, languidly echoing to the roof from the padded dais where the Lord High Chancellor looks into the lantern that has no light in it and where the attendant wigs are all stuck in a fog-bank! This is the Court of Chancery, which has its decaying houses and its blighted lands in every shire, which has its worn-out lunatic in every madhouse and its dead in every churchyard, which has its ruined suitor with his slipshod heels and threadbare dress borrowing and begging through the round of every man's acquaintance, which gives to monied might the means abundantly of wearying out the right, which so exhausts finances, patience, courage, hope, so overthrows the brain and breaks the heart, that there is not an honourable man among its practitioners who would not give – who does not often give – the warning, "Suffer any wrong that can be done you rather than come here!"

d. Stephen Gill, *Bleak House* Oxford University Press, [Oxford, 1998, pp. 11–13]. Future references to this edition will be abbreviated as *BH*, thus: (*BH*, 11–13).

As with the opening of *Hard Times*, this extract immediately grips the reader because of its distinctive and dramatic 'voice'. This time, however, the 'voice' is that of the author, not one of his characters. The first sentence is one word that denotes the story's place: 'London'. Sentence 2 tells us the time of year, 'Michaelmas Term lately over', but the reference to university and legal 'terms' connects us to the world of the law, confirmed by the Lord Chancellor 'sitting' in the Court of Chancery. As with *Hard Times*, then, the reader's deductive faculties are immediately engaged. The text leaves it to us to formulate assumptions (this novel will be about a legal case in Chancery) and develop further questions (Who will be involved in the case? What will it be about?). At the same time, we are listening to a strong voice. What are its characteristics?

First, this voice can be peremptory, as the first sentence tells us: there is no verb, just one word. The speaker typically begins his sentences in this way, with a one-word statement of subject: 'Smoke', 'Dogs', 'Horses', 'Foot passengers'. Then, verbs are mainly participles, starting with the Chancellor 'sitting'. This conveys a static situation in which there is no action or direction of effort. The participles do more than indicate stasis, however. If we list them, we see that they are increasingly about lack of control, and being stuck: 'waddling [Megalosaurus] … lowering [smoke] … jostling … losing … slipping … sliding [people] … adding … sticking … accumulating [mud]'. People are losing the ability to stand and come and go, and mud is gaining power.

Second, this opening paragraph contains a great deal of imagery and a wide range of allusion. The first simile is introduced 'As much mud … as if', then treats us to a biblical reference (to Noah's Flood) in neo-Old Testament style: 'the waters had but newly *retired from the face of the earth*' (my italics). This is followed immediately by a picture from a non-biblical concept of Earth's past: the comic grotesquery of a giant lizard 'waddling' up 'Holborn-hill'. Charles Darwin's *On the Origin of Species*, seen by many as a shocking attack on the truth of Genesis, was published some seven years after Dickens wrote the opening of *Bleak House*. Here, Dickens already suggests two pasts, one biblical, the other not. One refers to the Flood, a catastrophic punishment, specifically the work of a God who cares about mankind's sinfulness. The other conjures a bestial past, pre-civilisation, and describes a creature with a silly 'waddling' gait, enormous and foolish, missing any moral or intellectual purpose. So, right at the beginning of his novel, Dickens's imagery proposes two opposed theories of the world, and in doing so poses a question: is the world organised with reason and moral purpose, or is life the product of monstrous, muddy stupidity, like the megalosaurus? Any answer to such a question is, of course, of supreme significance, so we will bear it in mind as we continue to study *Bleak House*.

The third image, comparing flakes of soot to snowflakes 'mourning for the death of the sun' is startlingly effective, but its effect is hard to pin down. It has to do with two characteristics. First, that it comes at the end of its sentence, and is extremely concise in harnessing together several ideas: soot, snowflakes, funerals, the death of the sun. Second, a completely new idea bursts upon us suddenly at the end of the sentence: 'death of the sun' is unexpected, and adds a new element to the vision we conjure in our minds. There is another example of this technique at the end of the paragraph. We read about mud, which is sticky and growing deeper, so 'accumulating'; but we are surprised when Dickens suddenly combines standard and financial vocabularies. 'Compound interest' describes investment growth when interest is added to capital; but it is only after reading these final words that we think back to 'deposits' and 'accumulating' and realise that they also belong in both vocabularies. This end of the sentence is witty, but it also has its intensifying effect. The same two features characterise 'compound interest': the conjunction of real foul weather and real stuck people, with metaphorical foul financial practices, of which people are the trapped victims, is concisely expressed. The second feature – of surprise – we have already mentioned. Such sentence endings are a regular characteristic of Dickens's writing. We should notice them particularly because they often mix metaphoric and literal ideas in such a way as to create a further, suggested layer of meaning. This is a sort of half-symbolic meaning that hovers over the literal story. So Dickens establishes an interchangeable metaphor between money and mud such that he can write about each in terms of the other; just as, in the second paragraph, he writes about fog in such a way that it becomes interchangeable with the obfuscations of the law, and Chancery in particular.

This second paragraph is an obvious rhetorical tour de force. Dickens begins eleven descriptions in succession with the word 'Fog'; and the ensuing descriptions are also patterned in various ways. So there is fog 'up the river' and 'down the river', 'on' the Essex marshes, and 'on' the Kentish heights. As the paragraph develops, the fog takes on life in its verbs, 'creeping', 'lying', 'hovering', 'drooping', before, in a third phase, it attacks people: Greenwich pensioners, the 'wrathful skipper', and his ''prentice boy'. We remark that Dickens uses multiple *anaphora* here. However, it is so obvious that it can simply be called repetition, which creates a heavy drumming rhythm. The more subtle achievement of this paragraph is its three-phase development we have noted above. First, the fog is there, then it becomes active ('creeping', etc.), and, finally, it attacks (in 'eyes and throats', or 'cruelly pinching'). So, hostile 'fog' develops aggressively, throughout this paragraph.

Two further issues are raised in this paragraph. First, the contrast between 'green aits and meadows' upriver and 'defiled ... pollution ... dirty' downriver identifies London as the polluting city, the origin of all the dirt the Thames must carry down to the sea. Second, the paragraph's only imagery is a surprising picture of Londoners looking down into a 'nether sky', surrounded by fog 'as if they were up in a balloon, and hanging in the misty clouds'. This image hints at truths that *Bleak House* will portray. The 'nether sky' suggests that what you see in this fog-bound city is somehow all the wrong way up, and so makes no sense; then, 'up in a balloon' perfectly conveys the fantasy, even madness, of separation from reality, that afflicts numerous characters as the novel progresses. We mean Richard Carstone and Miss Flite, and the other victims of Chancery, of course. The meaning also hints at many others as well, such as the 'fashionable intelligence', Mrs. Jellyby, Mr. Chadband and Mr. Turveydrop. So, in one surprising simile, Dickens prepares us for a story in which almost all can be thought of as 'up in a balloon' and bamboozled by a 'nether sky'.

Three short paragraphs bring us to the author's target. In the first, gaslight through fog has a 'haggard and unwilling' look. In the second, the target is finally revealed. The parallelism of the first three clauses lends the idea of intoning a chant as we approach the 'rawest ... densest ... muddiest' centre, explicitly blamed as 'leaden-headed old', twice, both obstruction and corporation. Finally Dickens makes us wait through two subordinate clauses ('in Lincoln's Inn Hall, at the very heart of the fog') before landing on the decisive verb 'sits', and revealing the arch-villain of his novel's opening polemic: the Lord Chancellor and Chancery, which Dickens twice graces with the ironic adjective 'High'.

In the third short paragraph, the damning of Chancery begins with another parallelism: this time it is 'Never ... too thick, never ... too deep', while 'groping' and 'floundering' remind us of the people slipping and sticking in mud whom we have met throughout. There is, finally, no subtlety or mercy in Dickens's opinion of Chancery: it is 'most pestilent of hoary sinners ... in the sight of heaven and earth'.

Our author, then, within one and a half pages of opening his novel, has reached this climax: the utter condemnation of the High Court of Chancery, which he has ridiculed with the metaphors of fog and mud. We have analysed some splendid rhetorical devices, and noticed some more subtle effects (for example, the three-staged development of fog in paragraph 2), but we should also notice our author's tone. There is no question that he writes in indignation, disgust and contempt, and that his aim is to damn and ridicule his target. Is there any indication of irony? No. There is every reason to believe that this opinion and its attendant emotion belong to Charles Dickens himself. We should notice, then, that this is an unusually direct and barefaced opening for a novel, and that it is different from that of *Hard Times*, for example, which adopts the voice of Thomas Gradgrind, and where we have to deduce the author's opinion from his imagery and language.

The final paragraph of our extract provides further examples of the features of style we have been noticing from the start. We notice five distinct and prominent stylistic successes:

1. *Zeugma*[4] when 'some score' of barristers are made to perform a comic list of five actions, including 'tripping ... up', 'slippery', 'groping knee-deep', 'running their ... heads against walls of words'. The final 'pretence of equity' and simile of acting is a

---

[4] *Zeugma* refers to a figure of speech in which one single phrase or word joins different parts of a sentence, for example: 'You are free to execute your laws and your citizens as you see fit.'

more serious criticism of these lawyers, while several elements remind us of people unable to keep their footing or stuck in the mud.

2. The ten-item list of 'bills, cross-bills, ... etc', making up the 'mountains of costly nonsense' piled before the solicitors.
3. *Anaphora* as four successive clauses are introduced by 'well may the...'
4. A further sustained *anaphora* as it is said that Chancery is the court 'which has ... which has ... and its dead ... which has ... which gives ... which so exhausts...'
5. A more widely spaced, but significant *anaphora*, when the paragraph opens to say that the Lord Chancellor 'ought to be ... as here he is'; then later tells us that twenty or so barristers 'ought to be – as here they are'; and finally that the solicitors 'ought to be – as are they not?' also present in the court with their piles of legal documents before them.

Interlaced with these major effects are other, smaller features. For example, the *zeugma* we noted is in fact the second in the paragraph: the barrister with 'great whiskers, a little voice, and an interminable brief' is a delightful comic portrait, concisely expressed via *zeugma*. Our fifth feature tells us something about Dickens's self-confidence. The novel is beginning its move from generality and polemic, into actual fiction; so, Dickens draws our attention to this process by means of the *anaphora* which emphasises the move. Everybody knows that the Chancellor *ought* to be in court, and – well, what a surprise! There he is! To draw such unnecessary attention to his craft as he moves into the fiction, suggests a Dickens who is wielding his powers with enormous self-confidence. He begins by speaking to us directly, and bludgeoning us into agreement with him; he then deliberately moves into his fiction, telling us at each stage the deception he is practising upon us. At the same time, the picture of Chancery as a disgraceful and pestilential influence, its destructive effects apparent everywhere, is enhanced as the paragraph – and our extract – rolls to its frightening climax: 'Suffer any wrong that can be done you, rather than come here!'

Concluding discussion

We have now looked at the opening passages of our two novels in some detail. There are differences: for example, *Hard Times* begins in the voice of Gradgrind, in the classroom, in the fiction, while *Bleak House* begins as a polemic addressed to us by the author, and only starts to conjure the fiction as it moves from generalisations to the particular events of a particular day. On the other hand, there are also striking similarities. Both voices are powerful, assertive, dramatic, and both – Gradgrind and Dickens – are delivering a political speech, using a dense collection of rhetorical techniques and devices. So, if we listen to Gradgrind's patterned opening paragraph with its rigid diction of opposites, then hear Dickens's grand condemnation of Chancery, which:

> ' ... has its decaying houses and its blighted lands in every shire, which has its worn-out lunatic in every madhouse and its dead in every churchyard ...
>
> (*BH*, 13)

We can appreciate that in both cases we are listening to oratory: that is, we are listening to the kind of language we hear in public speeches or in sermons, and particularly when somebody wants to persuade us that they are right.

In both cases, irony is carried to the point where it can be called sarcasm. So, for example, when Gradgrind is described 'as he eagerly sparkled at them', or when the Chancellor is seen 'with a foggy glory around his head', or is described as 'High', the damning ridicule is so clearly ironic as to be obvious in both instances.

Also, in both extracts there is a range of imagery for us to interpret. In our analysis of the opening of *Hard Times* we found it useful to make a list of images, so that we could then look at the list, and notice groups of image-ideas. This led us to notice a dominating group of image-ideas that treat natural things as lifeless objects, such as the children described as 'pitchers'; and we drew conclusions critical of the 'fact' philosophy from this observation. In *Bleak House* we commented on the allusions to Noah's Flood and to a 'Megalosaurus' in the opening paragraph, suggesting that these propose two opposed views of human existence, at the outset of the novel. Simultaneously,

Dickens develops both fog and mud to such a pervasive point, during his description, that these two natural elements quickly take on a symbolic significance. The fog becomes an emblem of the intellectual confusion and impenetrable obscurity of the Court of Chancery; the mud signifies the helplessness and stuck situation of Chancery's victims. Dickens's punning on 'deposits', 'accumulating at compound interest', connects the mud to the financial world also. Just as fog and mud come to have symbolic significance in *Bleak House*, so the sunbeam joining Sissy Jupe and Bitzer, in *Hard Times*, indicates a nature that is ultimately more just, and more powerful, than Gradgrind himself. First, as we have remarked, the sunbeam 'perhaps' directs Gradgrind's finger; second, the sunbeam tells us the truth about the two children, adding colour and lustre to Sissy, and all but erasing the pale Bitzer. We have found imagery acting in three ways, then. First, to bring the scene being described vividly before us; second, to use the image-idea for further development of its interpretation, as happens in the case of Gradgrind's 'wall' and 'cellarage' face, or in the case of the children as 'pitchers', where the writer adopts the metaphor in place of the literal; and finally to develop the image as a symbol: that is, as a literal element of the story that retains both its real existence, and its symbolic significance. This is what happens to fog and mud in our *Bleak House* extract.

Diction has proved equally helpful and revealing to analyse. We noticed, for example, the cluster of absolute terms in Gradgrind's opening paragraph, and the collection of participles increasingly out of control as Dickens elaborates on 'fog' in *Bleak House*. Similarly, we noticed that Dickens inserts words from different vocabularies for a sudden comic or satirical effect. Of this kind are his use of 'compound interest', and the sudden insertion of 'mountains of costly nonsense' into a list of legal terms. We noticed that surprises at the end of a sentence are a typical feature of the style.

Most of all, however, we have been impressed by the rhetorical power and the dramatic presence of Dickens in the openings of both books. In both cases the author we meet is outraged and angry, and enlists our sympathy – and expresses his own – on behalf of the vulnerable, who are victims of whichever inhumanity is his target: whether that be the 'fact' or Utilitarian philosophy as misused in education, or the shames and cruelties of the Court of Chancery.

Dickens throws down a gauntlet

We can now attempt to summarise our first chapter highlighting the main points of what we have learned.

The style is exceptionally patterned with frequent, intensive and often sustained use of rhetorical techniques such as *zeugma* and *anaphora*, as well as lists, repetition, balanced double sentences and many other features. Two consequences of this are worth noting: first, that the style is, in itself, a feature, or in other words the style is noticeable; and second, such an exceptionally rhetorical style subjects the reader to considerable pressure because we are being fed a continuous diet of enriched, or as we have already described it, *patterned* language.

The style is decorated by widespread use of imagery. This ranges from brief metaphors (for example when Gradgrind 'sparkled' at the children) to elaborated similes (such as 'he seemed a kind of cannon loaded to the muzzle with facts'), to natural features developing symbolic significance (for example 'fog' for the law's delays and confusions in *Bleak House*, or the sunbeam ironically linking Sissy Jupe and Bitzer, in *Hard Times*). In addition, there is a particularly Dickensian technique whereby a figurative idea is referred to more than once, but on its second and subsequent appearances is treated as if it were the literal thing it represents. We find this, for example, in the case of Gradgrind's eyes, which find 'commodious cellarage in two dark caves', a metaphor later referred to as 'the cellarage before mentioned'; and we noted the same feature when Dickens refers to the children as 'little pitchers'. The frequency of figurative ideas is such that the story we read is nearly continuously embroidered with metaphorical fancies. Again, as with the 'patterned' style, this makes for a particularly rich diet to feed the reader.

The imagery is not mere decoration, however: many of **the figurative ideas call for us to interpret their meaning,** thus adding their significance to the meaning of the text. This is obvious in the case of pervasive natural symbols such as the fog and mud of *Bleak House*. We find it natural to interpret brief, passing images as well, however: see, for example, the echo of death in 'vault', used to describe the schoolroom in *Hard Times*; or the sudden idea of 'the death of the sun'.

We noticed **surprises, particularly at the ends of sentences,** as another technique typical of Dickens. In our *Bleak House* analysis, for example, we remarked on the sudden interjection of finance in 'accumulating at compound interest' when the subject has been mud, not money. This technique often also employs **puns,** adding to the reader's impression of richness as multiple potential meanings grow from the language.

The features of style we have remarked on in the passages we have analysed, all contribute to what we have described as **a 'rich' diet for the reader:** an intense and lively reading experience where we are expected to respond to multiple stylistic and linguistic stimuli in quick succession. We have observed that the reader is thus subjected to considerable pressure. We now return to our other comment on this subject: that the style is noticeable, is a feature in itself, and can be described as 'showy'. This raises a controversy, for there are those who argue that Dickens' was something of a show-off. There are readers who argue that his polemical passages (to which class both of this chapter's extracts belong) bludgeon the reader, telling us what to think and hammering at us until we are forced to agree. Others admire the style, drawing from it the linguistic richness and excitement it conveys, and enjoying the close relationship with the author that is engendered.

Dickens imposes his personality on the reader very strongly. In *Hard Times,* we notice the contempt and anger in the repeated 'square' of Gradgrind, and the heavy irony of 'little pitchers'; and so we absorb both the author's hatred of the 'fact' party, and his sympathy with the children. In *Bleak House* the author instructs our emotions directly, so that we share Dickens's outrage at the destruction and misery caused by Chancery, 'most pestilent of hoary sinners'. So, in the opening pages of both novels, we immediately feel ourselves to be in the company of a powerful friend who shares his feelings with us and expects us to join him, to feel the same way. This is a prominent feature of Dickens's writing. As we study further in these texts, we will find that Dickens accompanies us all the way through, nudging or directing our responses, cajoling or browbeating us into agreement, whether explicitly or by use of heavy ironies and powerful images. We have mentioned the 'dramatic' qualities of Dickens's fictions in the introduction above. The constant presence of Dickens himself, and his larger-than-life personality, is a significant element of that theatricality.

Methods of analysis

1. **Notice specific elements of the style,** such as repetition, *anaphora, zeugma*. Do not, however, simply identify and label these features: you must also describe what they contribute to the power and effect of the writing. Such rhetorical techniques are only interesting because of the effects they produce.

2. **Be alert to Dickens's choices of diction.** 'Diction' is everything about the language: in particular, the words chosen (for example the choice of the adjective 'square' in *Hard Times*), the vocabularies used whether specialised or class-specific (for example, we remarked the sudden use of a financial term 'compound interest' applied to mud, in *Bleak House*), and the tone including irony or sarcasm (such as the neo-biblical tone we noticed in 'retired from the face of the earth', in *Bleak House*).

3. **Notice and interpret imagery.** In this chapter we have met similes and metaphors, and we have remarked upon some symbolism. These texts are particularly rich in imagery, with image-ideas that invite interpretation: far from being merely decorative, the imagery plays a significant role in the meaning of the text. So, for example, that Sissy and Bitzer are connected by a sunbeam is both ironic (satirising Gradgrind's claim of impartiality), and has something important to tell us about nature's enduring power. It is a prominent feature of Dickens's imagery that he interweaves extended images, sometimes so extended as to appear from time to time throughout the text, and mixes them with brief metaphors and similes.

4. **Look at sentences and patterns of sentences.** Consider the uses and effect of paragraphing. In this chapter we noticed, for example, the opening paragraph of *Hard Times*, where Gradgrind uses single sentences, then symmetrical double sentences, then a double sentence that is really single, to exclude opposed opinions; and in *Bleak House* we remarked on interjected clauses delaying the verb 'sits' so that the Chancellor's fixity is emphasised. We also noticed that short paragraphs reveal Chancery, sandwiched between two rhetorical tours de force, the first about fog, then the paragraph leading to the climax '…rather than come here!'

5. **Formulate questions which are about the area in which you are interested.** In this chapter, the announcement of a central satirical target that will dominate the novel – in *Hard Times* the dogma of 'fact' or Utilitarianism; in *Bleak House* the confusion and delays of the Court of Chancery – and the manner of presentation of these satirical themes. As we asked questions about the polemical targets these two openings set up, and at which they shoot, we asked particularly about the author. How does he introduce himself? What relationship does he offer to the reader? How do we learn his opinions? Are they directly expressed, or do we learn them by understanding irony, or sarcasm, or by interpreting imagery? These questions led us to realise the powerful self-presentation Dickens undertakes in both our novels' openings, and the dramatic, even theatrical tone of the world he creates.

As we pursue further studies in *Hard Times* and *Bleak House*, we will continue developing our sense of Dickens's presence in his own novels, and our insights into the intimacy he seeks to establish with his reader. We will also continue to make observations in terms of the dramatic and theatrical nature of his imagination. We leave these topics now, but only to return to them in subsequent chapters.

Suggested work

Confirm, expand and develop the work of this chapter by carrying out detailed analysis of a second passage from the early part of each novel, as follows:

> *Hard Times:* pages 14–15: from the start of Chapter III to the end of paragraph 3, page 15, '…that the greedy little Gradgrinds grasped at?'
> In your analysis of this extract, notice repeated instances of repetition, lists, *anaphora*, *zeugma* and so forth, as we identified these features in our analyses above. Above all, however, notice the tone of Dickens's sarcasm, and the development of his style for a more overt comic effect. You will also find a rich fund of imagery to

interpret in this passage, of which, notice the development of the simile likening Gradgrind's forehead to a wall.

Bleak House: pages 14–15: From paragraph 2, page 14, starting 'Jarndyce and Jarndyce drones on', to the end of paragraph 1, page 15, ' … in some off-hand manner, never meant to go right'.

This extract is again filled with lists, examples of *anaphora* and *zeugma*: your analysis will be able to identify these and comment on the effects they achieve. However, in this case pay particular attention to the tones of voice between which Dickens's utterance fluctuates. Remember to pay close attention to imagery, but above all, attempt to describe how the text comes to express such contempt and bitterness, while ridiculing the court. For example, you may try to explain how the phrase 'Shirking and sharking' is so witty, and what is its effect. A number of other moments in this extract will be equally interesting to explore.

2

Characterisation (1): From Grotesques to Intimates

Grotesques

This chapter begins by examining how people are introduced into Dickens's world. We know, from having read the novels, that a number of the characters are caricatured: often, one feature of their personality is so exaggerated as to become ridiculous. Typically, Dickens will have fun at their expense, but in terms of characterisation these are the simplest and shallowest figures in the novels. They are so one-dimensional that we can call them **grotesques**. We begin by looking at the reader's first meeting with two of these figures in *Hard Times*. Here is the passage introducing Mrs. Sparsit, Bounderby's housekeeper:

CHAPTER VII

MR. BOUNDERBY being a bachelor, an elderly lady presided over his establishment, in consideration of a certain annual stipend. Mrs. Sparsit was this lady's name; and she was a prominent figure in attendance on Mr. Bounderby's car, as it rolled along in triumph with the Bully of humility inside.

For, Mrs. Sparsit had not only seen different days, but was highly connected. She had a great aunt living in these very times called Lady Scadgers. Mr. Sparsit, deceased, of whom she was the relict, had been by the mother's side what Mrs. Sparsit still called 'a Powler.' Strangers

of limited information and dull apprehension were sometimes observed
not to know what a Powler was, and even to appear uncertain whether
it might be a business, or a political party, or a profession of faith.
The better class of minds, however, did not need to be informed that
the Powlers were an ancient stock, who could trace themselves so
exceedingly far back that it was not surprising if they sometimes lost
themselves – which they had rather frequently done, as respected horse-
flesh, blind-hookey, Hebrew monetary transactions, and the Insolvent
Debtors' Court.

The late Mr. Sparsit, being by the mother's side a Powler, married this
lady, being by the father's side a Scadgers. Lady Scadgers (an immensely
fat old woman, with an inordinate appetite for butcher's meat, and a
mysterious leg which had now refused to get out of bed for fourteen
years) contrived the marriage, at a period when Sparsit was just of age,
and chiefly noticeable for a slender body, weakly supported on two long
slim props, and surmounted by no head worth mentioning. He inherited a fair fortune from his uncle, but owed it all before he came into it,
and spent it twice over immediately afterwards. Thus, when he died, at
twenty-four (the scene of his decease, Calais, and the cause, brandy), he
did not leave his widow, from whom he had been separated soon after
the honeymoon, in affluent circumstances. That bereaved lady, fifteen
years older than he, fell presently at deadly feud with her only relative,
Lady Scadgers; and, partly to spite her ladyship, and partly to maintain
herself, went out at a salary. And here she was now, in her elderly days,
with the Coriolanian style of nose and the dense black eyebrows which
had captivated Sparsit, making Mr. Bounderby's tea as he took his
breakfast.

If Bounderby had been a Conqueror, and Mrs. Sparsit a captive
Princess whom he took about as a feature in his state-processions, he
could not have made a greater flourish with her than he habitually did.
Just as it belonged to his boastfulness to depreciate his own extraction,
so it belonged to it to exalt Mrs. Sparsit's. In the measure that he would
not allow his own youth to have been attended by a single favourable
circumstance, he brightened Mrs. Sparsit's juvenile career with every
possible advantage, and showered waggon-loads of early roses all over
that lady's path. 'And yet, sir,' he would say, 'how does it turn out after
all? Why here she is at a hundred a year (I give her a hundred, which she
is pleased to term handsome), keeping the house of Josiah Bounderby of
Coketown!'

(*HT*, 45–46)

The opening paragraph offers two triple sentences, and, in each case, the third part reveals a new angle on the subject. So, Mrs. Sparsit's 'annual stipend' reminds us of vulgar economics after the grand vocabulary of 'presided' and 'establishment', while the idea of Bounderby as the 'Bully of humility' in his own 'triumph' is a sudden comic picture of his vainglorious and boastful progress through life. We are not yet told how Mrs. Sparsit acts as a 'prominent figure in attendance' on Bounderby. Two paragraphs giving a brief biography intervene before we learn how he flaunts her like a 'captive Princess'. Meanwhile, we have learned the name 'Sparsit'. Like many Dickensian names, this has possible close words, including 'spar' and 'parse'; but the closest is the word 'sparse', denoting the opposite of plenty, an absence of growth and fruitfulness.

The second paragraph tells us of Mrs. Sparsit's high connections. She has a titled relative, still alive ('Lady Scadgers'), and her husband comes from an old family, the 'Powlers'. Dickens is adding further ridiculous names: 'Scadgers' is very close to 'cadgers', slang for parasites – those who 'cadge' from the better-off. A 'Powler' is simply a silly word, so we laugh at the idea that anyone would be proud of it. This paragraph is composed in a voice dripping with irony, borrowing typical phrases from the diction of small-town gossip. With Dickens, we always ask ourselves: who is speaking? What sort of person has a voice like this, or uses a phrase like that, which is clearly not Dickens's own? In this paragraph we start with the euphemism 'seen different days' (i.e. had lost all their money), then, we find the redundant 'in these very times' and the pompous 'relict' before we arrive at the first of two grand definitions. People who are unaffected by snobbery of 'connections' are described as 'Strangers of limited information and dull apprehension', while those who are impressed by such foolish snobbery are described as 'The better class of minds'. We hear the snobs mention 'an ancient stock' before the paragraph ends in high comedy: Powlers sometimes lose themselves, which turns out to mean that they lose all their money on the horses, borrow from Shylocks,[1] and end in debtors' prison.

---

[1] Moneylenders were often depicted as typically Jewish, in Dickens. Fagin (*Oliver Twist*), although not a moneylender, is the most notorious example; but there is also Mr. Riah (*Our Mutual Friend*). Critics of Dickens still argue whether he was anti-semitic.

Even more openly scornful is the next paragraph, chiefly notable for its economy. We are informed of the circumstances and fate of Mrs. Sparsit's marriage and we are provided with three vivid physical descriptions, each a startling thumbnail sketch. Dickens is at his most mischievous, ending the picture of Lady Scadgers with her 'mysterious' leg which refuses to get out of bed; that of Mr. Sparsit with 'no head worth mentioning'; and rounding off with the 'Coriolanian style of nose and the dense black eyebrows' that gives us a vivid cartoon of Mrs. Sparsit. We should also notice some perfectly turned witty sentences as we read; see for example the *zeugma* where the subject is Sparsit's inheritance, first 'inherited', then 'owed', and finally 'spent ... twice over'; or Sparsit's death, 'scene ... Calais ... cause ... brandy'.

At the same time, this paragraph sketches a pathetic story. Lady Scadgers arranged the marriage that brought separation and poverty, between a stupid boy and a grotesque woman 15 years his senior. This utter disaster was the work of Mrs. Sparsit's 'high connections'. Dickens reveals this tragic history in the form of subordinate clauses interjected into his narrative. So we learn that Sparsit was 'just of age' when married; that they 'separated soon after the honeymoon'; and that she was 'fifteen years older than he'; all pieces left for us to put together, and uttered in apparent innocence.

Our final paragraph in this extract brings us back to the present and to Bounderby. The first sentence proposes the simile of Bounderby's triumphal procession and Mrs. Sparsit as a captive Princess being exhibited to the people, another visual idea of high comedy. The second and third sentences, with their balanced construction, describe Bounderby's strategy: exaggerating simultaneously his own deprived childhood and Mrs. Sparsit's favoured upbringing. 'Just as ... so', and 'In the measure that ... he' are the two frames. The final words tell us the point of it all, which is, of course, the reversal of fortunes that leaves Josiah Bounderby, as her employer, victorious owner of her 'high connections'. In this final paragraph there is an influx of plenty: the word 'flourish' stands out, as does the picture of a 'procession', and we are treated to the image of Bounderby who 'showered waggon-loads of early roses all over that lady's path'. The abundance of his boasting makes a contrast with her 'sparse' name and history.

As Mrs. Sparsit plays her part in *Hard Times*, we realise that Dickens has nearly completed her characterisation within these four paragraphs. The 'Coriolanian' nose and black eyebrows are frequently mentioned, and we come to know little else about her appearance. Her 'high connections' and tragic marriage are also referred to regularly, particularly when Bounderby boasts of them. Even when hatred leads her to chase Louisa through a rainstorm, Mrs. Sparsit remains a shallow figure, capable only of ill feeling and ridiculous appearance. So, at the end of her pursuit, soaked by the rain in Coketown station, Dickens tells us that Mrs. Sparsit 'exulted hugely' over what she supposes to be Louisa's fall. She feels clever and responsible: 'Could she, who had been so active in the getting up of the funeral triumph, do less than exult?' (*HT*, 199). When she realises she has failed, for she has lost Louisa's trail, Dickens describes her with reference to her simple and recurrent character motifs: on the previous page the rain in 'rills ran from her ... Roman nose', and in the final paragraph she still has both a 'classical visage', and a 'highly connected back'. In short, Dickens continues to make cruel fun of Mrs. Sparsit, even in her moment of darkest misery.

Before we discuss the implications of this form of characterisation, let us examine another example. Here is the description of Slackbridge, the Union official who is responsible for sending Stephen Blackpool to Coventry:

Part Two: CHAPTER IV
'Men and Brothers'
'OH, my friends, the down-trodden operatives of Coketown! Oh, my friends and fellow-countrymen, the slaves of an iron-handed and a grinding despotism! Oh, my friends and fellow-sufferers, and fellow-workmen, and fellow-men! I tell you that the hour is come, when we must rally round one another as One united power, and crumble into dust the oppressors that too long have battened upon the plunder of our families, upon the sweat of our brows, upon the labour of our hands, upon the strength of our sinews, upon the God-created glorious rights of Humanity, and upon the holy and eternal privileges of Brotherhood!'

'Good!' 'Hear, hear, hear!' 'Hurrah!' and other cries, arose in many voices from various parts of the densely crowded and suffocatingly close Hall, in which the orator, perched on a stage, delivered himself of this and what other froth and fume he had in him. He had declaimed himself into a violent heat, and was as hoarse as he was hot. By dint of roaring at the top of his voice under a flaring gaslight, clenching his fists, knitting his brows, setting his teeth, and pounding with his arms, he had taken so much out of himself by this time, that he was brought to a stop, and called for a glass of water.

As he stood there, trying to quench his fiery face with his drink of water, the comparison between the orator and the crowd of attentive faces turned towards him, was extremely to his disadvantage. Judging him by Nature's evidence, he was above the mass in very little but the stage on which he stood. In many great respects he was essentially below them. He was not so honest, he was not so manly, he was not so good-humoured; he substituted cunning for their simplicity, and passion for their safe solid sense. An ill-made, high-shouldered man, with lowering brows, and his features crushed into an habitually sour expression, he contrasted most unfavourably, even in his mongrel dress, with the great body of his hearers in their plain working clothes. Strange as it always is to consider any assembly in the act of submissively resigning itself to the dreariness of some complacent person, lord or commoner, whom three-fourths of it could, by no human means, raise out of the slough of inanity to their own intellectual level, it was particularly strange, and it was even particularly affecting, to see this crowd of earnest faces, whose honesty in the main no competent observer free from bias could doubt, so agitated by such a leader.

(*HT*, 131–132)

Here are three paragraphs. The first is in the Union orator's voice, and is the final passage of his speech. The second paragraph describes him at the moment when he reaches his impassioned finale. The third paragraph contrasts him with his audience. In short, we are given how he sounds, how he looks and how he compares with others.

We begin with the extract from Slackbridge's speech. The apostrophe 'Oh, my friends!' that opens the first three sentences thus makes an *anaphora*. A further *anaphora* comes in the six-times-repeated '… upon the' with which the speaker builds up to his final phrase '… the holy and eternal privileges of Brotherhood!' Dickens clearly expects us to recognise that the speaker's rhetoric is overblown, and he includes some bathos to amuse us at the speaker's expense. So, for example, after 'fellow-sufferers' and 'fellow-workmen' comes the bathetic 'fellow-men' – a tacit admission that the Union man does not actually work with them in their factories. The finale is also undercut, for 'Brotherhood' is a let-down after 'God-created' and 'holy and eternal'.

We are expected to read this paragraph as low-quality and exaggerated rhetoric, typical of a political activist stirring up his working-class audience. Furthermore, we know from reading the next two paragraphs, and from our knowledge of *Hard Times*, that Slackbridge is a villainous figure in Dickens's eyes: he orchestrates the ugly mob hysteria that ostracises and indirectly kills the innocent and morally fastidious Stephen. On the other hand, reading with our present-day perspective, we can see that Dickens's Union man touches some resonant chords. In particular, he is right to insist that they 'must rally round one another as One united power'. A basic tenet of the entire Socialist movement has always been the need to act together, to show unity, in order to exert the greatest pressure on the owners of capital. Similarly, Slackbridge is right to describe their conditions as 'an iron-handed and a grinding despotism', and their bosses as 'oppressors' who live off the hard work of the operatives. What example of a mill owner do we have in *Hard Times* to help us be judges of the type? Only Bounderby, a character who bears out all Slackbridge can say about him and his kind. The Union man's speech, then, is somewhat ambivalent: it is boiling and common rhetoric, its comic bombast bathetic and ripe for our scorn. On the other hand, Slackbridge tells some truth about the plight of workers in the industrial north in the nineteenth century.

Our second paragraph describes the speaker. The author refers to the speech scornfully as 'this and what other froth and fume he had in him', and then launches into a series of clauses telling us of the speaker's exhaustion. Each picture is mildly ridiculous, and they are strung together as yet another *anaphora*: five clauses introduced by 'By dint of ... ', with a verb of effort in each: 'roaring ... clenching ... knitting ... setting ... pounding'. The other element Dickens emphasises here is heat. The hall is 'suffocatingly close' and Slackbridge is in 'a violent heat' and 'hot' with a background of 'flaring gaslight' and the need for water. This paragraph suggests that Slackbridge must be foolish, for he has roared himself silent.

The third paragraph of our extract is where Dickens is most personally present. It is founded on a comparison between Slackbridge and his audience, which we are told directly, and at the outset, is 'extremely to his disadvantage'. There are minor instances of the author's habitual constructions, such as the *anaphora* in the fourth sentence, but these are not as marked as we have become used to. Instead, most of the paragraph takes the form of statements, until we arrive at the very lengthy double idea in the final sentence (it is always strange to see the superior led by the inferior), which Dickens couches in 83 words. This is, then, quite a different tone from our passage concerning Mrs. Sparsit, or either of the passages we analysed in Chapter 1. In the middle of this paragraph, Dickens asks us to judge Slackbridge by 'Nature's evidence', and asserts that he was 'in many great respects ... below' his audience. There follow two sentences that supposedly give this 'Nature's evidence' to determine our judgement. First, we hear about Slackbridge's character. He is less honest, manly, good-humoured and simple, and has less 'solid good sense' than the people he is addressing. On the contrary, he is cunning and passionate. Next, we learn about his appearance: he is 'ill-made, high-shouldered ... lowering' and his features are 'crushed into an habitually sour expression'. Here, we find Dickens wielding the power of an author over his character, for Dickens can do anything he wants to Slackbridge. On the other hand, this diatribe raises some awkward issues. What is that 'Nature' by whose measurement Slackbridge is so inferior? Was he born with a 'naturally' evil character, cunning, dishonest and so forth? Can we accept such an arrogation of Nature in the same novel where Louisa Gradgrind's 'nurture' leads her to marry the appalling Bounderby? Conversely, is 'Nature' responsible for Slackbridge's ugliness, for his being 'ill-made'? More pertinently, is any of this his fault (for we are certainly encouraged to blame him for being the way he is)?

These are awkward questions because they strike at the heart of the problem of characterisation. Characters are not real people, and we must never treat them as such. They are elements the author has created as part of the pattern in his novel. Here, our author seems to make exactly this mistake: Dickens is with us in this extract. He sees Slackbridge, hates him and tells us to hate him as well; but the awkward questions about 'Nature's evidence' remain unresolved. Dickens

has, at least partly, failed to justify his opinion. What can be our critical stance in such circumstances?

The two characters we have looked at as 'grotesques' have elements
in common. Both are described with telling details of their ugliness, and Dickens expresses his dislike for both of them. However,
we have found irony and complexity in the history of Mrs Sparsit,
whose tragic marriage and pathetic submission to her grand relative's
plans may enlist some of our sympathy despite being simultaneously
ridiculous. Mrs. Sparsit is also given some interior narrative, which
emphasises the viciousness of her jealousy, as well as numerous occasions when she shamelessly flatters Bounderby or manipulates Bitzer.
These details, added to the constant refrain about her nose, eyebrows,
and being 'highly connected', are enough to cement our dislike, so
we can join Dickens in enjoying her journey through the rain and
in crowing over her ultimate defeat. Mrs. Sparsit is introduced as
a grotesque and she remains a grotesque: she is a shallow or two-
dimensional character, capable of no variety or development, and
bound firmly to the one social and two visual motifs with which she
is introduced. The consequence of this kind of characterisation is that
Dickens is set free from any compassionate constraint or compunction towards his creation. The author is free to judge, punish, torture
or ridicule, and he invites us to join in the fun. Mrs Sparsit's is a kind
of characterisation which brings us into Dickens's unrestrained company, often for the delight of his outrageous comic inventions.

Slackbridge, on the other hand, is introduced with virtually no
irony, and Dickens's direct declaration of his low character seems
to push us towards condemnation of the man, while the evidence
Dickens adduces to his opinion confuses the ideas of nature and
judgement as they appear elsewhere in *Hard Times*. We can connect
Slackbridge's appeal for the workers to 'Unite', with the Gradgrind
philosophy's insistence on lumping people together as all the same –
see, for example, the children as rows of 'little pitchers'. So, we can
understand that Dickens hates the Union's philosophy because it
focuses on the mass and ignores individuality. We clearly regret and
condemn the outcome of Slackbridge's speech, when the social group
turns on the individual and Stephen Blackpool is persecuted. On the
other hand, many readers find Stephen's reason for pitting himself
against his fellow workers, that he has 'passed a promess' (*HT*, 139),

too highly strained to justify his actions.[2] These considerations lead
into a broader topic that we will discuss in Chapter 4: the question
of Dickens's opinion of industrial disputes and of the Chartists and
the nascent socialist activities of the time. For the present, we should
notice that Slackbridge is presented in a direct and declamatory style.
If there is humour, it is conveyed as a rather bitter form of scorn, and
there is assertion rather than irony. Slackbridge, then, is a figure of
hate, pure and simple, a slightly different form of characterisation
from that of Mrs. Sparsit.

Our next port of call takes us to *Bleak House*, where we meet two
exaggerated characters, each grotesque in his own way, but who serve
a purpose in the novel as a whole that is different again from that of
Mrs Sparsit or Mr Slackbridge. Here is a description of Mr Skimpole:

> Mr. Skimpole was as agreeable at breakfast as he had been overnight.
> There was honey on the table, and it led him into a discourse about
> bees. He had no objection to honey, he said (and I should think he had
> not, for he seemed to like it), but he protested against the overweening
> assumptions of bees. He didn't at all see why the busy bee should be
> proposed as a model to him; he supposed the bee liked to make honey,
> or he wouldn't do it – nobody asked him. It was not necessary for the
> bee to make such a merit of his tastes. If every confectioner went buzz-
> ing about the world banging against everything that came in his way
> and egotistically calling upon everybody to take notice that he was going
> to his work and must not be interrupted, the world would be quite an
> unsupportable place. Then, after all, it was a ridiculous position to be
> smoked out of your fortune with brimstone as soon as you had made
> it. You would have a very mean opinion of a Manchester man if he
> spun cotton for no other purpose. He must say he thought a drone the
> embodiment of a pleasanter and wiser idea. The drone said unaffectedly,
> 'You will excuse me; I really cannot attend to the shop! I find myself in
> a world in which there is so much to see and so short a time to see it

---

[2] This is a particularly ineffective reason for Stephen's refusal to join the other
hands, since Dickens cancelled the passage when the promise was made that
explains Stephen's actions. In a passage left out of the published novel, Stephen
promises Rachael that he will 'let such things be', as the failures of reforms, after
Government inquiries into injuries in factories. The cancelled passage is printed in
the notes to the World's Classics edition (*HT*, 292–293), and the question of how
this omission spoils the themes of *Hard Times* is more fully discussed in Chapter 4.

in that I must take the liberty of looking about me and begging to be provided for by somebody who doesn't want to look about him.' This appeared to Mr. Skimpole to be the drone philosophy, and he thought it a very good philosophy, always supposing the drone to be willing to be on good terms with the bee, which, so far as he knew, the easy fellow always was, if the consequential creature would only let him, and not be so conceited about his honey!

He pursued this fancy with the lightest foot over a variety of ground and made us all merry, though again he seemed to have as serious a meaning in what he said as he was capable of having.

(*BH*, 106–107)

Our passage explains the analogy between Mr. Skimpole and a drone bee. Two short sentences set the scene, at breakfast with honey. Mr. Skimpole is still 'agreeable' and enters upon a 'discourse'. We already know that these two characteristics are typical of him: that he has a great deal of charm, and that he chooses a topic and talks, habitually constructing a clever and beguiling 'discourse' on whatever subject takes his fancy. The remainder of the long paragraph is couched in reported speech, except for the direct speech of Skimpole's imagined drone. The arguments against the busy bee – that he likes making honey or he would not do it; that if all 'confectioners' went around boasting of their busy-ness the world would be intolerable; that the bee is smoked out as soon as the honey is ready – are ingenious. The character-sketch of the drone who believes it is right 'to be provided for by somebody' because he wishes to 'look about him', and who is always willing to be on good terms with those who work, is amusing and charming.

The short paragraph then tells us that Mr. Skimpole 'pursued this fancy' and 'made us all merry', making it clear that his listeners do not take him seriously: the drone idea is a 'fancy', an amusing 'discourse' to pass the time. However, Esther concludes with the teasingly ambiguous assessment that 'he seemed to have as serious a meaning in what he said as he was capable of having'. This remark exposes the heart of the Skimpole dilemma. As we discover during the remainder of the novel, he does have a 'serious' meaning when he advocates the drone's philosophy: so serious that he ignores or resists the heartfelt pleas, anger and hostility of both Esther herself and Mr. Jarndyce on several occasions, rather than concede an inch of his freedom from their morality. In another sense, 'serious' may itself connote 'moral', so that Esther's comment tells us that Skimpole is not capable of becoming more 'serious', or moral. This idea is frequently expressed by Skimpole himself, as when he asserts that he knows 'nothing of the value of money' because he is 'a mere child' and may have 'come into the world expressly' to promote other people's generosity to him, while he is 'incapable' of their 'worldly' concerns.

We find in Skimpole another example of a 'grotesque' characterisation, by which term we mean a person figuring in the novel who has a limited number of caricatural qualities that are repeatedly referred to and demonstrated; who does not develop from such a two-dimensional depiction, but remains a shallow and exaggerated cipher. Just as Mrs. Sparsit has her nose and eyebrows, Mr. Skimpole has his innocence and amoral philosophy. He never departs from this characteristic, and although Dickens devotes a great deal of invention to Skimpole in a variety of situations, he only ever expresses and follows his single philosophy, except in the one uncharacteristic instance of the cutting remark about Jarndyce that Esther finds in his memoirs. This remark is very unlike Skimpole: we suppose that Dickens includes it in order to prove Skimpole's villainy, and therefore to settle our dilemma, at the end.

We now turn to Skimpole's opposite, Boythorn:

> 'There never was such an infernal cauldron as that Chancery on the face of the earth!' said Mr. Boythorn. 'Nothing but a mine below it on a busy day in term time, with all its records, rules, and precedents collected in it and every functionary belonging to it also, high and low, upward and downward, from its son the Accountant-General to its father the Devil, and the whole blown to atoms with ten thousand hundredweight of gunpowder, would reform it in the least!'
>
> (*BH*, 131–132)

We remember that Skimpole was 'agreeable' in the evening and at breakfast, while his bee is described as 'overweening' and his drone as an 'easy fellow' ready to be 'on good terms' with the bee. Skimpole's speech not only digresses into an amusing but utterly unreal fancy, it also uses a moderate range of language, rendering bee and drone both into a world where they are 'fellows' who really ought to be able to get along together. The world Skimpole imagines and portrays is a sort of jolly little nonsense.

As soon as we hear Boythorn, we realise that he is Skimpole's opposite. The language is extreme, filled with absolutes and exaggerations. So 'never' is the second word from our extract, while the imagery for Chancery is about Hell, an 'infernal cauldron' and having 'its father the Devil'. The absolutes continue: there is nothing like it 'on the face of the earth', and 'nothing' but a mine to blow 'all' of it 'to atoms' could reform it. Notice that Dickens takes every opportunity to overwrite Boythorn: all-inclusive phrases abound ('high and low, upward and downward') and it cannot even be reformed 'in the least', or even blown sky-high by no less than 'ten thousand hundredweight of gunpowder'.

Skimpole and Boythorn remain caricatures throughout the novel, and they provide Dickens with numerous opportunities to elaborate both the gentle fancies with which Skimpole feeds his unshakeable cheerfulness, and the grandiose and absolute violence of language with which Boythorn approaches every subject. So, near to the end of *Bleak House*, we hear that 'war rages yet' (*BH*, 907) between Boythorn and Sir Leicester, while Esther's last meeting with Skimpole finds him 'in excellent spirits' and entertaining her with 'a variety of delightful conversation' (*BH*, 864) as is his wont. Skimpole and Boythorn, then, are limited figures who do little more, as they act their parts in the narrative, than to represent a single quality each: Skimpole fanciful innocence and Boythorn exaggerated irascibility. They are shallow and unreal, then. So, what is the point of their characterisation?

To answer this question we have to think about their roles in the novel as a whole, in particular asking: how do they affect other, more central characters? And, how does their two-dimensional caricature contribute to the novel's serious concerns? Even as we only begin to review Skimpole's and Boythorn's roles in our minds, it becomes obvious that they have a role to play on a complex level of the novel's construction. We will only mention some examples briefly, from the contributions these two characters make, before we move on to consider the functions of Dickens's *'grotesques'* more broadly.

Think of the incident during Skimpole's first visit, when Richard and Esther pay his debt. Look back at the aftermath of this event (see pages 92–95). Mr. Jarndyce is very upset when he learns that Skimpole has taken their money. A little later, however, Esther refers to his childishness, and Jarndyce tells himself off for forgetting this aspect of Skimpole. Eventually, much happier, he takes his 'craftier head' to his 'more worldly pillow'. Esther thinks that her guardian tries to avoid having to 'depreciate or disparage anyone', and that this motive is the origin of his blaming the east wind. This episode, placed firmly at our first meeting with Skimpole, already indicates the dilemma his character presents to others. We notice that our central characters have undergone a test: Richard and Esther have been found to be generous, and not retentive of money. Similarly, Jarndyce has often paid debts for his friend. On the other hand, the unlimited 'childish' demand Skimpole imposes upon his friends is already seen to be an immoral imposition. His willingness to take their only money from the young pair, leaving them penniless, is objectionable to Jarndyce, who exclaims, 'Oh, dear me, what's this, what's this!' (*BH*, 92). Skimpole, then, has highlighted a positive quality in the two young people, that will be explored and more precisely defined as the story develops, showing Esther's financial generosity as a higher quality than Richard's financial carelessness and optimism. At the same time, we have learned a subtle level in Mr. Jarndyce's character: his desire to find and enact goodness, even in a world containing so much evil, which explains his friendship with the parasitic Skimpole. So, although Skimpole is entirely two-dimensional within his supposedly innocent childishness, we find that his effect is to reveal to us serious and complex levels of character in the more rounded and realistic central characters of the novel.

Our brief example has shown how a 'grotesque', even because of his simplicity, can provide subtle insights into other, more rounded characters, by demanding and setting off their qualities. If we now consider Boythorn and Skimpole together, in relation to the themes of *Bleak House*, it is immediately obvious that they represent two extreme responses to the flawed world presented in the novel. This is the world where Chancery exists, where Joe the crossing sweeper lives and dies, where Krook goes up in smoke, the Smallweeds prosper, Tulkinghorn lurks and the Dedlocks lead the fashionable world. In other words, it is a world full of greed, evil, ignorance and violence. It is the world of Mrs. Jellyby, Mr. Turveydrop and Borrioboola-Gha, a world often seemingly ruled by stupidity or absurdity. One question the novel poses to the reader is: what is the proper response to such a world? Looking for an answer in *Bleak House* brings us to Mr. Jarndyce, whose measured responses to good and evil offer something like an answer. Flanked by, and reacting to, the two extremes presented by Skimpole and Boythorn, Mr. Jarndyce's judicious blend of perception, judgement, intelligence and generous feelings, is set off against Boythorn's extreme of critical judgement and worldly activity on the one hand, and Skimpole's unlimited unworldliness on the other. A little thought will then tell us that these themes are worked into the novel's ending. So, Jarndyce eventually ceases to tolerate Skimpole, not for financial reasons, but because he mistreated Richard and accepted the bribes from Bucket and from Vholes. Thus, the so-called child, who Esther has several times suspected of a very un-childlike strategy, is eventually discarded. Boythorn, meanwhile, reveals a history and sensitivity that belie his manner. He remains a valuable person in Dickens's casting up of judgements at the end.

Discussion of grotesques. We chose to consider Skimpole and Boythorn for their clear and symmetrical contribution to the novel's themes. Their role in the novel is easy to approach because they stand at either side of Jarndyce, and they cancel each other out. We will now think more broadly about other grotesque characters, in a brief discussion before we move on to consider the central, more naturalistic, characterisations.

In *Hard Times* we have looked at Mrs. Sparsit and Mr. Slackbridge. Other 'grotesque' characters who are recognisable by their motifs would include the pale Bitzer, Tom Gradgrind ('the Whelp'), Bounderby with the constant myth of his childhood and Thomas Gradgrind up until Louisa's escape, with his rigid Utilitarian outlook. These characters remain simple and two-dimensional, recognisable from the repeated references to their ruling motifs. Just as we found that Mrs. Sparsit, for example, is recognisable by her Roman nose and 'high connections', so we find that Bitzer is regularly evoked via his 'white eyelashes quivering, his colourless face more colourless than ever ... ' (*HT*, 263). We do not include Sleary in this list. His peculiarity is the lisp in his speech; but if we attend to the perceptiveness of what he says, rather than amusement at how he says it, we will not mistake him for a shallow figure. These, then, are the 'grotesques' of *Hard Times*. Other characters such as the later Gradgrind, Louisa, Harthouse, Stephen, Rachael and Sissy, all belong to the central group.

In *Bleak House,* we meet a much larger cast of grotesques, so that the construction of various groups of figures, and the ways in which the plot enables members of different groups to interact, can be difficult to think about, let alone to integrate into a coherent view of this huge and varied novel. We have considered only Skimpole and Boythorn. Other distinctive caricatures include Volumnia, the Smallweeds, Miss Flite, Guppy, Jobling, Mr. and Mrs. Snagsby, Guster, the Chadbands, Krook, Phil, Conversation Kenge and Vholes. Then, there is a second rank of background figures such as Little Swills, Mrs. Pardiggle, Quale, the debilitated cousin, Mrs. Piper and Mrs. Perkins: a series of brief, sharp satirical portraits that populate what we might call the novel's middle-distance, so that Dickens creates a depth of absurdity and high colouring as far as we can see, behind the characters who occupy the foreground at any given moment.

Thinking about the population of *Bleak House,* we find a much more extreme level of caricature than Dickens permits himself in *Hard Times.* Bitzer, for example, may be a pale young man, and this aspect of his appearance is repeatedly mentioned. On the other hand, paleness is a natural feature, while in *Bleak House* the motifs are more exaggeratedly unnatural. Miss Flite, for example, keeps her birds up in the roof; Mr. Tulkinghorn is watched by his ceiling; old Mr. Smallweed throws his cushion at his wife and needs "plumping up" in his chair each time; Guster has her fits; Krook takes on and secretes some foul and greasy substance, which eventually catches fire. These are all contributions to the imagery of the novel, and they depict a world where physical attributes and symbolic imagination meet and mingle among the grotesque population Dickens has created; and in *Bleak House,* Dickens allows much freer rein to his symbolic imagination than in *Hard Times.* Of course, in *Bleak House* he has much more room to indulge his invention.

We have discussed Skimpole and Boythorn, who present opposite extremes. As we study the themes of *Bleak House* we can place these two characters at each end of a worldly/unworldly axis, or an easygoing/irascible axis. If we now turn our attention to the theme of the law, we find that the cast of grotesque characters Dickens has created to populate this theme is far more varied and numerous and would provide material for a major study. Consider the lawyers we meet: Kenge, Vholes, Tulkinghorn; then the clerks Guppy, Jobling, Small, and those others connected to the law; Snagsby, Captain Hawdon who becomes a law-writer, Krook, old Mr. Smallweed, Judy and even perhaps the warder in the prison where Trooper George is held; and finally the victims of the law: Richard and Ada Clare, Miss Flite, the man from Shropshire, Tom Jarndyce, who blew his brains out, and Trooper George. This veritable crowd represents different styles of legal practice, various relationships dependent on the law, and the effects of the law blighting people's lives. Each of these characters provokes us to think about a particular aspect of the theme, and calls upon our moral judgement. So, for example, the Shropshire man is trapped by his lawsuit, unable to stop it despite trying to withdraw: so, once the law has its hands on you, it will never let go. Similarly, Vholes exemplifies the hypocrisy of a lawyer's devotion to his client, where the truth is that the lawyer becomes the client's parasite, not his servant. We also judge all of these characters. We judge the Shropshire man kindly: he was unwise, but the grasping hands that take hold of him and wring his life from him, the dead hands of Chancery, are evil in the extreme. We condemn Vholes, recognising his hypocrisy, and feeling sympathy for Richard, his victim. This discussion takes only two examples and is limited to brief remarks about them. If we consider the range of elements of the theme represented by this crowd of shallow figures and the wide array of moral judgements we are called upon to sanction, we quickly realise how Dickens has brought together a numerous and complex spread of grotesque characters in order to bring his theme to the reader.

The theory we are developing is that Dickens populates a kind of 'panorama' with a range of moral or social simplifications. On their own, these characters are ridiculous caricatures or 'grotesques'; and, as we have commented, the cast of *Bleak House* is more unnatural and extraordinary than that of *Hard Times*. However, when considered as a 'whole' population, these shallow 'grotesques' provide a full range of moral and social contrasts, comparisons and distinctions which inform the novel as a 'whole' work. At the same time, they also contribute to educating our moral judgement, as we are encouraged to assess their value through their interactions with others.

There is something more to the effect of Dickens's shallow 'grotesque' characterisations, a particular effect that we have come across

in the short passages we have looked at. We have been studying simplified characterisation based upon dominant motifs (e.g. Bitzer: paleness and Tulkinghorn: secrecy). In this chapter we have met Mrs.
Sparsit and Mr. Slackbridge, each with clear, dominant motifs, and
each one a satire upon a certain kind of person. Then, we have listened
to Skimpole and Boythorn, again aware that each is a satire upon an
attitude. Our suggestion is that it is this very simplicity, the very shallowness of these characterisations, that operates upon the world of the
novel in a similar manner to the way Dickens's literalised similes work.
Just as the figurative side of a simile becomes habitually treated as literal, so the dominant characteristic of a caricature becomes the whole
figure. In this way we are induced to accept that the grotesque takes
over from reality. In short, there is a strange form of alchemy taking
place, by which we are induced to accept that a range of extreme,
satirical motifs arrayed before us is a kind of reality. If we think about
it, this way of perceiving people in more and more simplified terms,
the less we know of them, right down to the background people you
pass in the street, is beguiling because it reminds us of life.

Dickens achieves this effect in *Bleak House* by means of a very large
cast of characters, at different distances from us and different levels
of detail therefore: people who interact in groups that are sometimes
socially divided, sometimes connected by geography, coincidence or
self-interest. How does Dickens orchestrate his crowd of characters,
and manage them so that they interact within a single narrative?

Managing the crowd

How does the author manage the crowd? This is a huge and complicated question, just as *Bleak House* is a huge and complicated novel.
In order to think about the crowd of characters, and how they interact, we must bring the complexity down to a manageable level. We
can do this by dividing the crowd into groups. Here is our suggestion
as to how the characters can be organised:

1. **Bleak House:** Mr. Jarndyce, Esther, Ada Clare and Richard
   Carstone belong to this group, although Richard leaves. Of secondary characters, Skimpole, Boythorn and the maid, Charley,
   belong here.

2. **Dedlocks:** Sir Leicester Dedlock and Lady Dedlock, Mr. Tulkinghorn. Of secondary characters, the maid, Hortense, Rosa, Mrs. Rouncewell, Watt Rouncewell and Volumnia belong here.
3. **Cook's Court:** Mr. Snagsby, Mrs. Snagsby, Guster, Mrs. Perkins, Mrs. Piper, Krook, Miss Flite, Jo, Mr. Chadband, the law-writer and Mrs. Chadband aka Mrs. Rachel. Of secondary characters, Little Swills, the Coroner and the Beadle, Tony Jobling and later the Smallweeds, all can belong in this group.
4. **The Jellyby group:** Mr. Jellyby, Mrs. Jellyby, Peepy, Caddy, Caddy's sister, Mr. Quale, Prince Turveydrop and Mr. Turveydrop.
5. **The George Group:** Trooper George, Phil Squod, Mr. Bagnet, Mrs. Bagnet, Woolwich, Quebec and Malta Bagnet.
6. **The Chancery Group:** Conversation Kenge, Mr. Tulkinghorn, Mr. Vholes, Miss Flite, Mr. Gridley, Mr. Guppy, Mrs. Guppy, Mr. Weevle (aka Tony Jobling), Bartholomew Smallweed, Grandfather Smallweed, Mrs. Smallweed and Judy Smallweed.

Sorting Dickens's characters into these groups seems to make sense. However, you will notice that several characters are not mentioned and that some appear twice. Of those not mentioned, the most important are the brick-makers' wives, Inspector Bucket and Allan Woodcourt. Those mentioned twice indicate how difficult it is to distinguish between Cook's Court and Chancery itself. We have decided that it would be unnatural to exclude Tulkinghorn, Miss Flite or Tony Jobling, from both groups. Mr. Snagsby and Mr. Krook, on the other hand, belong in Cook's Court, despite their links with the law.

Now let us try out our groups on a portion of the text of *Bleak House*. We will study character organisation in Chapters 4–10, by leafing back through those chapters and noting the characters involved:

Chapter 4 *Telescopic Philanthropy* (Esther)
- 1 (Esther, Ada, Richard), 6 (Kenge, Guppy)
- 1 (Esther, Ada, Richard), 4 (Mr. and Mrs. Jellyby, Caddy, Peepy, Mr. Quale)
- 1 (Esther, Ada)
- 1 (Esther), 4 (Caddy)

End of the episode published March 1852

Chapter 5 *A Morning Adventure* (Esther)
- 1 (Esther), 4 (Caddy)

- 1 (Esther, Ada, Richard), 4 (Caddy), 3 (Miss Flite, Mr. Krook)
- 1 (Esther), 4 (Mrs. Jellyby, Caddy, Peepy)

Chapter 6 *Quite at Home* (Esther)
- 1 (Esther, Mr. Jarndyce, Richard, Ada)
- 1 (Esther, Mr. Jarndyce, Richard, Ada, Mr. Skimpole)
- 1 (Esther, Richard, Mr. Skimpole),* (Coavinses)
- 1 (Esther, Richard, Ada, Mr. Jarndyce)
- 1 (Esther, Ada)

Chapter 7 *The Ghost's Walk* (Author)
- 2 (Mrs. Rouncewell, Watt Rouncewell)
- 2 (Mrs. Rouncewell, Watt Rouncewell, Rosa), 6 (Mr. Guppy)
- 2 (Mrs. Rouncewell, Watt Rouncewell, Rosa)
End of the episode published April 1852

Chapter 8 *Covering a Multitude of Sins* (Esther)
- 1 (Esther)
- 1 (Esther, Mr. Jarndyce, Mr. Skimpole, Ada, Richard)
- 1 (Esther, Mr. Jarndyce)
- 1+* (Esther, Ada, Richard, Mrs. Pardiggle, her five sons, the brick-makers and their wives, and Jenny's baby)
- 1+* (Esther, Ada, Richard, the brick-makers, their wives, the dead baby)

Chapter 9 *Signs and Tokens* (Esther)
- 1 (Esther, Ada, Richard)
- 1 (Esther, Ada, Richard, Mr. Jarndyce) 1/2 (Mr. Boythorn)
- 1 (Esther, Mr. Jarndyce)
- 1 (Esther), 6 (Mr. Guppy)

Chapter 10 *The Law-Writer* (Author)
- 3 (Mr. Snagsby)
- 2/6 (Mr. Tulkinghorn)
- 3 (Mr. Snagsby), 2/6 (Mr. Tulkinghorn)
- 3 (Mr. Krook), 2/6 (Mr. Tulkinghorn)
End of the episode published May 1852

We have constructed our notes in the form of a list, broadly recording the different scenes between different people. Do these notes show up how Dickens organises his characters?

First, notice that Esther narrates five of these seven chapters. This is not typical. In the whole of *Bleak House*, the author narrates 34 chapters to Esther's 33: they take virtually an equal share of the story. However, in this section it is noticeable that the author narrates the end of two of the episodes. What is more, both of the author's chapters are dramatic and portentous: the first being where Guppy first notices the resemblance between Esther and Lady Dedlock, an event whose drama is enhanced by darkness, rain and the superstition of the Ghost's Walk; and the second leading up to the flagrant 'cliff-hanger' as Mr. Tulkinghorn hesitates outside the law-writer's door. The author's two chapters, then, build the melodramatic mood as a foretaste of later events.

We also notice that Esther has confidential dialogues with several other characters: she talks one-to-one with Ada, Mr. Jarndyce, Caddy Jellyby, Krook and Mr. Guppy; and this brings her into closer relation to groups 3, 4 and 6, as well as making her a conduit for Mr. Jarndyce's opinions, and the repository for Ada's and Richard's confidences. Esther takes Caddy under her wing when the younger girl elects her to be her mentor and protector, a development that establishes a more permanent connection between Esther and the Jellybys. Then the pseudo-Jellyby, Mrs. Pardiggle, arrives at Bleak House so that Esther can make the all-important visit to the brick-makers' wives. We can already see, therefore, how Esther's one-on-one intimacies are setting up her consciousness as the central sensitivity in the world of *Bleak House*.

Another noticeable feature of our list of notes is that Mr. Guppy makes three appearances. He is a minor employee of the lawyer Kenge, yet he is chosen to meet Esther on her arrival; he escorts the young people to the Jellyby house (and is active in setting Peepy free from the railings). Then, by chance, he happens to visit Chesney Wold, being suddenly 150 miles from London on unspecified legal business, an excuse used for a second time when he happens to be sent to Bleak House on business for Mr. Boythorn, and takes the opportunity to propose to Esther.

The point about Guppy is to see how Dickens uses his character as a joining-piece, giving weak explanations for his ability to turn up in different contexts. It is noticeable that his presence on three occasions provides a common element between our domestic Esther and Mr. Jarndyce in **Group 1**, Chesney Wold and the Dedlocks in

Group 2, the fringes of the law in Cook's Court in **Group 3**, the Jellybys (**Group 4**) and Chancery in **Group 6**. Looking at our notes, we see that no other character is so ubiquitous, and is used in so cavalier a fashion as the young clerk Guppy. At this stage of the story, Guppy knits it all together. Later in the novel, you will find that Inspector Bucket, Allan Woodcourt and Esther herself, play similar roles, bridging the divides.

Realising Guppy's function in these chapters, highlights Dickens's blatant use of coincidence throughout *Bleak House*. Notice, for example, that Laurence Boythorn is both a schoolfriend of Mr. Jarndyce, and the Dedlocks' neighbour, while Sir Leicester is a distant relative of Ada and Richard; that Mrs. Smallweed is Krook's sister; that Mrs. Rachel becomes Mrs. Chadband; that Trooper George is Mrs. Rouncewell's son; and that she is housekeeper at the Dedlocks' place in Lincolnshire. Think of how we meet Jo in Cook's Court, at the cemetery, at Bleak House and at Tom-all-Alone's; or our repeated meetings with the brick-makers' wives, and their meetings with Esther and her mother. Think of the chances that bring Jo and Allan Woodcourt from Tom-all-Alone's to George's shooting gallery. Dickens's manipulation of coincidence in the complexities of *Bleak House* might be thought too cavalier. However, combining so many coincidences does create the impression of a life of shape and purpose, a 'novel' life as opposed to the chaotic and shapeless real lives we all live outside the pages of a book.

More rounded characters

We begin considering more rounded characterisations with a final point about grotesques: there are characters who begin in a caricatural or 'grotesque' mode, then develop into more complex or sympathetic figures. Thinking about our two novels, we quickly realise that this happens in the case of Thomas Gradgrind in *Hard Times,* and with both of the Dedlocks in *Bleak House*. Remember that nothing could be more shallowly satirical than Gradgrind's 'fact' speech which opens *Hard Times,* unless it is Lady Dedlock's vanity, satirised mercilessly in Chapter 2 ('In Fashion', *BH*, 17–23); or Sir Leicester's figure as seen in Chapter 40 ('National and Domestic', *BH*, 589–602). We will look at the development of all three of these figures, in this section.

We begin with *Hard Times*, by looking at the relationship between Louisa Gradgrind and her father. Here is the passage when they discuss Bounderby's proposal of marriage to Louisa:

> Silence between them. The deadly statistical clock very hollow. The distant smoke very black and heavy.
> 'Father,' said Louisa, 'do you think I love Mr. Bounderby?'
> Mr. Gradgrind was extremely discomfited by this unexpected question.
> 'Well, my child,' he returned, 'I – really – cannot take upon myself to say.'
> 'Father,' pursued Louisa in exactly the same voice as before, 'do you ask me to love Mr. Bounderby?'
> 'My dear Louisa, no. No. I ask nothing'.
> 'Father,' she still pursued, 'does Mr. Bounderby ask me to love him?'
> 'Really, my dear,' said Mr. Gradgrind, 'it is difficult to answer your question – '
> 'Difficult to answer it, Yes or No, father?
> 'Certainly, my dear. Because;' here was something to demonstrate, and it set him up again; 'because the reply depends so materially, Louisa, on the sense in which we use the expression. Now, Mr. Bounderby does not do you the injustice, and does not do himself the injustice, of pretending to anything fanciful, fantastic, or (I am using synonymous terms) sentimental. Mr. Bounderby would have seen you grow up under his eyes, to very little purpose, if he could so far forget what is due to your good sense, not to say to his, as to address you from any such ground. Therefore, perhaps the expression itself – I merely suggest this to you, my dear – may be a little misplaced'.
> 'What would you advise me to use in its stead, father?'
> 'Why, my dear Louisa,' said Mr. Gradgrind, completely recovered by this time, 'I would advise you (since you ask me) to consider this question, as you have been accustomed to consider every other question, simply as one of tangible Fact. The ignorant and the giddy may embarrass such subjects with irrelevant fancies, and other absurdities that have no existence, properly viewed – really no existence – but it is no compliment to you to say, that you know better. Now, what are the Facts of this case? You are, we will say in round numbers, twenty years of age; Mr. Bounderby is, we will say in round numbers, fifty. There is some disparity in your respective years, but in your means and positions there is none; on the contrary, there is a great suitability. Then the question arises, Is this one disparity sufficient to operate as a bar to

such a marriage? In considering this question, it is not unimportant to take into account the statistics of marriage, so far as they have yet been obtained, in England and Wales. I find, on reference to the figures, that a large proportion of these marriages are contracted between parties of very unequal ages, and that the elder of these contracting parties is, in rather more than three-fourths of these instances, the bridegroom. It is remarkable as showing the wide prevalence of this law, that among the natives of the British possessions in India, also in a considerable part of China, and among the Calmucks of Tartary, the best means of computation yet furnished us by travellers, yield similar results. The disparity I have mentioned, therefore, almost ceases to be disparity, and (virtually) all but disappears'.

'What do you recommend, father,' asked Louisa, her reserved composure not in the least affected by these gratifying results, 'that I should substitute for the term I used just now? For the misplaced expression?'

'Louisa,' returned her father, 'it appears to me that nothing can be plainer. Confining yourself rigidly to Fact, the question of Fact you state to yourself is: Does Mr. Bounderby ask me to marry him? Yes, he does. The sole remaining question then is: Shall I marry him? I think nothing can be plainer than that?'

'Shall I marry him?' repeated Louisa, with great deliberation.

'Precisely. And it is satisfactory to me, as your father, my dear Louisa, to know that you do not come to the consideration of that question with the previous habits of mind, and habits of life, that belong to many young women'.

'No, father,' she returned, 'I do not'.

'I now leave you to judge for yourself,' said Mr. Gradgrind. 'I have stated the case, as such cases are usually stated among practical minds; I have stated it, as the case of your mother and myself was stated in its time. The rest, my dear Louisa, is for you to decide'.

From the beginning, she had sat looking at him fixedly. As he now leaned back in his chair, and bent his deep-set eyes upon her in his turn, perhaps he might have seen one wavering moment in her, when she was impelled to throw herself upon his breast, and give him the pent-up confidences of her heart. But, to see it, he must have overleaped at a bound the artificial barriers he had for many years been erecting, between himself and all those subtle essences of humanity which will elude the utmost cunning of algebra until the last trumpet ever to be sounded shall blow even algebra to wreck. The barriers were too many and too high for such a leap. With his unbending, Utilitarian, matter-of-fact face, he hardened her again; and the moment shot away into the plumbless depths of the past, to mingle with all the lost opportunities that are drowned there.

Removing her eyes from him, she sat so long looking silently towards the town, that he said, at length: 'Are you consulting the chimneys of the Coketown works, Louisa?'

'There seems to be nothing there but languid and monotonous smoke. Yet when the night comes, Fire bursts out, father!' she answered, turning quickly.

'Of course I know that, Louisa. I do not see the application of the remark'. To do him justice, he did not, at all.

(*HT*, 94–96)

This scene is a crucial crisis in the lives of two of the central characters. It is also an exploration of a central theme of *Hard Times*: Gradgrind's Utilitarian philosophy. To begin with, think about what leads up to this scene, and what follows. There have been a number of hints that Mr. Bounderby finds Louisa attractive, and that Gradgrind plans their marriage, starting with Gradgrind's 'what would Mr. Bounderby say?' (*HT*, 18), when he finds his children peeking into the booth of the horse-riding show. We have therefore been anticipating the moment when Louisa will face this proposition, since the beginning of the book. Dickens then prepares the scene by titillating our anticipation: Gradgrind notices his daughter's maturity, and sets an appointment in his study for the next morning. Louisa knows what is coming, but in the meantime discusses the idea with her brother Tom. So, by giving us advance notice, then interposing a delay, Dickens heightens tension, building up our expectations. Now, what are the consequences of this scene? Louisa's marriage to Bounderby, the near-affair with Harthouse, her escape to her father, his understanding of his errors, and all the outcome of the story as affecting the Gradgrinds and Sissy. So the scene we are studying is pivotal, and even before it starts, it is heavily laden with anticipation and tension. Dickens teases us with Louisa's enigmatic statements throughout the first 14 chapters, balancing her awareness of a world of emotions and imagination, beyond her father's philosophy, against her devotion to her selfish brother. We do not know what will happen, but we anticipate a collision between Louisa's emotions and her father's rigid, inhuman dogma.

Now, we can turn to the extract itself: what does this long-anticipated scene give to us? Certainly it is not what we expect, or what Mr. Gradgrind expects.

Louisa speaks almost entirely in monosyllables, and her speeches are all short. Her speeches are, in order, 8, 9, 9, 8, 11, 20, 4 and 5 words long. Her only longer (20 words) speech ironically adopts Gradgrind's euphemism, calling 'love' ' ... the term I used just now? The misplaced expression?' Louisa's contributions are very direct, using a plain, even minimal vocabulary. See, for example, that she does not even expect Bounderby to 'demand', 'request', 'require' or 'expect' love from her: instead she uses the shortest word that will convey the meaning, 'ask'.

In contrast to his daughter's, Gradgrind's speeches are filled with a more elaborate and multisyllabic vocabulary, as well as more complex constructions. His sentences are far longer than Louisa's and contain numerous subordinate clauses. So, for example, the sentence beginning 'Now, Mr. Bounderby does not do you the injustice ... ' is 29 words long, and is followed by another of 41 words. In the first of these sentences, nine of the words are three syllables long and the sentence is constructed from six clauses including the three attempts to find a term for 'love', the interjection in brackets asserting that all three words have the same meaning anyway, and the parallel constructions 'do you the injustice' and 'do himself the injustice'. In the next paragraph, and typically, Gradgrind begins one of his sentences with a participle clause 'In considering this question', then proceeds to a double negative 'it is not unimportant to take into account' – a convoluted and pedagogic opening, supposedly justifying his digression into the statistics of marriage. In other words, Gradgrind's speech style is much as we would expect: pompous, over-elaborate and bombastic, and in vivid contrast to Louisa's. This contrast is all in Louisa's favour – we are impressed with her direct outspokenness, while we feel contempt at her father's replies and recognise the poor style Dickens has allotted to this character.

What do we know about the inner life of these two people? Dickens provides us with authorial information about the unspoken inner life of Mr. Gradgrind, on three points; and informs us about Louisa's inner life, once. We learn that Gradgrind is 'extremely discomfited' by Louisa's first question; that he fails to understand her remark about the Coketown smoke; and that he fails to see the 'one wavering moment' in her, because of his long-ingrained habits of mind and behaviour, which have erected 'barriers' between them.

About Louisa, we learn more about her 'one wavering moment' when Dickens tells us that she might have been 'impelled to throw herself upon his breast, and give him the pent-up confidences of her heart'. Louisa has been questioning her father, first about love, then about what she should substitute for it, since, according to him, love is 'absurdities that have no existence, properly viewed – really no existence'. Dickens implies here that there was a moment when Louisa might have broken down, but that Gradgrind's face is too 'unbending, utilitarian, matter-of-fact' so that looking at him 'hardened her again'. We should notice a slight difference in the author's stance, in relation to these two characters. With Gradgrind he is not in doubt: he *is* 'discomfited' by the first question; he 'did not' see the application of Louisa's remark, and his 'barriers were too many and too high' for him to notice Louisa's weaker moment. With Louisa, on the other hand, Dickens is more tentative. We hear her pursuing her questions, but we are not quite sure what she thinks. The crucial description is couched within '*perhaps* he *might have* seen' (my italics). In context, the reader is encouraged to believe that such a 'wavering', and the 'pent-up confidences of her heart', were really there in Louisa. However, Dickens preserves some of the mystery surrounding her motives, by his tentative wording, when he dips into her inner life.

We have looked at this extract to analyse the contrast between the two characters involved, we have found both their styles of speech to be opposite extremes, and Dickens's treatment of their inner selves to be noticeably different. Now we should consider the content of the scene. Gradgrind's speeches are no surprise to us, as they are merely a further revelation of his 'fact' philosophy. His ridiculous use of statistics, which prove only the opposite of his argument, indicating instead that most marriages have too great a disparity in age, also belongs with Dickens's long-running satire on Utilitarianism. The crux of the question in this scene, however, is the existence or non-existence of love. Gradgrind makes a major contribution to the analysis of Utilitarianism, when he treats 'love' as something 'fanciful, fantastic, or (I am using synonymous terms) sentimental'; describes those who believe in it as 'The ignorant and the giddy'; and finally asserts that love is 'irrelevant fancies, and other absurdities that have no existence, properly viewed – really no existence'. We should note that he fails to answer Louisa's final question: having dismissed love, he does not say what term could be used in its place.

These elements of the scene are direct developments in the major theme of Utilitarianism, so our scene makes an important contribution to the intellectual content of *Hard Times*. From the point of view of characterisation, however, Gradgrind's speeches could equally well come from the absurd, shallow 'grotesque' caricature we met in the opening chapters. What makes Mr. Gradgrind more interesting in this scene is that Dickens attributes to him a potential for change. We find that Louisa is 'wavering' one minute, then 'hardened' the next, simple metaphors showing a moment of softening emotion. Gradgrind, on the other hand, is treated to an elaborate, rolling and changing metaphor, beginning with the idea that he must have 'overleaped at a bound the artificial barriers' of his habits of mind. These cut him off from 'subtle essences of humanity which will elude the most cunning of algebra'. These 'essences of humanity' will always escape from Gradgrind's 'algebra', until the 'last trumpet' sounds, ending the world – including algebra. This knot of images is completed by the statement that 'The barriers were too many and too high for such a leap', so Gradgrind fails to make contact with his daughter's momentary weakness, and the opportunity is lost. Dickens turns to metaphor again, telling us that the moment 'shot away into the plumbless depths of the past' where 'lost opportunities' lie 'drowned'.

All of these image-ideas come in one paragraph: a surprising cluster of melodramatic ideas in a scene where the outward dialogue remains so subdued. The sudden whirligig of image-ideas (barriers, leaping, last trumpet, wreck, shot, plumbless depths, drowned) depicting Gradgrind's failure at this moment has the paradoxical effect of hinting that he might have succeeded: that he has the potential to change.

Finally, notice the setting of this scene. Our extract begins with a reminder of two motifs associated with Gradgrind's study: the 'statistical' clock (previously given an association with death), and the view of Coketown chimneys through the window. At the end of our extract, Louisa remarks on the smoke, that it may seem to be 'languid and monotonous', but 'when the night comes, Fire bursts out, father!' What does she mean? We are told in the next line that Gradgrind does not understand her. We have to presume that she speaks prophetically. What she says is a warning to Gradgrind: she may appear to be under control of her reason, like a 'languid' or 'monotonous' person, but there will come a time when her passions will burst out. Dickens comments that 'To do him justice he did not [understand], at all'. This marks a new departure for Gradgrind's characterisation: here, Dickens expresses sympathy, and is sad about his character's failings.

Louisa and Thomas Gradgrind, then, both show the potential for change. In Louisa's case, we are not sure what she thinks and feels, so that her motives in accepting Bounderby remain partly obscure; while we are told that there was a weak moment when she felt 'compelled to throw herself upon his breast'. In the case of Gradgrind, Dickens describes his inner character in a cluster of melodramatic ideas that both switches our view of him (he has become the prisoner of the barriers he has erected), and suggests that he might, at some future date, 'overleap' all the barriers that stand between him and a more humane understanding of life. These, then, are characters drawn more sympathetically than the simple grotesques, with their exaggerated, repeated motifs, who have no potential for development. These characters are given a psychological and emotional life. We will postpone until later in this chapter the question of how far we accept Louisa's psychological story. For the moment, her motives remain partly obscure.

Turning to *Bleak House*, we analyse a passage of first-person narrative to gauge how Dickens handles the characterisation of Esther Summerson. In this extract, she discusses Allan Woodcourt, while describing his mother's visit to Bleak House:

> I believe – at least I know – that he was not rich. All his widowed
> mother could spare had been spent in qualifying him for his profession.
> It was not lucrative to a young practitioner, with very little influence in
> London; and although he was, night and day, at the service of numbers
> of poor people and did wonders of gentleness and skill for them, he
> gained very little by it in money. He was seven years older than I. Not
> that I need mention it, for it hardly seems to belong to anything.

I think – I mean, he told us – that he had been in practice three or four years and that if he could have hoped to contend through three or four more, he would not have made the voyage on which he was bound. But he had no fortune or private means, and so he was going away. He had been to see us several times altogether. We thought it a pity he should go away. Because he was distinguished in his art among those who knew it best, and some of the greatest men belonging to it had a high opinion of him.

When he came to bid us good-bye, he brought his mother with him for the first time. She was a pretty old lady, with bright black eyes, but she seemed proud. She came from Wales and had had, a long time ago, an eminent person for an ancestor, of the name of Morgan ap-Kerrig – of some place that sounded like Gimlet – who was the most illustrious person that ever was known and all of whose relations were a sort of royal family. He appeared to have passed his life in always getting up into mountains and fighting somebody; and a bard whose name sounded like Crumlinwallinwer had sung his praises in a piece which was called, as nearly as I could catch it, Mewlinnwillinwodd.

Mrs. Woodcourt, after expatiating to us on the fame of her great kinsman, said that no doubt wherever her son Allan went he would remember his pedigree and would on no account form an alliance below it. She told him that there were many handsome English ladies in India who went out on speculation, and that there were some to be picked up with property, but that neither charms nor wealth would suffice for the descendant from such a line without birth, which must ever be the first consideration. She talked so much about birth that for a moment I half fancied, and with pain – But what an idle fancy to suppose that she could think or care what MINE was!

Mr. Woodcourt seemed a little distressed by her prolixity, but he was too considerate to let her see it and contrived delicately to bring the conversation round to making his acknowledgments to my guardian for his hospitality and for the very happy hours – he called them the very happy hours – he had passed with us. The recollection of them, he said, would go with him wherever he went and would be always treasured. And so we gave him our hands, one after another – at least, they did – and I did; and so he put his lips to Ada's hand – and to mine; and so he went away upon his long, long voyage!

I was very busy indeed all day and wrote directions home to the servants, and wrote notes for my guardian, and dusted his books and papers, and jingled my housekeeping keys a good deal, one way and another.

I was still busy between the lights, singing and working by the window, when who should come in but Caddy, whom I had no expectation of seeing!

(*BH*, 255–256)

Esther's first-person narratives alternate with Dickens's own voice in *Bleak House*. It was not the first time he adopted a character to tell the story, but it was the first interweaving of first- and third-person writing, and the first time Dickens wrote as a woman. Our question, in analysing the above extract, is: how does Dickens use the form as a means of investigating and developing Esther's character?

First, we look at Esther's sentences in this extract. The first sentence pauses for a correction at the third word: 'I believe – at least I know' – precedes the information that Woodcourt is 'not rich'. Esther's re-phrasing suggests that this information affects her. By correcting her expression she gives the impression that perhaps she is embarrassed to know such a down-to-earth fact about a gentleman, or that the information itself is distressing. The reader can believe that Esther's modesty shies away from being too explicit about money. We also recognise her distress, however: Woodcourt's poverty prevents him from marrying, and she is in love with him. Dickens has given us a broad hint about Esther's feelings, merely by giving her an uncharacteristic break and fumble in her sentence.

Looking at the rest of the extract, we find that this kind of break or self-correction in Esther's sentences happens a further seven times. First, she mentions his age but then apologises – 'Not that I need mention it'– because it is not relevant to anything. Next, she fumbles the beginning of her next paragraph: 'I think – I mean, he told us' how long he had been working. This is similar to our first example. Just as then the vague 'believe' changes to 'know', this time the vague 'think' changes to 'he told us'. In the meantime, she has dismissed her knowledge of his age. Clearly, Esther knows much more about Woodcourt than she wants to display. The next problem is that Esther begins a new sentence with the subordinate clause starting 'Because'. Her sentence has no main clause, which is unlike her usual correct constructions. Next, we find Esther distressed at Mrs. Woodcourt's speeches, but failing to complete her own thought. This time she truly stops herself, and suppresses her own ideas: 'for a moment I half fancied, and with pain – But what an idle fancy … ', whereas Esther has, of course, correctly interpreted Mrs. Woodcourt's pointed and cruel discourse, warning her away from Allan and making covert reference to Esther's presumed illegitimacy. The final three examples are, first, the repetition 'the very happy hours – he called them the very happy hours – he had passed with us', which only serves to betray the load of emotion this parting carries for Esther; then, the two occasions when she tries to write herself out of the parting, but then corrects and includes herself: 'we gave him our hands … they did – and I did'; and finally 'he put his lips to Ada's hand – and to mine'. All of these examples where Esther's writing is most uncharacteristically mixed and disturbed, show us how deeply she is distressed, and how turbulent her emotions are, at parting from the man she loves.

Further evidence comes in the short switches of subject of which Esther is guilty: when she mentions Woodcourt's age, for example; or when she moves from his reasons for going away, to remark that 'He had been to see us several times'. Previously, Esther has mentioned that he will be away a 'long, long time'. Her forlorn feelings are again apparent when she repeats this sad repetition, his 'long, long voyage!'

Finally, Esther throws herself into her housekeeping duties in order to prevent herself from giving way to her emotions. She becomes 'very busy indeed' in order to keep her mind occupied with everyday things. Notice that she strings together four clauses, each starting with 'and', so that her busy-ness seems to come in waves until the bathetic final phrase 'one way and another'.

In this extract, then, Dickens has succeeded in conveying an event that arouses powerful emotions in his narrator, enabling the reader to hear these emotions in the rhythms, broken, self-censoring, self-correcting or surging of the writing; in the tendency of the narrative to drift aside; and at the same time giving virtually no explicit expression to Esther's emotion. All, in short, is done by suggestion, reticence, allusion and embarrassment. The character revealed to us by means of this first-person narrative, is extremely shy, self-effacing and with a low estimate of her own value. She sets a high standard of courtesy and is humble in manner. Dickens's technique here, using diversion, denial and self-deprecation to reveal rather than to hide Esther, is psychologically true. We may find Esther's character a little too self-effacing, too humble, or we may join several critics in accusing her of the indirect boast when she celebrates her humility; but Dickens's skill in rounding out her inner story is clear.

Further examples from more rounded characters

Before we discuss the two distinct forms of characterisation we have studied, we will look at Stephen Blackpool (*Hard Times*) and the Dedlocks (*Bleak House*).

Stephen Blackpool. In the depiction of Stephen, Dickens sets himself a particular challenge. When he is first introduced, Dickens insists that Stephen is not clever. He has qualities – he is 'a good power-loom weaver, and a man of perfect integrity', but 'What more he was, or what else he had in him, if anything, let him show for himself' (*HT*, 65). Here Stephen pleads with Mr. Bounderby, seeking divorce:

> 'I ha' paid her to keep awa' fra' me. These five year I ha' paid her. I ha' gotten decent fewtrils about me agen. I ha' lived hard and sad, but not ashamed and fearfo' a' the minnits o' my life. Last night, I went home. There she lay upon my har-stone! There she is!'
> In the strength of his misfortune, and the energy of his distress, he fired for the moment like a proud man. In another moment, he stood as he had stood all the time – his usual stoop upon him; his pondering face addressed to Mr. Bounderby, with a curious expression on it, half shrewd, half perplexed, as if his mind were set upon unravelling something very difficult; his hat held tight in his left hand, which rested on his hip; his right arm, with a rugged propriety and force of action, very earnestly emphasizing what he said: not least so when it always paused, a little bent, but not withdrawn, as he paused.
>
> (*HT*, 72)

In the first paragraph we hear Stephen speaking. Dickens has given him a Lancashire accent and some dialect features (in this instance, 'fewtrils', which means small possessions or trifles; the expression 'ha' gotten'; and 'har-stone' for hearth stone). However, Stephen speaks in short bursts, shown by his first three sentences that are 9, 7 and 8 words long respectively. Also, notice how his narrative consists of simple statements, one after another, without conjunctions: 'I went home … There she lay … There she is!' To Stephen, each event is a simple, separate thing. Rachael also speaks in the local accent and dialect, but what she says is more fluent and complex.

The second paragraph is Dickens's description of Stephen. He stands with a stoop, although for a moment he 'fired … like a proud man'. We are given a precise account of his arms and hands, one holding his hat and the other making gestures; and Dickens describes the expression on his face in a way that conveys to us Stephen's intellectual limitation: he is 'perplexed' and trying to unravel 'something very difficult', so he wears a 'curious' expression. His stoop is the only characteristic 'motif' we could compare to that of a Dickensian 'grotesque', a detail repeatedly mentioned. The picture of his arms, how he stands, his momentary pride, and his mixed expression, as he struggles to think clearly – all of these tell us something about his thoughts and feelings, unlike, for example, Mrs. Sparsit's Roman nose, which does not tell us about her thoughts at all. Also, unlike Mrs. Sparsit, there is nothing ridiculous in Stephen's appearance. Dickens simply mentions his hands, his arm, his stance, his expression, without suggesting that he has misshapen hands, arm or face.

This characterisation, then, allows each reader's imagination to picture Stephen. The stoop gives a visual clue, but we are free to paint Stephen Blackpool each in our own way, rather than being provided with the vivid details we are given in many of Dickens's portraits. It is as if Dickens allows Stephen to 'show for himself' what 'more he was' or what qualities he 'has in him'. We may speculate that the writer deliberately created an ordinary industrial worker, not an exceptional one, in order to see for himself what the outcome would be, so that *Hard Times* may read like a kind of experiment in social engineering, but in literary form.[3] At the same time, the focus of Dickens's characterisation is firmly upon Stephen's inner life, rather than his external appearance.

---

[3] Many critics regard the characterisation of Stephen as one of Dickens's failures. For example, we will meet Stephen J. Spector's 'Monsters of Metonymy: *Hard Times* and Knowing the Working Class' in Chapter 9 below. Spector argues that Dickens recognised his inability to characterise the industrial working class, and gave up that project half-way through *Hard Times* (See Chapter 9).

The Dedlocks. In *Bleak House* we meet Sir Leicester and Lady Dedlock as cardboard caricatures. Few of Dickens's characters appear to be as satirically drawn, or as hopelessly shallow, as do this couple on their first appearance. Lady Dedlock is first mentioned in the language of a paragraph in the gossip column of a newspaper:

> My Lady Dedlock has returned to her house in town for a few days pre-
> vious to her departure for Paris, where her ladyship intends to stay some
> weeks, after which her movements are uncertain. The fashionable intel-
> ligence says so for the comfort of the Parisians, and it knows all fashion-
> able things. To know things otherwise were to be unfashionable. My
> Lady Dedlock has been down at what she calls, in familiar conversation,
> her 'place' in Lincolnshire.
>
> (*BH*, 17)

The satire of the world of fashion is clear from the diction, starting with the possessive 'My Lady ... ' and including the tone of phrases such as 'her ladyship intends', all in the voice of a toadying journalist, turning out gushy little paragraphs about self-important people. Later in this same second chapter, Dickens expands upon the vanity and shallow appearance of 'fashion', Lady Dedlock included:

> She supposes herself to be an inscrutable Being, quite out of the reach
> and ken of ordinary mortals – seeing herself in her glass, where indeed
> she looks so. Yet every dim little star revolving about her, from her maid
> to the manager of the Italian Opera, knows her weaknesses, prejudices,
> follies, haughtinesses, and caprices and lives upon as accurate a calcula-
> tion and as nice a measure of her moral nature as her dressmaker takes of
> her physical proportions.
>
> (*BH*, 21)

It would be hard to find a less auspicious first appearance in the novel, and we would be justified in expecting nothing more from Lady Dedlock other than vanity and extravagance. This impression is further fortified when we realise that her husband is such a self-important windbag, another of the Dickens caricatures in which we can hear his satirical laughter:

> His family is as old as the hills, and infinitely more respectable. He has a
> general opinion that the world might get on without hills but would be

done up without Dedlocks. He would on the whole admit nature to be a good idea (a little low, perhaps, when not enclosed with a park-fence), but an idea dependent for its execution on your great county families.

(*BH*, 18–19)

There is broad laughter here, where Dickens is enjoying some good verbal jokes at Sir Leicester's expense, including the idea that Dedlocks are 'infinitely more respectable' than hills; and the adoption of the pompous nobleman's diction, saying that the world 'might get on' without hills but 'would be done up' without Dedlocks. In such writing, Dickens is witty, merciless, and laughs loudly.

In the Dedlocks, then, it seems that we have a pair of self-important, vain and rich vacuities, mere sport for the author's satire. For the present, there is little indication that this couple will become anything more. Dickens does sound indulgent, however, when listing Sir Leicester's weaknesses, almost as if he likes the old buffer despite everything: Sir Leicester is 'an honorable, obstinate, truthful, high-spirited, intensely prejudiced, perfectly unreasonable man' (*BH*, 19).

We know, of course, that this was a naïve expectation on our part. By the end of the book, both Sir Leicester and his Lady have revealed deeper, more complex and much more appealing qualities. Both have become more interesting characterisations than the simple grotesques they appeared to be at first. Here is Lady Dedlock at a moment when she is most revealed:

'To bless and receive me,' groaned my mother, 'it is far too late. I must travel my dark road alone, and it will lead me where it will. From day to day, sometimes from hour to hour, I do not see the way before my guilty feet. This is the earthly punishment I have brought upon myself. I bear it, and I hide it.'

Even in the thinking of her endurance, she drew her habitual air of proud indifference about her like a veil, though she soon cast it off again.

'I must keep this secret, if by any means it can be kept, not wholly for myself. I have a husband, wretched and dishonouring creature that I am!'

These words she uttered with a suppressed cry of despair, more terrible in its sound than any shriek. Covering her face with her hands, she shrank down in my embrace as if she were unwilling that I should touch her; nor could I, by my utmost persuasions or by any endearments

I could use, prevail upon her to rise. She said, no, no, no, she could only speak to me so; she must be proud and disdainful everywhere else; she would be humbled and ashamed there, in the only natural moments of her life.

(*BH*, 535–536)

This is a very different figure from the lady of 'fashionable intelligence'. What do we notice about the way the writing has changed? First, there is no satirical voice to hear in this passage. Dickens writes seriously, with no adoption of ridiculous diction, or any satirised style. The direct speech we hear is that of Lady Dedlock, but she speaks from emotion, not vanity. Her style is mannered and rhetorical, reminiscent of a speech from a theatrical melodrama, with its, 'From day to day, sometimes from hour to hour', and the exclamatory 'wretched and dishonouring creature that I am!' Listen, for example, to this from *The Frozen Deep*, a play in which Dickens acted: 'There is something dreadful! I feel it, though I see nothing. I feel it, nearer and nearer in the empty air, darker and darker in the sunny light. I don't know what it is. Take me away!'

In our extract, Lady Dedlock's emotion is vividly externalised, as in melodrama, and it is expressed in highly dramatised language, but with regard to her character, there is no doubt that we are meant to take her seriously, and the vain caricature of 'In Fashion' is a figure of the past.

Second, there seems to be a theme that recurs in the vocabulary, phrases and figures of speech, which acts like a motif of mood surrounding Lady Dedlock. She begins this herself by mentioning her 'dark road', and that she often cannot 'see the way before my guilty feet'. The idea is then continued, as her habitual air is likened to a 'veil', a word with overtones of death, as well as the recurrent idea of darkness, and she utters a 'suppressed' cry. Next, she is seen 'Covering her face', whereupon she 'shrank down'. This is a short extract, but within this little space we have found six references to darkness, covering or withdrawal from the light. Also within this short space, Lady Dedlock's habitual external manner is mentioned twice: as 'proud indifference' and as 'proud and disdainful'.

This, then, is an intense and effective characterisation; and of course it is taken from one of the most emotional scenes in the novel, when Esther and her mother meet and speak to each other, their relationship revealed. There is one further point to notice: we remember that when she is first introduced, Lady Dedlock is 'inscrutable' and depends on 'seeing herself in her glass, where indeed she looks so', that is, unrevealing. Dickens told us from the start that this is a false belief: all the servants and services know her weaknesses and foibles very well. Notice that the theme of a secret and hidden inner life, and an attempt to control the world by means of a fortified outside appearance, is still an insistent part of Lady Dedlock's characterisation as she is revealed to her daughter. Dickens seems to have altered his attitude, in fact. He no longer laughs at the energy she expends in maintaining her superior manner; now, he pities her. In short, Lady Dedlock has grown out of her shallow characterisation, and as she has done so she has become a vehicle for a more serious theme: the theme of shallow public appearances, unnatural manners and class pretentiousness. Dickens is now using this theme to ask some very different questions from those his laughter posed at the start. Now he asks: how can an individual escape from the prescribed shallowness, the artificial straitjacket, of society and social expectations? This development of theme is one of the outcomes of Dickens's characterisations, when grotesques grow into complexity and depth.

Sir Leicester is similarly redeemed from his laughable absurdities. Here is Dickens's comment, after Lady Dedlock's disappearance, when Sir Leicester declares that he is on 'unaltered' terms with her:

> His formal array of words might have at any other time, as it has
> often had, something ludicrous in it, but at this time it is serious and
> affecting. His noble earnestness, his fidelity, his gallant shielding of her,
> his generous conquest of his own wrong and his own pride for her sake,
> are simply honourable, manly, and true. Nothing less worthy can be seen
> through the lustre of such qualities in the commonest mechanic, nothing
> less worthy can be seen in the best-born gentleman. In such a light both
> aspire alike, both rise alike, both children of the dust shine equally.
>
> (*BH*, 828)

Sir Leicester still speaks in a pompous and formal style, but Dickens points out that his speech at this juncture is 'serious and affecting', not 'ludicrous'. The compliments from the author continue in an overwhelming wave of approval: 'noble ... fidelity ... gallant ... generous ... honourable ... manly ... true ... worthy ... lustre of such qualities ... shine'. There is no restraint in this language: Dickens is finding and stringing together the strongest expressions of value and approval he can frame. Finally, the author points out that the selfless qualities Sir Leicester shows at this crucial juncture in his story may exist without reference to class, whether shown by 'the best-born gentleman' or 'the commonest mechanic'. Calling these two supposed characters 'both children of the dust' who 'shine equally' incorporates a strong echo of the bible[4] into Dickens's comment. Sir Leicester has not only shown his positive human quality; what he demonstrates by his loyalty to his wife, is a high Christian virtue also.

Sir Leicester's case, then, may stand as another way in which a shallow, 'grotesque' character may grow in the course of their existence in one of Dickens's novels. We can suggest that some of the characters, who eventually reveal complexity and a more rounded personality, do so because they acquire Christian traits, in particular those of self-sacrifice and forgiveness. Here, we think of Sir Leicester's forgiveness of his wife, and his loyalty to her which is also a victory over his pride. In *Hard Times*, Gradgrind is similarly humanised by his remorse, and his consequent suffering, when he realises his former errors.

Concluding discussion

In this chapter, we have analysed samples of Dickens's characterisations, concentrating our attention on the ways in which the author conveys a 'person' to the reader. We began by sampling some of Dickens's shallow, caricatural figures, noticing certain recurring techniques. These include repetitive motifs such as Mrs. Sparsit's nose; metaphors subsequently becoming literal, such as naming Tom Gradgrind 'the whelp'; and exaggerated descriptions or speech, such as the bible-satire of Slackbridge's style. Many of these cardboard characters stay within their narrow confines to the end, and we raised some questions about Dickens's attitude towards these figures, many

---

[4] This is probably a reference to Psalm 103, verses 13 and 14: 'The LORD pitieth them that fear him; for he knoweth our frame; he remembreth that we are dust'.

of whom are satirised without mercy. Nonetheless, we noted that the background of each novel is populated with a wide range of vivid, single-feature and easily recognisable figures, so that their very simplicity gives the whole group a semblance of naturalism. By presenting the whole range, Dickens induces us to accept the exaggerated as a kind of reality. Furthermore, we noted that these caricatures, or 'grotesques', illustrate and develop Dickens's themes. So, in *Bleak House,* Skimpole and Boythorn work with Jarndyce to explore an appropriate response to a flawed society, while a number of figures populate the theme of the law, its practitioners and victims. Considering the crowded population of *Bleak House,* we also looked at Dickens's management of groups of characters, seeing how they are connected into one narrative.

In the second half of the chapter we have looked at several characters who are drawn in a more complex manner, that we have called a more 'rounded' characterisation. We noticed that Dickens maintains a mystery about Louisa's motives, and attributes potential to both her and her father, and we analysed how he handles Esther's first-person narrative using her awkward self-betrayals to portray her emotional state, despite her reticence. Our final analyses focused upon Stephen Blackpool from *Hard Times,* and the Dedlocks in *Bleak House.* These samples show further different means of characterisation employed by Dickens. We will return to discussion of Stephen within our discussion of the industrial theme in *Hard Times,* in Chapter 4 below. Here, we reached the suggestion that Dickens set himself a difficult challenge, and perhaps conceived of Stephen as a kind of literary and social experiment. With the Dedlocks, we found that Dickens uses an intensive style in each case: an intensive motif of darkness, hiding and theme of inner truth, versus external appearance, in the case of Lady Dedlock; and an intensive wave of admiration and approval, leading to echoes of the Bible, in Sir Leicester's case. In fact, we have found Dickens using a number of different techniques to portray his more rounded characters, often suiting his means to the particular moment, or to his own relationship with that character. The author's purpose in these characterisations, however, can be considered.

More interior or 'rounded' characterisation seems to arrive at the same time as integration with Dickens's ideals concerning compassion, self-sacrifice, endurance, suffering and a proto-Christian 'humanity'.

This calls on our sympathy equally for both the downtrodden victims of circumstances, as well as understanding for those who have been oppressors. Such a conclusion might indicate a dogmatic novel with a Christian 'message'. However, there are departures where the author maintains our hostility and where compassion is withheld – indeed, we are even urged to enjoy a character's downfall. For example, little sympathy is shown for Tulkinghorn or Krook: their motives remain dark and selfish to their ends. As we have seen, the comic entertainment provided by Skimpole becomes progressively less and less forgivable; Vholes is uniformly revolting, and there is no good excuse for the existence of the Smallweeds. In *Hard Times,* Dickens never forgives Bounderby, or Bitzer, who are apparently beyond redemption; and we enjoy the comedy of Mrs. Sparsit's desperate journey, laughing at her discomfiture.

This discussion, then, returns to a point we noticed in the previous chapter: that Dickens is an author who is unusually present on his own page, He not only keeps us company with his depiction of people and scenes, and his narrative voice, but he also exposes us to his opinions and emotions, urging us to adopt his attitudes because he is so constantly in our company. Who is so close to tears as Louisa and Gradgrind miss their opportunity to understand each other? Why, Dickens. Who feels no compunction for the Roman nose and bushy brows, as the rain falls and Louisa escapes? Hard-hearted Dickens. Who enumerates the faults of Sir Leicester Dedlock, but with an indulgent smile? Why, Dickens. Finally, who likens Sir Leicester to Christ in a shockingly overwritten paean of praise? Dickens, of course.

We have remarked previously that these novels are dramatic, or 'theatrical', in many ways. This 'theatrical' effect is partly due to the vivid use of scenery, the extraordinary variety and naturalness of dialogue, and the rhetorical style. However, at least half of the 'theatricality' of *Hard Times* and *Bleak House* lies in having the company of Dickens by our side all the time, like the literary incarnation of an impresario, or a master of ceremonies describing and controlling each performance.

One consequence of being in the author's company is that we are frequently made aware of his opinions: in these novels, the characters and their actions are judged for us and we are expected to concur in that judgement. It is worth pausing for a moment to consider the implications of this statement. What it amounts to is that Dickens's characters are sorted into the good and the bad, so that by the end of the novel they exist as two 'batches'. So, in the ending of *Bleak House*, George, Mrs. Rouncewell, Sir Leicester, Caddy, etc., are firmly ensconced among the 'good'; while the oddly interjected visit from Bucket with the Smallweeds, then from Guppy, his mother and his friend, are slightly squeaky plot devices that dispose of some unethical leftovers. There is even a valedictory paragraph putting Skimpole in his ('bad') place, which we have remarked seems out of character. It is hardly too strong to say that Dickens creates a form of paradise at the end of his novel, to be inhabited by the deserving, and a kind of hell of failure into which the rejected can fall.

Now consider some other nineteenth-century fictions: do any of them depend upon such explicit and simple calls for judgement of the moral qualities of the characters? For example, are we asked to make a judgement of the 'goodness' or 'wickedness' of Emily Brontë's Cathy? Even in the case of Heathcliff, the author is reticent about judgement and urges understanding. Does Thomas Hardy ask us to judge Tess or Angel Clare, or Wildeve or Captain Troy, however violent the passion of the one, and shallow the vanity of the other? In George Eliot's *Middlemarch*, surely Lydgate, Fred Vincy and even Nicholas Bulstrode present personalities far too complex to be subjected to a Dickensian simplicity of judgement.

Thinking about *Hard Times* and *Bleak House*, we can perhaps identify characters who present a problem stubborn enough to call a simple moral judgement into question. One such is Richard Carstone. Put briefly, we are asked to sympathise with Richard as a victim of Chancery, who is increasingly unable to free himself from the baleful influence of the Suit. Furthermore, Richard's death is described in shining language:

> A smile irradiated his face, as she bent to kiss him. He slowly laid his face down upon her bosom, drew his arms closer round her neck, and with one parting sob began the world. Not this world, O not this! The world that sets this right.
>
> (*BH*, 904)

In this passage the word 'irradiated' gives a foretaste of the mention of paradise: Richard is posed as a baby in Ada's maternal arms, and his death is sweetly silent. Dickens here acts the part of God, effectively giving Richard a place among the blessed. However, we can be excused if we have not completely forgotten the opportunities Richard has squandered and the heartaches he has caused, when every good influence has been brought to bear on his behalf. We may say that he has no excuse for leaving Ada a penniless widow. It is the dominating addiction to Chancery, then, that creates a more stubborn ethical problem in the case of Richard than with any of the other characters. On the other hand, we may be setting our judgement of Richard up against that of Dickens. Perhaps we should accept the man's death as a joyful escape from this vale of tears, as it is presented in the text?

The case of Richard, then, illustrates one of the difficulties we may have with an author such as Dickens, who sorts and judges his characters and allocates our judgements on our behalf. Put simply, we may disagree.

Here are some of the conclusions we can draw from our analysis of characterisation:

1. People, from caricatures to rounded psychological stories, populate these novels and provide a full range of moral and social comparisons.
2. Characteristics or 'motifs' dominate much characterisation, becoming 'real' in the same manner as do similes, so that we come to inhabit a world with a kind of vivid cardboard reality among its people as well as its places, events, practices and mores.
3. Our study of groups of people in *Bleak House* revealed how Dickens develops the centrality of Esther's consciousness by casting her into one-on-one dialogues, often on deeply personal topics, with people from different character-groups. We noticed, for example, that she has such dialogues with Caddy Jellyby and Mr. Guppy, as well as with those we would expect, such as Mr. Jarndyce, Ada and Richard.
4. However, the most surprising revelation was the role of Mr. Guppy, who, apparently by accident, happens to be present three times, and acts as a kind of coincidental glue, linking different character-groups in the early part of the novel. Mr. Guppy's

role in Chapters 4–10 alerted us to other characters who perform a similar linking function later on, for example Inspector Bucket and Allan Woodcourt.

5. Some characters within the central group become more rounded. They have a psychological story, and they can inadvertently reveal inner selves (e.g. Esther being busy).
6. However, the psychological stories are all relatively simple. Compare, for example, Louisa Gradgrind with Jane Eyre or Becky Sharp. In short, there is dramatic grandeur, but not subtlety or complexity in Dickens's more naturalistic mode of characterisation.
7. In Dickens's more natural or 'rounded' characterisations, revelation is often founded upon a tension between inside and outside. So, for example, the outside appearance and behaviour of the Dedlocks is peeled away by events later in the novel, which reveal previously hidden 'inner' personalities in both of them. Similarly, Esther's first-person narrative is revealing as it describes her efforts to hide her inner feelings, and maintain her external behaviour.

Methods of analysis

1. As described in Chapter 1, when approaching the extracts for detailed analysis.
2. Decide what kind of characterisation you are studying: is this a grotesque, or a psychologically rounded person? Consider what you are learning about the person, and ask whether it is internal or external.
3. Notice the character's motif; then identify the motif in later references to the character. This may be as obvious as Mrs. Sparsit's Roman nose, or it may be as natural as Esther's 'busy-ness'.
4. In addition: compare conclusions from close analysis, with your knowledge of the text, to identify and choose secondary and further passages to study, relevant to the character in whom you are interested.
5. In particular, identify an early appearance of the character you are studying, and find the last mention of them, to remind yourself of how they are disposed of at the end of the novel.

Suggested work

To enlarge upon this chapter's focus and develop your insight into Dickens's characterisation, study further relevant episodes, such as:

In *Hard Times,* study:

- The passage between page 33 para. 5, beginning 'Before Mr. Bounderby could reply ... ' as far as page 34, line 2 up, ' "... missing his tip," Mr. E. W. B. Childers answered.' Here we meet two caricatures in comic contrast to Gradgrind and Bounderby. Bear in mind that these latter characters are still grotesques at this point.
- The passage between page 261, para. 4, 'They all three went in ... ' and page 263, where Tom says to Louisa, "Not you. I don't want to have anything to say to you!" This passage provides a direct parallel to the father-daughter interview analysed above. Consider how Dickens provides direct means of measurement of Tom against Louisa, both disillusioned about their upbringing, and of Gradgrind's moral progress, in the comparison between the two scenes.

In *Bleak House,* study:

- Page 208, from line 1, 'Just then, there appeared from a side-door, old Mr. Turveydrop, in the full lustre of his Deportment,' as far as page 209, line 5 up, ' ... looked up to him with veneration on the old imaginary pinnacle'. This passage introduces a grotesque who is and remains morally ambivalent. Study the standard features of Dickens's characterisation of a grotesque, found in this passage.
- Page 856, from the beginning of para. 3, 'We sat down to dinner ... ' and as far as the end of page 857, ' ... always liked him, and – and so forth'. This passage is rich in more natural psychology, blending the consistent theme of the Chancery suit with the sympathetic characterisation of Richard as well as Esther's own suppressed love. Consider Dickens's handling of the scene: how complete is the characterisation of Richard at this point, not long before his death?

3

Characterisation (2): Women

This chapter looks at Dickens's female characters, in an attempt to distinguish between characterisation that uses gender-specific language or stereotypes, and the more general picture of women as part of each novel's population. As soon as we think about the female populations of *Hard Times* and *Bleak House*, we may start considering three groups. First, many of the women are filled with vanity, jealousy, spite, greed, ignorance and foolishness. Then, in stark contrast, there are good women such as Mrs. Bagnet and Mrs. Rouncewell, or Louisa Gradgrind/Bounderby. Finally, there are angelic women of infinite loyalty, love and patience, the obvious examples being Ada in *Bleak House*, and Rachael in *Hard Times* (as well as Sissy Jupe, who plays an active role in the final chapters). It is with these paragons, therefore, that we begin our investigation.

Angelic women: Rachael, Ada, Sissy

Here is the scene when Stephen returns home to find Rachael looking after his sick and drunken wife:

> From the outside of his home he gloomily passed to the inside, with suspended breath and with a slow footstep. He went up to his door, opened it, and so into the room.
>
> Quiet and peace were there. Rachael was there, sitting by the bed.
>
> She turned her head, and the light of her face shone in upon the midnight of his mind. She sat by the bed, watching and tending his wife.

75

That is to say, he saw that some one lay there, and he knew too well it must be she; but Rachael's hands had put a curtain up, so that she was screened from his eyes. Her disgraceful garments were removed, and some of Rachael's were in the room. Everything was in its place and order as he had always kept it, the little fire was newly trimmed, and the hearth was freshly swept. It appeared to him that he saw all this in Rachael's face, and looked at nothing besides. While looking at it, it was shut out from his view by the softened tears that filled his eyes; but not before he had seen how earnestly she looked at him, and how her own eyes were filled too.

She turned again towards the bed, and satisfying herself that all was quiet there, spoke in a low, calm, cheerful voice.

'I am glad you have come at last, Stephen. You are very late.'

'I ha' been walking up an' down.'

'I thought so. But 'tis too bad a night for that. The rain falls very heavy, and the wind has risen.'

The wind? True. It was blowing hard. Hark to the thundering in the chimney, and the surging noise! To have been out in such a wind, and not to have known it was blowing!

'I have been here once before, to-day, Stephen. Landlady came round for me at dinner-time. There was some one here that needed looking to, she said. And 'deed she was right. All wandering and lost, Stephen. Wounded too, and bruised.'

He slowly moved to a chair and sat down, drooping his head before her.

'I came to do what little I could, Stephen; first, for that she worked with me when we were girls both, and for that you courted her and married her when I was her friend – '

He laid his furrowed forehead on his hand, with a low groan.

'And next, for that I know your heart, and am right sure and certain that 'tis far too merciful to let her die, or even so much as suffer, for want of aid. Thou knowest who said, "Let him who is without sin among you cast the first stone at her!" There have been plenty to do that. Thou art not the man to cast the last stone, Stephen, when she is brought so low.'

'O Rachael, Rachael!'

(*HT*, 81–82)

The scene opens by underlining Stephen's reluctance to face his wife: he enters the house 'gloomily' and the room 'with suspended breath and with a slow footstep', which sets up the contrast Rachael's presence effects. What are the qualities Rachael displays in this scene?

Dickens uses a three-part sentence, delaying and anticipating her effect, and two short, largely monosyllabic sentences linked by the parallelism ' ... were there ... was there' to emphasise that 'Quiet and peace' are attributes of Rachael. The next touch takes the exaltation of Rachael further, when 'the light of her face' is said to have 'shone in upon the midnight of his mind'. Both of them find their eyes filled with tears during the next paragraph, but we must also notice the veins of language that accompany Rachael. She is 'watching' and 'tending' his wife, and Stephen cries 'softened' tears while she regards him 'earnestly'. So far the passage emphasises sympathy and shared sorrow. At the same time, the foul wife is 'screened', the 'disgraceful garments' have been 'removed', and 'Everything was in its place and order', 'trimmed' and 'swept'. When Rachael speaks, her voice is 'low, calm, cheerful'.

We have not yet catalogued the full range of qualities Rachael brings into Stephen's lodging, but it is worth pausing at this point to summarise. There seem to be three strands: first, Rachael brings 'Quiet and peace', her voice is 'low' and 'calm', and she brings order. This 'everything ... in its place' includes a housewife's tidying and cleaning duties: trimming the fire and sweeping the hearth. Second, Rachael puts the ugliness away: the dirty clothes and the dirty woman are 'removed' and 'screened' so that Stephen is protected from the sight of them. Finally, the light of Rachael's face has the ability to shine, lighting up the 'midnight' in Stephen's mind. Their mutual sympathy and suffering is part of this effect, as she looks at him 'earnestly' and her eyes fill with tears. Thus far, then, Rachael has hidden the most upsetting sights, been a good housewife, brought 'quiet and peace' and in these ways, she has 'shone' into Stephen's mind. What will this influential woman do next?

The second half of our extract begins with an equivocal statement, where Rachael remarks that he has come 'at last' but is 'very late'. Dickens does not seem to think this is a reproach, although a lot of men in Stephen's position might. The moment passes, however, as they discuss the weather. Then begins Rachael's homily, which is in three parts, interrupted by Stephen sitting down, then laying his head down and groaning, and finally exclaiming 'O Rachael, Rachael!' First, she says that this is her second visit to care for his wife, and emphasises how helpless the woman was, 'wandering ...

lost ... injured ... bruised'. Stephen sits down. Rachael then gives two reasons for helping: first, that they had once worked together, and second that they were friends when Stephen married her. Stephen lays his head down and groans. Finally, Rachael gives what she calls her third reason for helping the sick woman. This is, that she knows Stephen would never leave his wife to die or suffer, without trying to help her. In support of this theory, Rachael quotes the scripture: 'Let him who is without sin among you cast the first stone at her!' and asserts that Stephen is too merciful to cast the last stone at his wife.

This is an interesting final cause of Rachael's intervention, for several reasons. First, we reflect that Stephen has shown no sign that he can cope with his wife's reappearance on his own. He went out, and stayed out; he asked Bounderby for help and advice; he has avoided the problem, needing Rachael's interference to help him both by tidying up his lodging and by shining on him with her face. Second, Stephen's physical movements suggest that Rachael's speech does act as a reproach, which makes Stephen feel ashamed as he sat 'drooping his head before her'. His low groan may be no more than the memory of courting and marrying the wrong woman; but when he bursts out 'O Rachael, Rachael!' we are free to suppose that the homily has struck home, and that Stephen has learned a lesson. If you now read further in the same scene (see *HT*, 82) you will find even more self-sacrificing virtues proceeding from Rachael, and further examples where Stephen cannot cope with the 'horror' of his wife.

Hard Times's final account of Rachael completes her characterisation as a perfect woman. She has 'a pensive beauty', is 'sweet-tempered', 'serene' and 'cheerful'. She is the only person to have 'compassion' upon Stephen's widow, and she is 'working, always working', as if this is 'her natural lot, until she should be too old to labour any more' (all from *HT*, 273). Here are Rachael's qualities again. 'Pensive' and the other adjectives remind us of the quiet manner she shows throughout the novel; her 'compassion' for the broken-down drunkard is continuing proof of her Christian selflessness; and she works, doing her duty until unable to carry on. Her association with light is also emphasised in *Hard Times*'s final scenes, for Stephen talks of the star he could see from the bottom of the pit, which made him think of Rachael, and which Dickens tells us 'had shown him where to find ... God' (*HT*, 253) as he dies.

In these extracts, then, we have found that Rachael has acted as a combination of a good housewife, a spiritual instructor and example, and an influence of peace associated with shining light. It is now time to turn to our other paragon, Ada Clare. In the following extract, Ada explains her devotion to Richard:

'When I married Richard I was not insensible to what was before him. I had been perfectly happy for a long time with you, and I had never known any trouble or anxiety, so loved and cared for, but I understood the danger he was in, dear Esther.'

'I know, I know, my darling.'

'When we were married I had some little hope that I might be able to convince him of his mistake, that he might come to regard it in a new way as my husband and not pursue it all the more desperately for my sake – as he does. But if I had not had that hope, I would have married him just the same, Esther. Just the same!'

In the momentary firmness of the hand that was never still – a firmness inspired by the utterance of these last words, and dying away with them – I saw the confirmation of her earnest tones.

'You are not to think, my dearest Esther, that I fail to see what you see and fear what you fear. No one can understand him better than I do. The greatest wisdom that ever lived in the world could scarcely know Richard better than my love does.'

She spoke so modestly and softly and her trembling hand expressed such agitation as it moved to and fro upon the silent notes! My dear, dear girl!

'I see him at his worst every day. I watch him in his sleep. I know every change of his face. But when I married Richard I was quite determined, Esther, if heaven would help me, never to show him that I grieved for what he did and so to make him more unhappy. I want him, when he comes home, to find no trouble in my face. I want him, when he looks at me, to see what he loved in me. I married him to do this, and this supports me.'

I felt her trembling more. I waited for what was yet to come, and I now thought I began to know what it was.

'And something else supports me, Esther.'

She stopped a minute. Stopped speaking only; her hand was still in motion.

'I look forward a little while, and I don't know what great aid may come to me. When Richard turns his eyes upon me then, there may be something lying on my breast more eloquent than I have been, with greater power than mine to show him his true course and win him back.'

Her hand stopped now. She clasped me in her arms, and I clasped her in mine.

'If that little creature should fail too, Esther, I still look forward. I look forward a long while, through years and years, and think that then, when I am growing old, or when I am dead perhaps, a beautiful woman, his daughter, happily married, may be proud of him and a blessing to him. Or that a generous brave man, as handsome as he used to be, as hopeful, and far more happy, may walk in the sunshine with him, honouring his grey head and saying to himself, "I thank God this is my father! Ruined by a fatal inheritance, and restored through me!"'

Oh, my sweet girl, what a heart was that which beat so fast against me!

(*BH*, 858–859)

In this scene, Ada tells Esther that she is pregnant. Richard has just been prevailed upon to take an evening walk with Allan Woodcourt, and the two women are left alone, sitting together at the piano on which Ada has just been playing. It is a moody and sentimental setting, directly following a depressing meal with Mr. Vholes, when Esther has observed the decline in Richard's mental and physical condition.

We have met Rachael and noted what she does for Stephen: she presides over his home, bringing peace and quiet, and order. Ada takes this female virtue further: when Richard comes home, she manufactures his surroundings, including her own behaviour, so as to become what she imagines Richard wants. When he comes home, he is 'to find no trouble in my face' and 'to see what he loved in me'. Above all, she will never show him 'that I grieved for what he did and so to make him more unhappy'. In the case of Stephen Blackpool, the insoluble problem of his life is present in his home; and Rachael does more than bring domestic peace and quiet, for she tells Stephen how to behave, bringing advice derived from scripture. In Richard's case, on the contrary, the Chancery suit is outside his home. He has brought it home in the person of Vholes, and brings it home in the form of his own obsession. Ada hides her distress, and appears loving, cheerful and above all, uncritical. We hear that Ada was always 'quite determined' to do this, because she 'married him to do this'; and she insists that she was well aware of the problem, and the danger of Richard continuing on his destructive course, when she married him.

She had some 'little hope' that being married might change him; but unfortunately marriage has had the opposite effect, for he pursues the suit 'all the more desperately for my sake'. Now that she is pregnant, Ada hopes that the baby may be 'more eloquent than I have been, with greater power than mine to show him his true course'. Ada has failed, and she hopes the baby may succeed; but what if that does not happen? What if, with a wife and a child, Richard still pursues his disastrous course? In her final confession to Esther, Ada shows her determination: however obstinate Richard's obsession proves, she will 'look forward' (she uses this phrase three times). She imagines Richard as an old man, cared for and honoured by a grown-up daughter or son.

We can question whether Ada's devotion is either sensible, an honest treatment of Richard, or morally sound; and it is likely that most modern readers will feel at least some uneasiness at her suppression of all criticism and her pretence of carefree love. Ada herself, however, calls for God's aid, 'if heaven would help me', seeming in no doubt that the Almighty will approve her strategy; and Esther exclaims admiringly 'what a heart was that which beat so fast against me!' while Ada explains that absolute support for her wrong-headed and financially catastrophic husband, is her virtuous duty.

So far we have picked out Ada's determination, her insistence that she has always known what she is doing, and her perseverance in looking 'forward', all of which are signs of strength. At the same time, this passage adds some details of Ada that are softer, or we might say, more 'feminine'. So, for example, Ada's hand shows only a 'momentary firmness' when she declares her devotion to Richard, a firmness 'dying away' with her words. Otherwise, her hand is 'never still' hovering over the keyboard. Then, Esther describes Ada's voice as 'She spoke so modestly and softly' (we remember that Rachael's tone is 'low' and 'calm') while her hand is 'trembling' with 'agitation', before Esther 'felt her trembling more', and mentions that her hand still moves above the keys without touching them. Eventually, the two women embrace each other for Ada's final speech. So, Dickens emphasises Ada's trembling and her agitated movements, while at the same time she declares her strength and purpose. We can suppose that Dickens creates this strength-and-weakness contrast to depict an admirable woman. Maintaining a pretence of cheerfulness to her husband requires an almost superhuman emotional strength, and this is even more emphatically drawn in contrast to her 'feminine' physical weakness.

These two extracts show Rachael from *Hard Times* and Ada from *Bleak House*, two women who are presented as paragons of self-sacrifice and a high, even spiritual morality. In both extracts there are references to heaven, with the clear implication that these women are angelic examples of goodness. We will consider this kind of feminine perfection, and the troubling questions it raises, later in this chapter, but first we will look at a paragraph from *Hard Times*, in which Sissy Jupe's goodness defeats all the wiles of the sophisticated Harthouse:

> Mr. Harthouse drew a long breath; and, if ever man found himself in the position of not knowing what to say, made the discovery beyond all question that he was so circumstanced. The child-like ingenuousness with which his visitor spoke, her modest fearlessness, her truthfulness which put all artifice aside, her entire forgetfulness of herself in her earnest quiet holding to the object with which she had come; all this, together with her reliance on his easily given promise – which in itself shamed him – presented something in which he was so inexperienced, and against which he knew any of his usual weapons would fall so powerless; that not a word could he rally to his relief.
>
> (*HT*, 214–215)

In the two extracts we have studied in this chapter so far, we have found that Rachael's dedicated work on behalf of Stephen and his wife is effective, but can only succeed to a limited extent: she brings comfort and calm to his home, instructs him in his duty, and nurses the foul and sick woman, his wife. Rachael cannot make divorce possible, however, and she suppresses her own feelings while nursing her rival. Ada, like Rachael, hides her own desires beneath a pretence of cheerfulness, in order to bring Richard relief from unhappiness. Ada's self-sacrifice, her absolute love that always puts Richard first, does not achieve what she hoped it would, which was 'to convince him of his mistake'.

In Sissy Jupe we meet another good woman, but on this occasion the battle between virtue and vice ends with a decisive victory for the good. Dickens spells it out for us: Sissy employs 'child-like ingenuousness', 'modest fearlessness', 'truthfulness' and a complete absence of 'artifice'. Then, she behaves, as do Rachael and Ada, with 'entire forgetfulness of herself' and maintains her 'earnest quiet holding to the object' of her visit, so that Harthouse is unable to divert her. Finally, he is trapped by his own promise, which 'shamed him' because he had never intended to keep it. Dickens introduces the metaphor of battle with mention of 'his usual weapons' which are powerless against Sissy. Harthouse, then, fights with his usual amused cynicism and immoral witticisms; but we are told that Sissy 'presented something' Harthouse could not withstand. What that 'something' is we already know: it is the combination of qualities already described, which could be said to constitute a 'something' called goodness, or virtue, which in this scene exercises a decisive power over vice. A large element of this victorious quality consists of honesty, referred to as Sissy's 'ingenuousness' and 'truthfulness'. The other dominant idea is Sissy's 'entire forgetfulness of herself', which matches the self-abnegation we have found in both our angelic females.

It may be helpful to summarise what these female characters demonstrate, in order to define the ideal of femininity Dickens holds up for our scrutiny. Here is an attempt to describe the angels of *Bleak House* and *Hard Times*.

1. All three suppress or sacrifice themselves so their behaviour is completely altruistic. There is no self-interest at all. Rachael nurtures Stephen and his wife; Ada nurtures Richard; and Sissy acts on behalf of Louisa.
2. All three are superior to the men in question. Sissy obtains the most obvious victory for femininity over the masculine wiles and vices of Harthouse. Rachael's superiority is shown when she copes with the return of Stephen's wife more courageously, and with more compassion, than does Stephen. Ada puts Richard first, while he thinks of nothing but the Chancery suit. The moral seems to be that men need support and direction from these angelic women, in order to help them bear the hardships of their

lives. In the cases of both Stephen and Harthouse, the women act as guarantors of a higher, more virtuous behaviour than the men would achieve on their own.

3. All three demonstrate qualities that bring order to the man's life. Even Sissy, who has no interest in Harthouse's domestic arrangements, shows a 'child-like' and 'modest' manner with an 'earnest voice (though so quiet)', bringing order when she visits. Rachael, as we have remarked, is a housewife who trims, tidies and sweeps, and who hides unpleasant sights from her man. She also speaks 'low' and 'calm'. Ada speaks 'modestly and softly' and Dickens again uses the word 'earnest' for her manner. Ada also has restless hands, and she trembles.

It is clear that these women represent an ideal. Dickens proposes a picture of virtue that is supposed to be specifically feminine, when he highlights self-sacrifice, absolute devotion and calm determination. Furthermore, Dickens does not hide what he is doing: his angelic women are praised, are held up as paragons for the reader's approval, and no male character comes near to them.[1] All three are quietly spoken: but we should be careful not to assume that Dickens gives them all the same stereotypical qualities. So, for example, Ada is the only one who trembles; Sissy and Rachael are both physically strong.

Studying Dickens's angels has raised some troubling questions, which can be divided into two kinds. First, there are questions about Dickens's misogyny: did he really expect women to provide such almost miraculous spiritual guidance or Christian example? Is this really Dickens's ideal of femininity – suffering, self-denial and devotion? And, is it *because they are women* that these characters can attain such virtuous heights? These questions explore our reactions to gender as it is portrayed in *Hard Times* and *Bleak House*. Second, another group of questions concern the ethics revealed by these idealised characterisations: male or female, is it right and sensible to hide your feelings from your partner in life? Should you not rather try to save his life and your marriage?

---

[1] With the possible temporary exception of Allan Woodcourt saving lives when shipwrecked. However, Dr. Woodcourt's heroics happen offstage and are reported briefly. Otherwise, he seems to exist in the background of *Bleak House* as a shadowy figure rather than a hero.

Both Rachael's and Sissy's episodes raise similar questions about marital breakdown, a subject Dickens is not shy of discussing openly in Chapter XI (*HT*, 69–75). Both the marriages involved – Stephen's to his drunken wife, Louisa's to Bounderby – are irretrievable. We will discuss such problematic issues more fully later in the present chapter. Before we do so, however, we should take Dickens's depiction of women into account, in a more generalised and wider-ranging form.

The female populations of *Hard Times* and *Bleak House*

Rather than selecting specific passages for analysis, this discussion will survey the range of other women who appear in *Hard Times* and *Bleak House*. Of the former, there are very few: Mrs. Gradgrind is treated very briefly and as a background figure; Bounderby's mother, Mrs. Pegler, is predominantly used to sustain the mystery of his boasting, and to lead up to his unmasking; and there is Mrs. Sparsit who merits some further discussion as her vanity and her jealous spite against Louisa can be considered as 'gender-specific' faults. Aside from these three, there are Louisa herself, the brief appearance of her sister Jane, and Sissy Jupe and Rachael, who have already been discussed.

Mrs. Gradgrind remains a caricature as 'little, thin, white, pink-eyed' and 'of surpassing feebleness, mental and bodily' (*HT*, 20). Her stupidity, ignorance and hypochondria are her consistent character motifs until the scene of her death, when she declares that she had something to say, but cannot recover whatever it was. Mrs. Pegler, on the other hand, is provided with a detailed physical description, but her character consists of little more than the pride she takes in her bully of a son. Louisa, victim of her father's system, and suffering from her fatal attraction to Harthouse, falls into a faint imploring Gradgrind to save her. Mrs. Sparsit nurses her spiteful jealousy, lives upon her boast of 'high connections' and ends in a sordid old age shared with Lady Scadgers. In *Hard Times*, she acts as the comic foil to the selfish hypocrite Bounderby. Her qualities, including her ridiculous vanity and touchiness concerning nose and eyebrows, present several aspects of a feminine stereotype: jealousy, vindictive vengefulness, ridiculous vanity, snobbishness.

If we consider this group of women as a whole, it is clear that Dickens employs a range of different ways of writing about women. Mrs. Sparsit and Mrs. Gradgrind only ever speak to earn the reader's ridicule, and their comedy owes a lot to gender-clichés about snobs, female hypochondria, false vanities and so on; Rachael and Sissy always speak, and act, to earn the reader's admiration. Louisa, unable to bear the conflict between lust and virtue, faints like a 'typical woman' and begs her patriarch to save her. On the other hand, Sissy takes on a man – and one from a higher class, to boot – and shows herself to be the stronger. Stronger, however, in her gendered, feminine way: in her 'truthfulness', 'honesty' and quiet determination. We can conclude, then, that there is a variety of women and Dickens provides them with a variety of circumstances and qualities; but he repeatedly dips into the bucketfuls of gender stereotypes left over from tradition and cliché, whenever he wishes to use such gender-shorthand for his angels or his comic stupid women.

The female population of *Bleak House* is extensive, as is to be expected in such a huge novel with so many interlocking lines of plot, and we do not have the space for a detailed assessment of each character. When you are faced with such a varied and complex topic, and it is difficult to hold the entirety in your mind, it can be helpful to break the subject down into categories. In this case, the categories are quite obvious. We can list all the dreadful women, then, all those good women who are also caricatures or eccentric, and finally, there are the actual or near angels. Here are the groups:

1. *Dreadful women*: Miss Barbary, Mrs. Jellyby, Mrs. Snagsby, Mrs. Rachael/Chadband, Mrs. Woodcourt, Judy Smallweed and Grandmother Smallweed, Mrs. Guppy, Mrs. Pardiggle, Mlle. Hortense.
2. *Good women who are caricatures or eccentric*: Guster, Miss Flite, Jenny and Liz (Brickmakers' wives), Mrs. Piper, Mrs. Perkins, Volumnia, Rosa, Caddy Jellyby, Charley, Mrs. Rouncewell, Mrs. Bagnet.
3. *Angels*: Ada Clare/Carstone, Esther Summerson.

Lady Dedlock is the only woman who does not fit comfortably within any of these categories. As we remarked in Chapter 2, she develops from being an object of satire for her 'fashionable' vanities, to attracting our sympathy and pity both when we learn her secret, and as we watch her long duel with Tulkinghorn.

The group we have called 'dreadful women' can be further subdivided, because their dreadfulness veers towards either cruelty or stupidity. So, Mlle. Hortense, Miss Barbary, Mrs. Snagsby, Mrs. Chadband, Judy Smallweed and even Mrs. Woodcourt are all capable of being vicious and hurtful; while Mrs. Jellyby, Mrs. Pardiggle and Mrs. Guppy are stupid, and Grandmother Smallweed is demented. This said, we could see cruelty in the Jellyby and Pardiggle forms of foolishness, because their families, particularly the children, suffer. Thinking about the group we have called 'good women', we are faced with a wide variety of extreme types, from Miss Flite and her birds, who is almost an allegorical or symbolic figure; to the sentimentally evoked victims of violent husbands, Jenny and Liz; to natural figures such as Rosa or the gossips Mrs. Piper and Mrs. Perkins; to Caddy and Charley who provide detail and variety in Esther's life; and finally to the dominant matriarch Mrs. Bagnet, her husband's 'old girl'.

Together with the two 'angels' and Lady Dedlock, this makes a bewilderingly varied group. How far are we justified in seeing gender stereotypes in the way Dickens portrays these characters? Or, is this female population a confection made from the author's misogyny? Here we are faced with a more complicated task than in *Hard Times*. We could certainly argue that Dickens is even-handed when it comes to attributing wickedness or stupidity between the sexes: for every Judy Smallweed, there is a Small; for every Mrs. Chadband there is a Mr. Chadband; and so on through the large population and many events of the text. The peculiarities of speech are also allotted equally to both men and women: Miss Flite's 've-ry honored' is no more necessarily feminine than Mr. Bucket's 'You know me and I know you' is masculine. Then, the characterisations of Mrs. Jellyby and Mrs. Pardiggle can be read as a satire on the limited roles society makes available to women: they could become charitable, but other forms of work were not open to them. When it appears that female roles are (or are supposed to be – see Mrs. Jellyby) those of nurturing, or of victims, we can argue that nothing else was possible in a novel of the time. Indeed, we can point out that Dickens was brave to have sympathised with the 'fallen' woman Lady Dedlock, treating her as a tragic heroine and casting the illegitimate Esther as his protagonist. According to these arguments, Dickens has done enough: no reader could be expected to believe in a modern, emancipated woman, set within a society that so restricted her actions and so prescribed her attitudes.

There are two points that weigh against such a conclusion and suggest that the situation is a great deal more complicated. First, we must remember our analyses of the angels: Rachael and her influence over Stephen; Ada and her devotion to Richard. To this we can add the scene where Esther rejects Allan Woodcourt's proposal; and bring to mind her coyness when Woodcourt's mother visits.[2] The angels, their virtues and willingness to sacrifice their own interests, are depicted as perfect and ideal: Ada and Rachael, and to a lesser extent Sissy and Esther, represent an ideal of femininity that is extremely sentimental, and overarched by a Christian pseudo-biblical rhetoric that is hard to defend from the charge of bad taste.

The second point on which Dickens is vulnerable to the accusation of gender-stereotyping derives from perhaps the boldest decision he made when planning *Bleak House*: his decision to tell half of the story in Esther's first-person narrative. How successfully does Dickens carry off this ambitious plan? Rereading the final paragraph of the novel is instructive:

> I did not know that [that I was prettier than ever]. I am not certain that I know it now. But I know that my dearest little pets are very pretty, and that my darling is very beautiful, and that my husband is very handsome, and that my guardian has the brightest and most benevolent face that ever was seen, and that they can very well do without much beauty in me—even supposing ....
>
> (*BH*, 914)

The subject matter is stereotypically feminine, of course: Esther is worrying about how pretty she is. What is more, the coyness, or 'arch' manner with which she signs off 'even supposing—' can strike the reader as rather sickly. Then, 'pets', 'darling', 'very pretty', 'very

---

[2] See the analysis of this scene in Chapter 2.

beautiful', 'handsome', 'brightest and most benevolent': the paragraph is in danger of having too sugary a taste. Several critics accuse
Esther of recording her shy humility too often, and of harping on
other characters' compliments to her too frequently. In their view she
is guilty of the indirect boast, and of really being smug, not humble
at all. Such a reading may make the mistake of treating her as a real
person, however, when she is actually a character in a book. A different reading sees her repeated self-deprecations as necessary, because
they are Dickens's way of characterising her as truly shy and humble.

Thinking about Esther's narrative as a whole, we may then take
note of her jolly jangling bunch of housekeeping keys, and her happy
housewifely nicknames of Dame Durden, little woman, and such-
like. The suggestion is that Dickens has created the first-person narrative of a woman whose mind works as a man would like it to work;
who thinks as a man imagines she must think. Esther is charming,
shy and a little bit twee, right up to the final paragraph; but there is
no doubt that she was created by a man.

Concluding discussion

We are not able to settle the whole question of gender-representation
in *Hard Times* and *Bleak House*, then. There remain some arguments
on each side. Here are some of the more reliable conclusions that can
be drawn:

1. **Domestic virtues:** devotion to husband and children, and nur-
    turing and holding together the family are seen to be the duties
    of a woman. Mrs. Bagnet in particular exemplifies this quality:
    she saves her family, while at the opposite pole, Mrs. Jellyby, by
    ignoring her domestic duties, destroys her family. The Gradgrind
    family in *Hard Times* ironically comes to rely upon Sissy Jupe
    for their cohesion and domestic order, while Rachael tidies and
    sweeps for Stephen, and insists on his relationship to his wife.
    There are several examples in the two novels, where a woman's
    domestic virtue and her domestic insight are superior to a man's.
    In this chapter, we have met this in Stephen and in Richard
    Carstone. It is also broadly lampooned in Mr. and Mrs. Bagnet.

On the other hand, there are men who, variously, nurture and ignore their family duties – men such as Mr. Jarndyce and Mr. Skimpole, for example. Furthermore, one of the most cohesive families in either novel is the Smallweed family: hardly an example of female domestic virtues!

2. **Female angels:** Dickens's presentation of a feminine 'ideal' appears sentimentally immature when read in the context of present-day attitudes: even those with no 'feminism' will scarcely believe the ladling on of sugar of which Dickens was guilty when he indulged in characters such as Rachael and Sissy in *Hard Times* or Ada, Caddy Jellyby and sometimes Esther herself, in *Bleak House*. In particular, the aura or halo of quasi-divinity with which these characters shine, and which enables them to spread a Christian influence in their path, is hard for the modern reader to accept, even when our eyes prick with sentimental tears at a death scene, due to Dickens's skill with the rhythms of the language.

3. We have discussed a variety of **other gender stereotypes** as they appear among the female populations of these novels. Fashion, vanity, jealousy, spite, hypochondria, foolishness, long-suffering victim-hood: all of these and more are depicted, and we have remarked that Dickens does not hesitate to draw upon the stereotyping tradition for features and details about the women he presents. However, we should also remember that many of the male characters are masculine stereotypes as well: Dickens is equally happy to draw upon traditional types for his masculine characters. See, for example, Mr. Bagnet, Guppy or the two drunken brick-makers with their mixture of aggression and slight embarrassment. Perhaps, rather than seeking a consistent answer about the author's attitudes towards gender, we should return to our discussion of grotesques in the last chapter. Just as we commented that a wide variety of one-dimensional caricatures creates a kind of naturalism when conveyed as a whole; so an equally varied plenty of gender stereotypes provides us with an illusion of humanity when mingled all together.

4. Awkward questions remain, in addition to the gender typing we have commented on in 1 and 2 above. If we actively compare different episodes and plot lines with each other, we may often find ourselves questioning the guidance our ever-present author

provides. So, for example: why is Mrs. Jellyby's obsession with
Borrioboola-Gha a matter for broad farce and the satire of absurdity, as well as explicit condemnation, while Richard Carstone
equally obsessively destroys his own marriage and his life, but is
treated with melancholy indulgence? Indeed, Richard has made
such an utter mess of his life on earth, that he has to be given a
second chance to 'start the world' in Heaven. Here we must stop:
we have already wondered whether Ada's pretence of cheerfulness
is honest, or sensible. Thinking about the rights and wrongs of
that household only leads us in circles.

Methods of analysis

1. As in previous chapters when undertaking **detailed analysis of
   the text;** but with a particular focus upon gendered text, including choices of simile and metaphor, as well as the diction (choice
   of adjectives, verbs, adverbs) that carries connotations of gender
   stereotypes.
2. Distinguishing **gender assumptions** from **non-stereotyped
   content.**
3. **Thinking about the text:** this is particularly difficult when studying Dickens, because his novels are generally so big, and contain multiple groups of characters and interlocking plot lines.
   However, there is no substitute for framing and asking yourself a
   series of systematic questions and attempting to answer them in
   your head. When specifically looking at the characterisation of
   women, as we have been doing in this chapter, we have considered the female populations of the novels we are studying. Two
   methods have helped:
   a. With *Bleak House* we broke the varied and large group of
      characters down into three smaller groups (dreadful women,
      good women, angels), then broke 'dreadful women' into two
      (dreadful and cruel; dreadful and stupid). This helped us to
      think about them more confidently. It also highlighted how
      truly exceptional is the characterisation of Lady Dedlock.
   b. Asking systematic questions.
      i. If Dickens uses feminine stereotypes, does he also use
         masculine ones?

ii. If Dickens presents idealised feminine angels, does he also present stupid and vain stereotypes?

c. These and other such questions are quite simple to frame. Answering them, however, is difficult, and forces you to think about the text in some detail and in a critical manner.

4. When studying one female character in particular, consider the female character you are studying, within the novel's character-group or population:

a. as one of the whole population, and

b. as one of the population of women.

Suggested work

In **Hard Times,** study page 210, where Louisa confesses her faults to Sissy as the two women reach a crescendo of sympathy and forgiveness until Louisa lays her head on Sissy's 'loving heart': 'O lay it here ... Lay it here, my dear!' Consider the elements of the conventionally feminine that appear here, displayed by both the young women.

In **Bleak House,** study the way in which Caddy Jellyby is presented on page 344 (from '"Prince has a pupil over the way ... "') to page 346 ' ... we went to Newman Street direct'. In this extract a slavish devotion to Mr. Turveydrop's unreasonable demands, and Prince's inability to confront them, are both treated with indulgent archness, as comic subjects (which they are not). When you have analysed Caddy in this passage, look for further passages in which she figures, including the final settlement on page 912, when we learn of Prince's lameness, and Caddy supporting the entire household.

Thinking about both texts: Sit down with a blank notepad, and try to construct lists in answer to the following questions:

1. What occasions can you find when men depend on women for their greater virtue?

2. What occasions can you find when men depend on women for their greater intelligence?

3. What occasions can you find when men appear effeminate?

4. How many occasions can you think of when a man uses patriarchal authority? Is it used wisely or not? What is the outcome?

There are many other such questions, most obviously the above, but turned around (e.g. 'What occasions can you find when women depend on men for their greater virtue?' etc.). Additionally, it will be useful if you frame at least two of your own questions, and make your own notes and lists, in order to practise thinking about the character groups for yourself.

4

Morality and Society

This chapter focuses on Dickens's portrayal of English society, which means that we will consider a wide variety of issues. These will include fashion, the law, industry, class, politics and economics. We will consider how these issues are played out by a wide variety of people, each with their own personal morality and placed into controversial circumstances. We will also look for the characters' own attempts to understand their predicament in society and the world, with Dickens's use of simple statements such as Jo the crossing sweeper's 'He was wery good to me' and 'I don't know nothink'. Our aim, having examined the society Dickens depicts, is to define the moral response the author gives to the social and political evils he describes.

At the same time, we will take the opportunity to pursue a question raised in Chapter 1, where we looked at the introductory diatribes with which both of these novels begin. In *Hard Times* Dickens set himself to expose and oppose Utilitarianism, and in *Bleak House* he begins with a withering attack on the Court of Chancery. We know that the 'factual' upbringing of Louisa and Tom leads to disaster for both of them, and that the Court of Chancery leads to Richard's decline and death. However, we still take this opportunity to ask: how successfully does Dickens follow through, develop and complete his declared political campaigns, in *Hard Times* and *Bleak House*?

A daunting range of aims for one chapter. Let us begin forthwith. Here is the start of the second 'Book' of *Hard Times*, entitled 'Reaping', as the author takes time at the start of the weekly episode for 27 May 1854, and on the occasion of a year's break in the action, to offer a panoramic overview:

A SUNNY midsummer day. There was such a thing sometimes, even in Coketown.

Seen from a distance in such weather, Coketown lay shrouded in a haze of its own, which appeared impervious to the sun's rays. You only knew the town was there, because you knew there could have been no such sulky blotch upon the prospect without a town. A blur of soot and smoke, now confusedly tending this way, now that way, now aspiring to the vault of Heaven, now murkily creeping along the earth, as the wind rose and fell, or changed its quarter: a dense formless jumble, with sheets of cross light in it, that showed nothing but masses of darkness: – Coketown in the distance was suggestive of itself, though not a brick of it could be seen.

The wonder was, it was there at all. It had been ruined so often, that it was amazing how it had borne so many shocks. Surely there never was such fragile china-ware as that of which the millers of Coketown were made. Handle them never so lightly, and they fell to pieces with such ease that you might suspect them of having been flawed before. They were ruined, when they were required to send labouring children to school; they were ruined when inspectors were appointed to look into their works; they were ruined, when such inspectors considered it doubtful whether they were quite justified in chopping people up with their machinery; they were utterly undone, when it was hinted that perhaps they need not always make quite so much smoke. Besides Mr. Bounderby's gold spoon which was generally received in Coketown, another prevalent fiction was very popular there. It took the form of a threat. Whenever a Coketowner felt he was ill-used – that is to say, whenever he was not left entirely alone, and it was proposed to hold him accountable for the consequences of any of his acts – he was sure to come out with the awful menace, that he would 'sooner pitch his property into the Atlantic.' This had terrified the Home Secretary within an inch of his life, on several occasions.

However, the Coketowners were so patriotic after all, that they never had pitched their property into the Atlantic yet, but, on the contrary, had been kind enough to take mighty good care of it. So there it was, in the haze yonder; and it increased and multiplied.

The streets were hot and dusty on the summer day, and the sun was so bright that it even shone through the heavy vapour drooping over Coketown, and could not be looked at steadily. Stokers emerged from low underground doorways into factory yards, and sat on steps, and posts, and palings, wiping their swarthy visages, and contemplating coals. The whole town seemed to be frying in oil. There was a stifling smell of hot oil everywhere. The steam-engines shone with it, the dresses of the Hands were soiled with it, the mills throughout their many stories oozed and trickled it. The atmosphere of those Fairy palaces was like the breath of the simoom: and their inhabitants, wasting with heat, toiled languidly in the desert. But no temperature made the melancholy mad elephants more mad or more sane. Their wearisome heads went up and down at the same rate, in hot weather and cold, wet weather and dry, fair weather and foul. The measured motion of their shadows on the walls, was the substitute Coketown had to show for the shadows of rustling woods; while, for the summer hum of insects, it could offer, all the year round, from the dawn of Monday to the night of Saturday, the whirr of shafts and wheels.

Drowsily they whirred all through this sunny day, making the passenger more sleepy and more hot as he passed the humming walls of the mills. Sun-blinds, and sprinklings of water, a little cooled the main streets and the shops; but the mills, and the courts and alleys, baked at a fierce heat. Down upon the river that was black and thick with dye, some Coketown boys who were at large – a rare sight there – rowed a crazy boat, which made a spumous track upon the water as it jogged along, while every dip of an oar stirred up vile smells. But the sun itself, however beneficent, generally, was less kind to Coketown than hard frost, and rarely looked intently into any of its closer regions without engendering more death than life. So does the eye of Heaven itself become an evil eye, when incapable or sordid hands are interposed between it and the things it looks upon to bless.

(*HT*, 105–106)

This passage is detailed and dense, and it is helpful to begin by summarising the paragraphs, so that we can achieve an overview. Our summary should indicate the mode in which a paragraph is written, and give some idea of its content. After the opening line, which tells us it is sunny and hot, the paragraphs are:

1. Descriptive. Smoke and haze both hide the town and reveal that it must be there.
2. Ironic/even sarcastic satire. The mill owners always complain about suggestions of reform, and threaten to throw everything into the sea.

3. Ironic/even sarcastic. The mill owners never do throw their property into the sea.
4. Descriptive. Heat, stokers, oil, 'melancholy mad elephants', 'whirr of shafts and wheels'.
5. Descriptive. Boys in rowing boat, polluted river and town 'engendering more death than life'.

This summary tells us how Dickens has structured his opening passage: he has included a bitter piece of sarcastic satire, targeting the mill owners for their inhumane opposition to safety measures (paragraphs 2 and 3), sandwiched between descriptions of Coketown on a sunny summer's day (paragraphs 1, 4 and 5). The descriptions are also structured by means of the developing viewpoint. In paragraph 1 we are clearly looking at Coketown from a distance, but we are on the same level, looking from on the earth. In paragraph 4 our observing eyes are taken into Coketown: Dickens underlines this move by imagining the sun dazzling the eyes of people in the streets. Then, he takes us through those streets and into the 'mills', depicting the atmosphere and noise within those 'Fairy palaces'. Finally, paragraph 5 opens at ground level in Coketown, where paragraph 4 left off, as we watch boys in a 'crazy' rowing boat on the polluted river, but this paragraph then takes us suddenly up above the earth as 'the sun itself ... looked' down upon the town. Then, 'the eye of Heaven itself [has] become an evil eye', and can only see the mill owners. The workers are hidden by a layer of their 'incapable or sordid' bosses.

Our summary of paragraphs, and our look at the structure of this paragraph, has therefore shown us something about Dickens's intention. He begins with a panorama, but from a human level. He then takes us through two necessary stages: his attack on the Coketown owners for their cruel hypocrisy, and his description of the town itself, which is filled with horror and revulsion. Finally, he has prepared the ground and is ready to combine moral outrage with vision. So he ends this set piece with the suggestion that Coketown is offensive to the sun, nature and God. At the same time, he whisks us off to a great distance, whence we can see the entire system: Heaven looking down, the 'sordid' bosses getting in the way, and the Hands who cannot be blessed, who live under an 'evil eye'.

The extract, then, is written in two modes: descriptive and ironic. We will look first at the ironic middle section, paragraphs 2 and 3. Dickens begins with a series of four sentences which drip with sarcasm. 'The wonder was', 'it was amazing how', 'surely there never was', 'Handle them never so lightly'. It is clear to us that these sentences are a withering attack upon the 'millers of Coketown', and we know, because we already know Bounderby, that the idea that such men are so fragile they might break in pieces at the slightest hurt, is an absurd idea. However, we are still not sure what Dickens's heavy irony is about. Clearly, there is an amusing triple meaning in the phrase 'you might suspect them of having been flawed before', which has the original ironic double meaning (they claim to be fragile but they are nothing of the kind) and the extra implication (Dickens implies that they are morally 'flawed'). However, we do not begin to follow the actual target of this attack until the *anaphora* on 'They were ruined' begins, this phrase being repeated twice and then varied to 'they were utterly undone', and alternating with suggestions for improved conditions and safety reforms. The Coketown owners moan about costs, and threaten to go out of business, while Dickens mentions a list of reforms that are of steadily increasing humanity. Here is the list:

1. Send workers' children to school;
2. Allow inspectors into their factories;
3. Stop chopping up workers with their machines;
4. Don't make so much smoke.

Dickens has built his irony to a crescendo with this four-part *anaphora*, and by this time the reader is well on board with the true meaning of the attack, and shares Dickens's contempt for the whingeing millers. The final part of the paragraph takes us a step further, however. We are familiar with Bounderby's 'golden spoon' idea that all the Hands want to live in impossible luxury. Now we hear another of the mill owners' fictions – that they would rather throw away their mills than institute the proposed reforms. The evil of this fiction is that it threatens the Home Secretary (what would happen to the country if industry stopped?), so the owners win and no reforms can be begun. Notice that Dickens is still writing in a witheringly sarcastic mode: the Home Secretary is 'terrified ... within an inch of his life', for example, and the threat is an 'awful menace', while all this happens if a Coketowner is held 'accountable for the consequences of any of his acts'.

Paragraph 3 crowns the irony by combining its two strands into a statement that makes us laugh. The self-pity and whingeing of the owners, combined with their threat to the politicians, leads to the assertion that they are 'patriotic' in holding on to their property. We arrive, in fact, at the laughable combination of ideas: that they are making profits and growing rich, not from greed but out of patriotic duty. Dickens here has created a wonderful piece of polemical satire. We notice that there have been intensive uses of irony and many examples of sarcastic phrases; that the four sentences at the start of Paragraph 2, and the four-part *anaphora* that ensues, structurally build our outrage and our comic contempt for the owners who are Dickens's target; and that the two subsequent stages – to the Home Secretary, and then to patriotism – each take the satire one stage further. So, we have charted and admired Dickens's satirical technique. However, perhaps the most effective element in this passage is his reticence in the middle of such grandiose irony. Dickens does not explain the direction of his attack: we have to interpret and catch up with him. Similarly, he declares the owners' patriotism and kindness in a bland and open tone, with only the phrase 'take mighty good care' reminiscent of the extravagant ironies we have been reading. So, by means of this reticence, and some restraint, Dickens provides us with that slight delay as we realise exactly what his comic idea is, and as we catch up with him. It is the written equivalent of what a comic would call 'dead-pan' delivery. This in turn provides the pleasure and amusement we enjoy from the witty idea, which would not have been as effective had the author hammered it home more explicitly.

This is a surprising effect for us to remark, because the passage we are studying appears to be overwritten, if anything. So we realise that Dickens has managed to combine an unrestrained and quite withering level of sarcastic overwriting, with some selective reticence, and has thus created both the intellectual pleasure normally gleaned from a more subtle form of satire, as well as the direct power of his rhetorical tour de force.

We now turn to the descriptive paragraphs. The first of these emphasises what cannot be seen, because of visual confusions and indistinctness. The vocabulary Dickens employs intensively builds this effect: 'shrouded', 'haze', 'impervious', 'sulky blotch', 'blur of soot and smoke', 'confusedly', 'murkily', 'a dense formless jumble', 'nothing but masses of darkness'. The sentences echo the progress of the paragraph. The opening two sentences are clear. The main clause of sentence 1 is the middle of three, then, sentence 2 is a two-part sentence with the main clause at the start. The third sentence continues for the rest of the paragraph. It begins with ten phrases which are all descriptive subordinate clauses dependent on 'A blur' and 'a dense formless jumble', before finally reaching the main clause 'Coketown ... was suggestive of itself'. It is hard to describe the effect of this structure: it is as if the third sentence, with its 'this way', 'that way', 'to the vault of Heaven', 'creeping', 'rose and fell', seems to wave a whole cloud of words in front of 'Coketown'; and, as we have remarked, a lot of these words denote confusion and indistinctness. This paragraph also contains a vein of revulsion against Coketown. So, for example, the town is a 'sulky blotch', and a 'jumble', or 'masses of darkness' on a sunny day. None of these are attractive descriptions.

So far, we have noted diction and the developments in sentence structure. However, as usual with Dickens, we should also be alert to imagery, whether explicit or implied by connotation. So, for example, 'shrouded' imports a connotation of death; 'sulky' is a personification, implying the town's grumpy temper, and personification continues, the smoke pictured 'aspiring' to Heaven, then 'creeping along the earth'. Certainly, the character imputed to Coketown in these hints is both confused and lacking any intelligent consistency.

We now come to paragraph 4, where Dickens returns to a descriptive mode after his anti-owners satire. We begin by noticing the sentences. The first two are both quite long but of plain construction. The stokers sit on a list of 'steps, and posts, and palings', the sentence lengths perhaps enhancing the sense of exhaustion, before suddenly, two unexpectedly short sentences that tell us about oil. These are followed by a three-part parallelism: the oil is on 'steam-engines', the clothes of the Hands and throughout the mills. We will return to the 'Fairy palaces' and 'mad elephants'. A further parallelism emphasises how the looms are always working, in 'hot weather and cold, wet weather and dry, fair weather and foul', before Dickens's final two sentences are constructed as a kind of inversely parallel pair. The first compares the looms' shadows to shadows of trees in a wood; the second reverses the comparison, saying that in place of the hum of insects, there is the whir of machinery. Both these comparisons, of course, emphasise the absence of natural surroundings, but thanks to Dickens's careful construction of them as a reversed pair, we seem to move out of the mill, away from the machinery to the woods, then, via the hum of insects, we are delivered back into the mill, back to the noisy machines.

The first half of this paragraph is purely descriptive and is almost entirely literal, in contrast to the highly suggestive evocations found in paragraph 1. This conveys the dullness and emptiness of Coketown when heat has reduced energy. Then, with the image of the mills as 'Fairy palaces' and the air as a 'simoom' – a hot and sandy desert wind – imagery bursts into the writing. 'Fairy palaces' is clearly a sarcastic image for the mills, but when the 'simoom' continues the Arabian allusion, this leads to a directly bitter comment, for the Hands toil 'in the desert', that is both the desert of the metaphor, and the desert of an industrial worker's existence. Next come the 'melancholy mad elephants' with 'their wearisome heads', which we know to be Dickens's simile for the machines, first mentioned on page 26. Typically, Dickens does not reiterate his image, but instead writes of the image (i.e. the elephants) as literal. Finally, the elephants' shadows lead us into the pair of images at the end of the paragraph: machine-shadows/tree-shadows, then insect-hum/machine-whir. With its evocation of a town frying in oil, and with its strangely exotic imagery of Arabian sand-storms, fairy palaces and mad elephants, as well as the contrast with summer's sights and sounds in other, more natural surroundings, this paragraph gives a strong impression of the exhausted, sweltering town. Certainly, we feel that working in one of those mills on such a day would be a form of torture.

Our last paragraph, however, brings together the different threads of the passage we have been analysing so far. The paragraph first imagines a man, called a 'passenger', walking through the town: a draining of energy is again emphasised, for the machines whir 'drowsily' and the mills were 'humming'. Next, apart from some wider streets that have been watered, everything bakes. Then, we see boys in a boat;

but the dominant idea is pollution: the river is 'black and thick with dye', the boat's wake is 'spumous', and the oars stir up 'vile smells' from the water. It is deadly hot, there is a draining of energy, and it is repulsively foul.

In the final two sentences, Dickens turns to the sun again, personifying its character: it is 'less kind to Coketown' despite its general beneficence. The more 'intently' it looks at Coketown, the more it is 'engendering more death than life'. Again, as at the end of the previous paragraph, Dickens doubles his statement. Just as the Sun engenders 'death', so the 'eye of Heaven' becomes an 'evil eye' when directed to Coketown. As we have seen, this is because of the layer of the 'incapable or sordid' which overlies and hides the more deserving people below. We should notice what this finale to Dickens's panoramic overview has achieved. It has established that Coketown is not only unnatural, unhuman, foul, dirty, polluted and ugly – all of which are powerfully evoked by straightforward descriptive means; Coketown is also morally foul, and creates and lives off a reversal of both nature, morality, and by implication, God himself. In particular, the cruel and greedy self-interest of the owners, and their hypocrisy, seems to reverse nature entirely: in Coketown, even the sun breeds death, and the eye of Heaven is an 'evil eye'.

Our detailed analysis of this passage is not quite complete: there are two references for us to check. First, we notice biblical vocabulary and style in the phrase 'And it increased and multiplied' at the end of paragraph 3. This is a reference to Exodus:

> And the children of Israel were fruitful, and increased abundantly, and multiplied, and waxed exceeding mighty, and the land was filled with them.
>
> (*The Bible,* Exodus 1:7. Authorised Version)

Recognising when Dickens refers to the Bible can help our understanding. Here, it is the Coketown owners' property that multiplies: in other words they become richer and richer. If we look at the context in Exodus, we find that the Israelites 'increased' and 'multiplied' while in captivity in Egypt. Indeed, their oppression seems only to have made them stronger and more numerous: verse 12 reads 'But the more they [Egypt] afflicted them [the Israelites], the more they multiplied and grew'. This is an amusing and appropriate comment, because Dickens has just shown how the owners complain loudly of being 'afflicted' or ruined, while at the same time their profits grow. Another reference in this passage is 'The eye of Heaven', which is a quotation from Shakespeare's Sonnet no. 18, 'Shall I compare thee to a Summer's day?'

Having looked at this passage in detail, our questions are: how far does this represent a Dickensian critique of society, and what are the features and grounds of such a critique? Then, bearing in mind that *Hard Times* opened with such an energetic attack upon the 'fact'-based philosophy of Utilitarianism, how far can we see the present passage as a continuation or development of that theme?

This passage is a strong attack on Coketown, its appearance, polluting dirt and smoke; and the harshness of, and absence of nature from, the industrial urban landscape. The constant noise of machinery is also attacked, and we are given a glimpse of the exhausted workers who are subject to this unnatural environment, when the stokers and weavers are mentioned. Workers are uneducated, chopped up by machinery, and breathe unhealthy smoke. Owners are greedy, hypocritical, and termed 'incapable and sordid'. They are blamed for hiding all the evils of an unchecked pursuit of profit from 'the eye of Heaven', and are ridiculed for their whingeing lies.

What should be done, then? And, what is to be blamed? By implication, Dickens would advocate education for all, cleaner and safer works, with protective shields around the machines; a clean town, river and air. He would presumably also ensure that some natural things would still thrive even in the town – perhaps by planting trees. As for blame, in this passage there is no doubt: the mill owners and manufacturers, like Bounderby, are to blame, together with the weakness of the political authority; and it is their hypocrisy and greed that is responsible for the evils of the industrial town. Very well, the bosses are the villains, the workers are victims, and the whole horrid system is designed to make whingeing, lying hypocrites richer and richer.

Thus far, Dickens's analysis of a northern industrial town in the mid-nineteenth century would have few detractors today. Broadly, we accept as historical truth, the cruelty and ugliness of the industrial revolution, and we accept the brutality of which the bosses were often guilty, as well as the unbounded greed of capitalism when unchecked.

Thus far, also, Dickens belongs with a benevolent element in his time. Philanthropists and campaigners, including Dickens, were working hard to bring about improvements. Dickens's attack on the industrial north is appealing: we share his sympathy with the workers, and his anger at the bosses. On the other hand, making the workers' lot safer and more humane, cleaning up the pollution and providing some greenery in their town, does not add up to a radical or even a trenchant agenda. It can be argued that Dickens enlists our emotions in the form of our sympathy and our anger, but that there is a fuzzy centre to his programme, an absence of analysis or any intellectual rigour. So, Dickens provokes us to feel a revulsion against industrial mechanisation and its attendant hardships, ugliness and dirt, but fails to analyse how such ills have come about, or how they could and should be dealt with.

What about the declared target of *Hard Times* – Utilitarianism? The passage we have just analysed stands at the opening of the second and middle 'Book', and is a panorama of Coketown. Furthermore, it leads to a ringing finale, a condemnation that implies the outraged agreement of God himself, or at least of Nature with a capital N. It begins the episode directly following Louisa's marriage, a crucial hiatus in the plot. This, then, is a prominent set piece. Why is the 'fact' faction not even mentioned? Bounderby is referred to, but only for his ridiculous Golden Spoon complaints, not for any adherence to 'facts' but on the contrary for the sheer fantasy of his lies. The rest of the owners are the same: they lie about being ruined, about throwing away their factories and about their 'patriotic' stewardship. This has nothing to do with Utilitarianism, Dickens's trumpeted theme. Instead, it has everything to do with good old-fashioned greed, cruelty, and therefore villainy.

Also, we remember the first set-piece description of Coketown, in Chapter 5, 'The Key-Note'. In that passage, close to the start of the novel, many of the same ills and evils of Coketown are mentioned; but on that occasion the villain is unequivocally the 'fact' faction. Politicians with 'tabular' evidence prove ridiculous things about the workers, their beliefs and their habits, and they know what is best for the lower class. In short, 'everything was fact between the lying-in hospital and the cemetery', while nothing else ever 'should be, world without end, Amen' (*HT*, 27). Dickens could hardly make a clearer accusation, and we recognise his habit of using a Christian reference in a heavily ironic context, to imply that his opponents' views are against God's will. Here, the reference is a quotation from the Book of Common Prayer.

In Chapter 5, then, the evils of Coketown are a consequence of Utilitarianism, an error shared by politicians, the owning and genteel classes of Coketown, and the misguided Thomas Gradgrind. In Chapter 17, by contrast, the evils proceed from villainously dishonest and greedy individuals, who abuse their power and exploit workers without mercy. In Chapter 17, the bosses' cover story is self-pity and scaremongering: there is no mention of the Utilitarian faction. It is difficult to reconcile these two very different analyses of an industrial system; and it is possible to argue that Dickens had forgotten, or was re-casting, his polemic from Chapter 5, when, nearly two months later, he came to write the opening overview for Chapter 17.

We will consider this question more fully in our concluding discussion, later in the present chapter. For the moment, having raised this issue through our detailed analysis of one passage, it is time to turn our attention to another detailed study, this time from *Bleak House*. Here is the opening of Chapter 40, where Sir Leicester Dedlock becomes involved in a General Election:

> England has been in a dreadful state for some weeks. Lord Coodle would go out, Sir Thomas Doodle wouldn't come in, and there being nobody in Great Britain (to speak of) except Coodle and Doodle, there has been no government. It is a mercy that the hostile meeting between those two great men, which at one time seemed inevitable, did not come off, because if both pistols had taken effect, and Coodle and Doodle had killed each other, it is to be presumed that England must have waited to be governed until young Coodle and young Doodle, now in frocks and long stockings, were grown up. This stupendous national calamity, however, was averted by Lord Coodle's making the timely discovery that if in the heat of debate he had said that he scorned and despised the whole ignoble career of Sir Thomas Doodle, he had merely meant to say that party differences should never induce him to withhold from it the tribute of his warmest admiration; while it as opportunely turned out, on the other hand, that Sir Thomas Doodle had in his own bosom expressly booked Lord Coodle to go down to posterity as the mirror of virtue and

honour. Still England has been some weeks in the dismal strait of having no pilot (as was well observed by Sir Leicester Dedlock) to weather the storm; and the marvellous part of the matter is that England has not appeared to care very much about it, but has gone on eating and drinking and marrying and giving in marriage as the old world did in the days before the flood. But Coodle knew the danger, and Doodle knew the danger, and all their followers and hangers-on had the clearest possible perception of the danger. At last Sir Thomas Doodle has not only condescended to come in, but has done it handsomely, bringing in with him all his nephews, all his male cousins, and all his brothers-in-law. So there is hope for the old ship yet.

Doodle has found that he must throw himself upon the country, chiefly in the form of sovereigns and beer. In this metamorphosed state he is available in a good many places simultaneously and can throw himself upon a considerable portion of the country at one time. Britannia being much occupied in pocketing Doodle in the form of sovereigns, and swallowing Doodle in the form of beer, and in swearing herself black in the face that she does neither – plainly to the advancement of her glory and morality – the London season comes to a sudden end, through all the Doodleites and Coodleites dispersing to assist Britannia in those religious exercises.

(*BH*, 589–590)

This is a gloriously funny passage. The names Coodle and Doodle are ridiculous, and Dickens's assertion that they are the only two people in the country is neatly undercut by the bracketed '(to speak of)'. The two phrases 'go out' and 'come in', followed by the mutual insults, which are then undercut by insincere compliments, give a ludicrous picture of political activity, where the actors seem to resign out of pique and recant their statements on a whim. Dickens achieves a further undercutting, from England being 'in a dreadful state' with 'no pilot', to the 'marvellous' anti-climax because 'England has not appeared to care very much about it, but has gone on eating and drinking and marrying and giving in marriage as the old world did in the days before the flood'.

Doodle is then depicted having 'condescended to come in', and throwing himself upon the country. The country actually receives, not Doodle himself, but a lot of sovereigns and beer as bribes for votes. Dickens then calls this Doodle in a 'metamorphosed state' and points out that he can thus 'throw himself upon a considerable portion' of the country all at once. Finally, there is a picture of mass 'pocketing' and 'swallowing' of money and beer respectively, and of the fashionable world also dispersing around the country, in order to take part. Finally, Dickens describes all this pocketing and swallowing as 'religious exercises'.

The phrase 'religious exercises' is ironic, of course. It even implies that a 'religion' is an absurd and foolish belief, while we know that to take or give bribes, whether money or beer, is not 'religious' at all. However, the more telling biblical reference is the near-quotation concerning the world before the flood. This refers to the following passage from the Gospel according to St. Matthew, Chapter 24:

34 Verily I say unto you, This generation shall not pass, till all these things be fulfilled.

35 Heaven and earth shall pass away, but my words shall not pass away.

36 But of that day and hour knoweth no *man*, no, not the angels of heaven, but my Father only.

37 But as the days of Noe *were*, so shall also the coming of the Son of man be.

38 For as in the days that were before the flood they were eating and drinking, marrying and giving in marriage, until the day that Noe entered into the ark,

39 And knew not until the flood came, and took them all away; so shall also the coming of the Son of man be.

(Matthew 24:34–39)

The reference is to verse 38, but we follow our usual practice of reading around a biblical reference enough for us to understand the context. In Matthew Chapter 24, the disciples ask Jesus about the end of the world. In these verses Jesus explains that nobody will be able to predict the Second Coming of Christ (i.e. and the end of the world): on the contrary, everybody will continue living their lives as normal, right up until the Apocalypse has already begun. Dickens's outrageous joke is to compare the temporary political crisis to the end of the world; and to compare Doodle's belated decision to 'come in', to the 'coming of the Son of man'. To bring together the empty triviality of politics (whose hollowness has just been shown by both Coodle and Doodle in their sycophantic retractions) and the coming of the 'Son of man', when 'shall the sun be darkened, and the moon shall not give her light, and the stars shall fall from heaven' before Christ comes to earth 'in the clouds of heaven with power and great glory' (*The Bible,* Matthew 24:29 and 30 respectively) is the most outrageous hyperbole possible to imagine. This satirical overstatement is simultaneously undercut, however, for people are paying no attention to the frightful crisis gripping the country: they continue to eat, drink, marry and so forth. What is the political crisis, then? Either, the end of the world, or (simultaneously), nothing at all.

Dickens's attack upon the political system had contemporary relevance. Both *Bleak House* and *Hard Times* were written between the first Reform Bill (1832) and the second (1867). While there was some overdue relief from reformist pressure, because one Reform had belatedly been enacted after the long reactionary stagnation that accompanied and followed the Napoleonic War, there was still recognition that the first Bill did not go far enough, and it was clear to most thinking people that there would have to be more. So, although most of the 'rotten borough' problems[1] had been addressed, the practices of bribery and 'treating' were still widespread. For example, in 1835 a commission on electoral bribery reported to the Commons that, in Stafford, £14 was paid for each vote. At Leicester in the same election, public houses were opened by each party, the voters were collected and locked in, and were thoroughly drunk by polling day. So, Dickens's picture of universal pocketing and swallowing was easily recognised at the time. The picture is completed by the laughable behaviour of Coodle and Doodle. We should also note that Coodle is a Lord, and Doodle is 'Sir Thomas': in other words, they both belong to the privileged upper class.

The remainder of Chapter 40 of *Bleak House* further elaborates Dickens's attack on the election. Volumnia makes the mistake of referring to bribes too openly; the cousin is a comic upper-class buffoon; and the attitude expressed by Sir Leicester Dedlock towards the new class of successful industrialists, and Mr. Rouncewell in particular, is representative of a reactionary, anti-reform class of political ostriches with their heads stuck firmly in the sand.

---

[1] For example the 1832 Reform Bill abolished the 'Rotten Borough' of Old Sarum, with its electorate of seven voters returning two MPs.

We have studied this passage because it is a fine example of Dickens's satirical writing, and there are several passages, on different topics, similarly successful in attacking society's faults or stupidities. We may think, for example, of Chapter 2, 'In Fashion', the powerful evocation of Jo's illiteracy, or the Coroner's inquests. On the other hand, what do such satires contribute to the central themes of *Bleak House*? When we consider plotting we may well ask whether this election passage is merely inserted to delay the confrontation between Tulkinghorn and Lady Dedlock, in order to stretch out and heighten suspense. Is the election satire simply padding, a target that offers Dickens an opportunity, a delaying digression on a topic that will be much more trenchantly treated via Gradgrind and Harthouse, in *Hard Times*, by Twemlow and Veneering, in *Our Mutual Friend*, or by the famous Circumlocution Office in *Little Dorrit*?

Our next question, however, is the same one that we put to *Hard Times*: how far does Dickens develop his declared target, the Court of Chancery, as a theme of the novel? We will consider this question in relation to both texts in our concluding discussion below. Before we do so, we will look at another extract where Dickens attacks social ills: the description of Tom-all-Alone's, the slum where Jo sleeps:

> Jo lives – that is to say, Jo has not yet died – in a ruinous place known to the like of him by the name of Tom-all-Alone's. It is a black, dilapidated street, avoided by all decent people, where the crazy houses were seized upon, when their decay was far advanced, by some bold vagrants who after establishing their own possession took to letting them out in lodgings. Now, these tumbling tenements contain, by night, a swarm of misery. As on the ruined human wretch vermin parasites appear, so these ruined shelters have bred a crowd of foul existence that crawls in and out of gaps in walls and boards; and coils itself to sleep, in maggot numbers, where the rain drips in; and comes and goes, fetching and carrying fever and sowing more evil in its every footprint than Lord Coodle, and Sir Thomas Doodle, and the Duke of Foodle, and all the fine gentlemen in office, down to Zoodle, shall set right in five hundred years – though born expressly to do it.
>
> Twice lately there has been a crash and a cloud of dust, like the springing of a mine, in Tom-all-Alone's; and each time a house has fallen. These accidents have made a paragraph in the newspapers and

have filled a bed or two in the nearest hospital. The gaps remain, and there are not unpopular lodgings among the rubbish. As several more houses are nearly ready to go, the next crash in Tom-all-Alone's may be expected to be a good one. This desirable property is in Chancery, of course. It would be an insult to the discernment of any man with half an eye to tell him so. Whether 'Tom' is the popular representative of the original plaintiff or defendant in Jarndyce and Jarndyce, or whether Tom lived here when the suit had laid the street waste, all alone, until other settlers came to join him, or whether the traditional title is a comprehensive name for a retreat cut off from honest company and put out of the pale of hope, perhaps nobody knows. Certainly Jo don't know.

'For I don't', says Jo, 'I don't know nothink'.

(*BH*, 235–236)

The first paragraph of this extract contains powerful description. The opening appeal to our sympathy is concise and effective – the correction that Jo's life is simply an absence of death up to now. Then the evocation starts, with 'ruinous', 'black, dilapidated', 'crazy', 'decay', 'tumbling' and 'misery'. As he builds our sense of the place, Dickens introduces and elaborates his image comparing the inhabitants to parasites or insects: they are a 'swarm' like the 'vermin parasites' that feed off a 'wretch' – presumably a person far gone into poverty and filth. These people are 'a crowd of foul existence that crawls in and out of gaps in walls and boards; and coils itself to sleep, in maggot numbers'. Notice that Dickens refers to the people as 'it', and gives a vivid impression that they are an infestation as they carry 'fever' and 'evil' back and forth. The image is powerful and repulsive; but then its effect is enhanced by the sudden contrast with foolish joke names, as the ineffectual political class makes its appearance: 'Coodle', 'Doodle', 'Foodle' and all the rest as far as 'Zoodle'.

The fact that Tom-all-Alone's remains unaffected by the politicians or by the rest of society, and that society is not affected by Tom-all-Alone's, is emphasised when two houses fall and the event gives no more than 'a paragraph' in the papers; and by the carelessness with which people look forward to several more houses coming down, because the crash might be 'a good one'.

Dickens then ties this slum in to his Chancery theme: for Tom-all-Alone's is 'in Chancery', as anyone would have realised just from knowing about it. Dickens then speculates about the name, and concludes that nobody knows who the 'Tom' who was 'all-alone' might have been. One of the suggestions tells us that this slum is 'in' Jarndyce and Jarndyce, so relating the place to the main plot of the novel. We remember the opening salvo attacking the Court of Chancery, 'which has its decaying houses and its blighted lands in every shire' (*BH*, 13), and we recognise Tom-all-Alone's as representatively blighted and decaying. Perhaps more importantly we may sense that Tom-all-Alone's is representative of all who are 'in Chancery'. So, we may see the doomed destruction of this street as a visible emblem of the destruction that is wreaked upon Miss Flite, Mr. Gridley, and eventually upon Richard. We can argue that Dickens proposes Tom-all-Alone's as a symbol: as an explicit, physical version of the effect being 'in' Chancery has upon a victim. According to this idea, we will watch later in the book as parts of Richard Carstone fall to pieces, and as Chancery like parasitical maggots lives on his decaying person.

The question of parasites is relevant because it returns us to the simile developed in the first paragraph. Certainly the idea of something feeding off another's life, first proposed as a simple description of Tom-all-Alone's, is directly suited to the analysis of Chancery Dickens proposes. We can easily see that Richard's fixation on the outcome of the suit feeds on his good qualities by obstructing his mind, so that his obsession is like a kind of parasite. Then, the Chancery suit is more literally parasitic because, in the end, the lawyers have sucked out all the money that was ever bequeathed. Finally, *Bleak House* provides us with a living parasite – the lawyer Vholes – who preys on Richard in his gruesome manner.

Concluding discussion

We have looked at some of the elements of society that attract Dickens's condemnation, but we should mention that he is also satirical about several other targets that we do not have time to analyse. In *Hard Times*, for example, there is the Trade Union and its orator, Slackbridge; and there is the boastful 'bully' Bounderby. In *Bleak House* there are fashion, illiteracy and the shameful condition of the poor, as well as reactionary Tory politics. In *Bleak House* there are a number of other lesser targets as well, as Dickens fills out the population and complicates the events of this very long novel. So, for example, there is the vanity of the footman Mercury, Miss Barbary's religious cruelty, Chadband's oily preaching, Skimpole's self-excuse, both the Jellyby and Pardiggle mistreatments of children, and a host of other elements in society and among people that receive a jolt of contempt or hatred from the author, in passing. In this discussion we limit ourselves to considering the themes of each opening salvo; then to looking at the moral response Dickens gives to the social and political evils he describes.

Facts and Utilitarianism as a theme of *Hard Times*

In this chapter we have referred to two extracts, both overviews of Coketown, and we were led to wonder whether Dickens changed his attack on the industrial town, forgetting his early focus on Utilitarian philosophy, and turning instead to the wickedness of greedy, lying bosses.

How far has Dickens developed *Hard Times* as a coherent attack upon the 'fact' or Utilitarian philosophy? There are a number of elements and passages in the novel that further elaborate the 'fact' theme, showing that Dickens maintains his hostile attack throughout. Here is a broad survey of the main elements of the theme.

First, the 'facts' education is thoroughly discredited, its consequences demonstrated in the adult careers of Louisa, Tom, Sissy and Bitzer. Probably the one whose adult life most effectively demonstrates the errors of her education, is Louisa. When she marries Bounderby, she is persuaded that love does not exist; and she marries having reached the conclusion that nothing matters, and she pleases her father when she says 'you have been so careful of me, that I never had a child's heart. You have trained me so well, that I never dreamed a child's dream' (*HT*, 98). In her second crucial interview with her father, Louisa makes similar statements, but with the opposite opinion: 'How could you give me life, and take from me all the inappreciable things that raise it from the state of conscious death?' (*HT*, 200). Pages 201 and 202 are a comprehensive indictment of Louisa's 'factual' upbringing.

She explains that she was in conflict with her education throughout her childhood, but eventually submitted to the despairing idea that life would soon pass so nothing mattered. Louisa then explains that her upbringing left her vulnerable to Harthouse: the emotions she was trained to suppress proved too strong, and took their revenge. Louisa, then, demonstrates that it is not possible or sensible to suppress all that is not 'fact'; and her devastating catechism somehow influences her father to change his philosophy completely. Louisa's story is complicated by her only motive in marrying, which is to benefit Tom. It is a poor motive, but relevant to the 'fact' theme because it is the only natural emotion she has left: Tom is the 'subject of all the little tenderness of my life', she says (*HT*, 202).

There are two difficulties about the outcome of Louisa's story. She twice tells her father 'I don't reproach you', but says 'I curse the hour in which I was born to such a destiny'! (*HT*, 201, 200). In fact, she accuses her father with such a devastating hatred of her childhood that her denial of reproaching him is ridiculous. This in turn may lead us to suspect that the emotion driving Louisa's critique is not really hers, rather it is Dickens's feelings that are being so cogently expressed: it is Dickens who wishes to bury the 'fact' faction so deeply in its own error, and who cannot resist driving the nails home in its coffin, despite his attempt to soften his desperate heroine (this is the girl who is about to swoon at her father's feet). The second difficulty we have mentioned depends very much on each individual reader's reaction: whether Mr. Gradgrind's sudden conversion is believable or convincing. Dickens has prepared us, to an extent, by making occasional moderating remarks about Gradgrind, such as, 'Mr. Gradgrind, though hard enough, was by no means so rough a man as Mr. Bounderby' (*HT*, 30). On the other hand, his appearance in the opening two chapters; together with the horrible discussion of love he conducts with Louisa in Chapter 15, 'Father and Daughter', have presented such a flinty personality that we can hardly believe that his world is turned upside down by the half hour during which he listens to Louisa before she faints. If we remember his forehead as a wall, above two eyes that are the 'cellarage'; and we still have a vivid picture of Stone Lodge, that cold, square building – how can this man, the very champion of 'facts', suddenly become gentle, regretful and ready to concede the error of his whole life? If we do doubt this character development, we may think both that Dickens is the victim of his own success, because Gradgrind's appearance at the start of the novel is so exceptionally memorable; and that Dickens is unfamiliar with the short format of *Hard Times*. In *Bleak House*, for example, Richard Carstone can be introduced as a charming, carefree, affectionate and even clever young man, and there is time for him to turn into an obsessed, self-absorbed, sick and dependent creature, broken and dying. This is because *Bleak House* is nearly a thousand pages long. *Hard Times*, by contrast, is only 274 pages, and Gradgrind's conversion must consequently be abrupt, in order to fit in.

It can be argued that the adult career of Tom Gradgrind is also an outcome of his upbringing in the 'fact' philosophy. This argument would rest upon the Utilitarian concept of self-interest: the belief that all activities are part of a deal, or a contract, and that people only do things in order to benefit themselves. This idea is represented and verbally argued by Bitzer and countered by Sleary (see *HT,* 269), and there is no doubt that Tom Gradgrind is overwhelmingly selfish and self-interested. On the other hand, we are not struck by Tom as a product of the Gradgrind School: that distinction belongs much more to Bitzer. Tom is rather presented simply as a grumpy and selfish lout or 'whelp', ill-mannered and with a criminal tendency. Indeed, Tom's financial improvidence is the opposite of the 'fact' faction's emphasis on arithmetic. We can conclude that any contribution to the 'fact' theme made by the characterisation of Tom is limited and somewhat tenuous. He was educated with only 'facts' and he grows up to be a selfish thief. That is about as much as can be said.

Sissy Jupe is a problematic character in relation to this theme. She is the example of a child on whom the 'fact' education seems to have no effect, from her initial attempt to define a horse, right through to her continuing, irrational hope that her father will come to fetch her, discussed between Gradgrind and Sleary on page 269. Three aspects of Sissy seem to be important: first, she has the innocence and moral strength to face down Mr. Harthouse, defeating him in their dialogue and forcing him to go away by sheer power of her personality. Second, Sissy seems to act as a sort of guardian angel in the final third of the novel, bringing happiness and pity so she 'shone like a beautiful light upon the darkness of the other [Louisa]' (*HT,* 210) in a repeat of the image we remember being applied to Rachael and her effect upon Stephen. Her dismissal of Harthouse, the rescue of Stephen, and her facilitating Tom's escape, all give a practical dimension to her benevolence. Third, Dickens repeatedly emphasises Sissy's educational failure. We know that she has not learned about horses, from Chapter 2; Gradgrind observes, in Chapter 14, that her continuing at school would be 'useless', and she agrees; and when Louisa returns, Sissy tells her, 'You knew so much, and I knew so little', clearly conscious of her comparative ignorance. We can argue that Sissy's humility in this respect shows her lack of pride, and her unassuming personality. On the other hand, Sissy's role in disposing of Harthouse, and the active and commanding part she plays both with Rachael and in rescuing Stephen, are not the behaviour of a shy personality at all. Furthermore, her speech is that of a person confident in her intelligence, expressing herself in educated language. Dickens clearly intends to show that it is the 'factual' education that has failed Sissy, not she who has failed educationally. She is so perfect in the final chapters, on the other hand, that some readers will find her unconvincing.

Bitzer is arguably the most relevant and explicit embodiment of the 'fact' theme. His significant appearances at the beginning and end of the novel provide us with a measure for the intervening events, and an example of the 'fact' theme undimmed by experience. Bitzer is the successful pupil, who knows to call a horse a 'graminivorous quadruped', and who, at the end of the story, answers the question whether he has a heart by saying 'The circulation, Sir, ... couldn't be carried on without one' (*HT*, 264). Bitzer's role in Book 3 Chapter 8, 'Philosophical', is to represent Utilitarianism, just as Sleary represents the opposite point of view: that of love, mercy, imagination and entertainment. The chapter gives full expression to Bitzer, who promulgates the philosophy he learned at Gradgrind's school; then gives full expression to Sleary's 'there ith a love in the world, not all Thelf-interetht after all' (*HT*, 269). The chapter is set up like a debate, to act as a conclusion to the novel's stated theme, and it fulfils that function successfully.

Aside from the four young people we have considered, the 'fact' theme appears fitfully in the text of *Hard Times*, as we found for example from looking at the overview of Coketown in Book 2 Chapter 1, where we would expect it to appear but where it seems to be unaccountably absent. However, Dickens can be said to have sown his Utilitarianism theme into the remainder of *Hard Times*, particularly through the story of Louisa's marriage and her flight; through formal structures such as the parallel meetings with Sleary at the start and the end of the novel; and the balanced debate between Bitzer and Sleary in the last-but-one chapter. Additionally, Dickens provides plentiful concise and precise definitions of his theme. So, for example, we read:

> ... which craving [i.e. for fancy and entertainment] must and would be satisfied aright, or must and would inevitably go wrong, until the laws of the Creation were repealed.
>
> (*HT*, 28)

Utilitarianism and other elements of *Hard Times*

Hard Times has been a controversial text ever since its publication: it is recognised as being different from Dickens's other novels, and it has inspired both admiration and criticism to an unusual degree. *Hard Times* was Ruskin's favourite Dickens novel;[2] the work of one who did not understand the politics of his time, according to Macaulay;[3] but, according to Walter Allen,[4] it provided an unmatched 'critique of industrial society'. In this section we will turn devil's advocate and outline two arguments critical of Dickens's achievement.

We have remarked that the ostensible aim of *Hard Times*, judging from that famous opening passage in the schoolroom, is as a moral fable about Utilitarianism. Our discussion of the development and conclusion of that fable has shown that Dickens follows through, and we can satisfactorily read such a moral fable in *Hard Times*. Nature, or 'the laws of Creation', as Dickens puts it, cannot be suppressed and denied: it inevitably bursts out, and takes its revenge on those who would confine it within a prison of fact.

---

[2] John Ruskin (1819–1900) was the leading British art critic of the Victorian age.
[3] Thomas Babington Macaulay (1800–1859), British historian and Whig politician.
[4] Walter Allen (1911–1995), literary critic and writer.

If we sit back, having finished the novel, and ask ourselves whether such a reading tells us enough about *Hard Times*, we are likely to answer no, for two reasons. First, that there is another group of concerns that are strongly represented in the text, that often seem to obscure Utilitarianism, and to push it out of the consciousness of the reader (and perhaps of the writer as well). These concerns are about the evils of an industrial town and its society. What do we remember most vividly about Coketown? Is it the argument between mathematics and imagination? Or, is it not rather the 'melancholy mad elephants' constantly dipping their heads, and the dust, oil, filth and hellish fires among which the Coketowners live and work? According to this argument, Dickens's chosen theme is a matter for philosophical argument and political demonstration, while the theme of industrial society appeals to us on a direct naturalistic level, as well as enlisting our outrage and our pity because it is a theme involving humanity and injustice. Consequently, while we read with our intellect about the 'fact' faction, we are engaged and moved on a more personal level, when we read of the Coketown mills, and an industrial society.

The second critical argument we outline, concerns the plot of the robbery from the bank. This is the main story driving the characters' thoughts and actions through the second half of the novel, and it has the virtue of bringing the Gradgrinds and Bounderbys into the same action as Stephen, Rachael and Bitzer, after the breakdown of Louisa's marriage has played itself out. The critical argument says that this plot, with its complicated set-up, the framing of Stephen, the subterfuge of Tom, suspicion and gradual revelation of clues, is a simple crime thriller, dependent on all the usual props, clues and tricks of suspense of any story of that genre.

These two arguments charge that Dickens fails to write a moral fable against Utilitarianism, because we remember *Hard Times* as a deeply affecting evocation of life in an industrial city with its lurid fires, smoke, black dust and oil, its injuries, suffering, and unremitting noise and labour; and because we have been gripped by a thrilling crime story with its attendant clues, detection and suspense – a story only very loosely connected to the Utilitarianism theme.

The Court of Chancery as a theme of *Bleak House*

Chancery is condemned in the opening pages, as the place which has 'its worn-out lunatic in every madhouse, and its dead in every church-yard' because it is 'most pestilent of hoary sinners' (*BH*, 13, 12 respectively). As with *Hard Times*, we should acknowledge straight away that Dickens does a conscientious job of weaving the Chancery theme into the characters and events of his novel. Aside from Chancery's 'decaying houses and blighted lands', represented by Tom-all-Alone's as we have remarked, the Court's main embodiment is in the lives of four of the characters: Miss Flite, Mr. Gridley, Mr. Jarndyce and Richard Carstone.

Miss Flite is Chancery's 'worn-out lunatic'. She has been driven mad by 'expecting a judgment' which she confuses with the last judgement, or the end of the world – an idea which seems to equate the Chancellor with God. Miss Flite appears several times. Apart from her obviously scrambled wits, her prattling about judgement, spending her days in Court and toting her bag full of 'documents', Miss Flite is significant because of her pet birds which act as a symbol of Chancery's effect. She keeps them caged, and their names are 'Hope, Joy, Youth, Peace, Rest, Life, Dust, Ashes, Waste, Want, Ruin, Despair, Madness, Death, Cunning, Folly, Words, Wigs, Rags, Sheepskin, Plunder, Precedent, Jargon, Gammon, and Spinach!' (*BH*, 852). She adds two new birds called 'the Wards in Jarndyce' when she appoints Richard to be executor of her will. Finally, after Richard's death, Miss Flite tells Esther that she has 'given her birds their liberty'. The picture of Miss Flite's birds flying out and up from her rooftop garret may bring to mind the tradi-tional picture of a soul leaving the body and rising to Heaven in the form of a dove. It is a bitter idea that Richard's death should set 'Hope, Joy, Youth, … Dust, Ashes, Waste' and the rest, free from their earthly cage: that these should represent Richard's soul. Miss Flite's birds are, then, a moving and effective symbol of the corrupt-ing effect of Chancery.

Mr. Gridley, the 'man from Shropshire' whose life has been ruined by an endless suit, is brought to despair and death. Although his spirit has finally been broken by Chancery and he admits 'I am worn out', he asks those who are witnessing his death to 'lead them [i.e. the lawyers, and so Chancery] to believe that I died defying them, consistently and perseveringly' (*BH*, 372). Previously, Gridley appeared as a version of Boythorn, constantly angry, expressing himself in violent terms and apologising to Mr. Jarndyce for allowing his temper to impair his manners.

Mr. Jarndyce keeps himself free from the Jarndyce and Jarndyce suit. Of necessity he employs a lawyer because he is 'in' Chancery. However, he has no expectation of gain or even good sense from the Court and he does what he can to help three young people, two of whom are wards in the case. Mr. Jarndyce finds the Court to be hopeless, idiotic and ineffectual, and the business of the law to be only hurtful, misleading and incomprehensible to those who become caught up in its toils. He is the one who coins the word 'wiglomeration' for the deliberations, delays, speeches and obfuscations of lawyers and the Court. We can argue that it is easier for Mr. Jarndyce to take this view than it would be, for example, for Mr. Gridley, because the former is a rich man, who can afford to keep his distance from the suit, while the law has truly ruined Gridley's livelihood. However, we cannot impeach Mr. Jarndyce for his opinions and practice: he represents an intelligent aversion to Chancery and its pernicious infections.

The three characters we have mentioned are embroiled in the Court of Chancery, so their stories present further iteration of that theme, and opportunities for Dickens to paint shocking pictures of the law's effects. Also, Miss Flite and her birds carry a symbolic significance relevant to the theme. However, the central claim *Bleak House* can put forward for having pursued the condemnation of Chancery through the whole text, rides upon the story of Richard Carstone. We watch him throughout his journey and we are treated to a series of detailed discussions between Richard and Esther, which carefully chart the gradual but steady disintegration of his purposes in life. In our discussion of *Hard Times* above, we commented that some readers find Mr. Gradgrind's conversion unconvincing because it is too sudden. There is no such problem attending Richard's steady decline, which is fully charted and fully expounded. That he becomes suspicious of Mr. Jarndyce's motives, becomes the victim of the ghastly lawyer Mr. Vholes, and foolishly keeps company with Mr. Skimpole, are developments we believe implicitly. Even Richard's death has been amply prepared by Esther's observation, together with contributions from Ada and Allan Woodcourt, and is convincing. We accept, then, that Richard's story is a fable with a moral, and that the moral points out the baleful, even deadly, influence of the High Court of Chancery.

The Court of Chancery and other elements of *Bleak House*

As we have remarked, there are numerous social themes in this very long novel, where Dickens seems to take the opportunity, intermittently, to take aim at some other bêtes noires, such as 'the fashionable intelligence' and bribes and treats in electioneering. However, there seems to be sufficient room for multiple social concerns in this huge text, so that the Chancery topic is not overshadowed, and we can be comfortable that the vituperative opening salvo has been followed by a fable of sufficient weight and seriousness in the remainder of the novel. We will, however, remember the arguments we put forward criticising *Hard Times*: that Dickens develops another social theme that is more powerful and emotive than the philosophical theory he initially attacks; and that the plot in the second half of the novel is driven by a conventional crime story, not related to any social or political critiques.

Does either of these arguments apply to *Bleak House*? First, we ask: do any of the many other social targets Dickens takes on, effectively overshadow the evils condemned in the Court of Chancery? This is a question to which different readers will give different answers. Clearly, Chancery remains a central issue, and it can be argued that the characterisations of the lawyers – Kenge, Tulkinghorn and Vholes – and the clerks – Guppy, Jobling and Small – add to and broaden this theme considerably. Even when the legal business has nothing to do with Chancery (as is the case with much of Tulkinghorn's activity), Dickens remains busy attacking the legal world. Furthermore, as we have remarked, there is sufficient space in this very large book for what we could consider the next most powerful social concern: Jo the crossing sweeper, his illiteracy and his lack of a place in society:

> He seems to know that they have an inclination to shrink from him, partly for what he is, and partly for what he has caused. He, too, shrinks from them. He is not of the same order of things, not of the same place in creation. He is of no order and no place; neither of the beasts, nor of humanity.
>
> (*BH*, 669)

Jo is lavished with some of the most powerful passages of writing in *Bleak House*, and for this reason the evils of a society where such ignorance and poverty are tolerated, becomes a moving strand in the novel. For another powerful passage about Jo, see the description of living illiterate, on pages 236–237, or the comparison to the butcher's dog, pages 237–238. This is equally an indictment of the society that allows such a life to be lived.

Our second observation with regard to *Hard Times*, was that Dickens drives the second half of the novel with a conventional crime story which has no particular relevance to Utilitarianism. We are therefore not concerned with Dickens's social and political critique, because the story is simply that of a selfish thief and the details of how he tries to escape detection by framing another man. It can be argued that *Bleak House* presents a similar problem, because the later stages of Richard's decline happen at the same time as the story of Lady Dedlock's scandal is building up towards its climax. The crisis occurs, and Esther and Bucket embark upon the pursuit that ends when Esther recognises her mother's dead body. In *Bleak House*, the most complicated, mysterious and exciting part of the plot begins when Lady Dedlock recognises Captain Hawdon's handwriting (*BH*, 23). From that moment on, the scandal of Lady Dedlock's secret becomes more and more complicated and draws in a variety of characters including Tulkinghorn, Snagsby, the law-writer, Guppy, Tony Jobling, the Smallweeds, George, Jo, Hortense, Bucket and Esther of course: in short, almost everyone. This is the main plot that drives events and motivates the characters. Other interludes such as visits to Boythorn, Richard's brief sojourn with the Bayham Badgers, or

Esther's visits to Caddy and the Turveydrops, are no more than that: interludes that provide some amusement and a rest from the intensity and drama of Lady Dedlock's secret. Of course we feel increasing sympathy for Richard and Ada as his decline becomes more pronounced, but Richard's story cannot compete with the high drama of a society scandal, including a murder and a detective, a secret hidden long ago, and the flight and pursuit of a beautiful lady who is found dead from despair. The point about Lady Dedlock's secret, which is undeniably the main plot of *Bleak House*, is that it is not in any way at all connected to the Court of Chancery. It is a plain old love story of passion and loss, with a surviving child long thought to be dead. Just as the theft in *Hard Times* is merely a crime story, so Lady Dedlock's scandal is merely a romantic melodrama, with murder added.

We may therefore conclude that Dickens has failed to integrate his social and political commentary into the plots of these two novels. There are powerful critiques of society; there are ways in which such social concerns impinge upon characters; there are regular polemic passages attacking social ills; but in both novels, the main plot that grips the reader with drama and suspense, is an ordinary plot that is not related to any of the highlighted social issues.

A moral response to society's ills

In our analysis of Coketown above, we considered what Dickens says should be done about the ills of an industrial society, and we came up with a list largely constructed as the antithesis of those elements he attacks as wrong. So, there should be education (but not Utilitarianism) including imagination; the machines should be safer; the town should be cleaner; bosses should be less greedy and more honest; the Union should not ostracise individuals; and the town and factories should not be denuded of natural things such as trees, a cleaner river, and so forth. In brief, this prescription adds up to saying that industrial production ought to be much nicer than it is. The main serious reform Dickens proposes is education for all, and that education should encourage the imagination. Otherwise, we hear a voice raised in outrage against the conditions in which the workers live, and an insistence that things must improve, but we are not given guidance into how such improvements can come about. Dickens is critical of both the social institutions that might undertake such a task: the Union on the one hand, and government and the politicians on the other. There is no doubt that *Hard Times* arouses our sympathy and anger. What it does not do is to propose a solution.

There is a shadowy suggestion, which amounts to the idea that nature itself, under the influence of God, will return in the end because the 'laws of the Creation' (*HT*, 28) will eventually prevail. Also, we studied Rachael in Chapter 3, commenting on the angelic virtues of self-sacrifice, mercy and endurance that make her life a pattern for others. Such virtues, however, do not pretend to alter the social reality: even at the end, Rachael is praised for 'working, ever working, but content to do it, and preferring to do it as her natural lot' (*HT*, 273), a phrase that even aligns nature on the side of the status quo.

Our final comment on the social themes of *Hard Times* is unavoidable: there is a serious problem with Rachael, Stephen and the Union. This is partly due to what seems to have been an ill-considered, or ill-executed revision on Dickens's part. When preparing the text for publication, the passage in which Stephen promises not to pursue complaints about injuries in the factory was cut. As a result, we do not know why Stephen 'passed a promess' not to join in Union action; to whom he gave the promise; or for what reason. Even knowing the cancelled passage, we only know that they were discussing Rachael's sister's death from having an arm torn off by the machine; that he promised Rachael, because such ideas 'only lead to hurt'; and therefore he will not take part in industrial action. Dickens has not provided an alternative explanation, so Stephen's motive is left as a mystery. Not only did Dickens leave his character twisting in the wind through this mistake, but also there is a further difficulty. We know that Rachael works in the same mill as Stephen. Does she take part in the action with the rest of the workers? If she does, why does she not set Stephen free from his promise? If she does not, why is she not also sent to Coventry by her fellow-workers? There seems no way out of this riddle, and the treatment of the whole episode that culminates in Stephen being ostracised, seems thin, even if you reinsert the 'promess' passage into pages 86–87. It is as if Dickens was determined to rule out the solutions offered by Trade Unionists and Socialism, so he attacked Slackbridge; but at the same time this left Stephen's character in an untenable position. The moral response to social ills is thus left as the contribution of angelic women, whose combination of virtues can be called a form of 'divine goodness' that influences everybody for the better.

In *Bleak House*, the two major social ills Dickens confronts are Jo's destitute illiteracy, and the 'most pestilent' High Court of Chancery. What should be done about these two evils? In the case of Jo and others like him, Dickens does propose a measure. He clearly believes that English society should pay for the education of destitute children, and that money should be available to train them for an occupation. This solution is seen in action in the novel, for the bailiff's three children are taken in hand by Mr. Jarndyce's charity: Charley becomes Esther's maid, Tom is sent to school and later apprenticed to a miller, and on Charley's marriage, little Emma becomes Esther's maid. It is a charming story, but of limited use to the thousands of destitute or near-destitute people whose hopeless and brutal lives Dickens describes in the persons of Jo, the Coavinses and the brick-makers. Dickens's contribution to the issue is to insist that England should clear up the obscenities and injustices in its own society, before sending charity abroad. He is outraged that Mrs. Jellyby can collect so much for Borrioboola-Gha, while there are still boys like Jo wandering London's streets and bedding down in London's slums.

With regard to Chancery, Dickens expresses his anger with great power, as we saw from our analysis of the opening pages of the novel. The Court and its lawyers are accused of creating delay and confusion, bleeding their clients dry, sustaining cases by creating mountains of papers and never reaching a judgement, and being a laughing stock to all reasonable people. Our anger and frustration are aroused, and our sympathy is enlisted on behalf of the Court's victims, and in particular Richard. On the other hand, Dickens's prescription for reform is similar to the improvements he proposes for Coketown. The Court should be faster at dealing with cases, less confusing, clients should have some money left, there should be fewer papers: in short, the whole institution should be speeded up and radically improved. In very short: there should be less 'wiglomeration'. That is Dickens's agenda.

This discussion is not a complaint. The attack on Chancery, which expands implicitly to indict the rest of the legal world as well, gives rise to several passages of fine rhetoric and is devastatingly successful. Our point is not a criticism, only an observation of what Dickens's critique of society does, and what it does not attempt to do. What Dickens does, perhaps better than any other writer, is to arouse our anger, indignation and outrage at suffering, injustice and idiocy in high places. What he does not do is to analyse and assign causes and solutions. Dickens works on the level of the emotions, appealing to the sense of fairness we may be said to feel in our 'gut'. If we are looking for a programme to address the ills of Victorian society, however, or a penetrating intellectual analysis of what was wrong, we will do better to read, for example, Mrs. Gaskell's *Mary Barton* (1848), or *North and South* (1855), or Karl Marx's *Capital* (Vol. 1, 1867). What Dickens will do is to rouse us up into a crowd, all ready to confront the authorities, and shout and stamp, insisting that things have to be better, in a civilised society.

Methods of analysis

1. As for the previous chapters, pay close attention to the way in which an extract is written, including such matters as vocabulary, diction, rhetorical or stylistic features, and imagery.

2. Consider the possibility that an image or a description may carry a symbolic significance that resonates through the text. We noticed, for example, that Tom-all-Alone's in *Bleak House* could be read as a symbolic description of the destruction wreaked upon a person by the baleful influence of Chancery.

3. However, in this chapter we have also allowed ourselves to frame and ask questions that are potentially critical of the novels, and then to consider the novels as wholes when framing answers.

4. Opinions and thoughts in answer to such critical questions can lead us back to the text to reread and assess relevant passages.

Suggested work

In *Hard Times*, study Mr. Sleary's role in the novel, his appearances at the beginning and the end. Consider particularly (a) how far Sleary can be said to articulate and represent a view of life robust enough to oppose that of Gradgrind and (b) how far Sleary's view is incorporated into other characters and events (such as Sissy Jupe?) in between his two crucial appearances.

In *Hard Times*, re-examine the scene between Louisa and Mr. Gradgrind in Chapter XV: 'Father and Daughter' (*HT*, 93–98); then make a close study of the matching opposite scene, that is, the interview between Louisa and Mr. Gradgrind when she has abandoned her marriage, in Book 2, Chapter XII: 'Down' (*HT*, 200–204). Consider these two dialogues as contributions to the critique of Utilitarianism in the novel. Pay particular attention to Louisa's descriptions of her thoughts and feelings at different times in her life, and to her ways of speaking to her father on these two occasions.

In *Hard Times*, study the scene between Rachael and Stephen on pages 86 and 87 (i.e. after Mrs. Blackpool is prevented from drinking poison), then read the passage about Stephen's 'promess' that was cut (this is printed in the notes of the World's Classics edition on pages 292–293); then study from the third paragraph on page 132 ('The orator having refreshed himself, …') to the end of paragraph 4 on page 136 (' … and left it, of all the working men, to him only'): the account of Stephen being sent to Coventry. How successful or unsuccessful do you find Dickens's treatment of this part of the narrative? Consider what difference it would make to your assessment, to reinsert the cancelled passage about the 'promess'.

In *Bleak House*, study the theme of hopeless poverty in the novel. Consider the role played by Jo the crossing sweeper; the two women from the brick-works; Charley and her siblings; and the passages set in Tom-all-Alone's. Consider how well these threads are integrated with the book's legal theme. This may lead you to return to the text to make a special study of the occasions when Tulkinghorn interviews Jo, and when Jo gives testimony at the inquest.

In *Bleak House*, study Chapter 15: 'Bell Yard', from its beginning on page 219 as far as the end of paragraph 2 on page 220 (' … in the east for three whole weeks'). Then compare this passage with the description of Mrs. Pardiggle's visit to the brick-makers' cottage (from page 118, paragraph 3, 'Mrs. Pardiggle, leading the way ... ', as far as page 123, the end of the first paragraph '... dealing in it to a large extent'). Consider the different ways in which Dickens adds to his critique of charity in these two passages, one narrative and the other reflective.

5

Rhetoric, Imagery
and Symbol

This chapter brings together the features of style, and the uses of metaphor, we have found during the detailed studies of extracts carried out in Part 1, so as to provide a fuller description of Dickens's characteristic prose style than any one of Chapters 1 to 4 could accommodate. To do this, we look at a further extract chosen from each of the novels we are studying, but we also refer back to passages we have met in previous chapters.

Patterns of language

Hard Times

We start with an extract from *Hard Times*: here is Dickens's manner of introducing Stephen Blackpool, which begins with the Coketown 'Hands' in general, before reaching Stephen himself:

CHAPTER X
STEPHEN BLACKPOOL
I ENTERTAIN a weak idea that the English people are as hard-worked as any people upon whom the sun shines. I acknowledge to this ridiculous idiosyncrasy, as a reason why I would give them a little more play.

In the hardest working part of Coketown; in the innermost
fortifications of that ugly citadel, where Nature was as strongly bricked
out as killing airs and gases were bricked in; at the heart of the labyrinth
of narrow courts upon courts, and close streets upon streets, which had
come into existence piecemeal, every piece in a violent hurry for some
one man's purpose, and the whole an unnatural family, shouldering,
and trampling, and pressing one another to death; in the last close
nook of this great exhausted receiver, where the chimneys, for want of
air to make a draught, were built in an immense variety of stunted and
crooked shapes, as though every house put out a sign of the kind of
people who might be expected to be born in it; among the multitude
of Coketown, generically called 'the Hands,' – a race who would have
found more favour with some people, if Providence had seen fit to make
them only hands, or, like the lower creatures of the seashore, only hands
and stomachs – lived a certain Stephen Blackpool, forty years of age.

Stephen looked older, but he had had a hard life. It is said that every life
has its roses and thorns; there seemed, however, to have been a misadventure
or mistake in Stephen's case, whereby somebody else had become possessed
of his roses, and he had become possessed of the same somebody else's thorns
in addition to his own. He had known, to use his words, a peck of trouble.
He was usually called Old Stephen, in a kind of rough homage to the fact.

(HT, 64)

The sarcasm is in the fourth word, 'I entertain a <u>weak</u> idea', and this
word immediately highlights the distinction between Dickens (and
us), and another group who think that any sympathy or kindness
shown to the workers, is weakness. We already know to whom this
refers: in Chapter 4 we have read about the opinions of Gradgrind
and Bounderby, that the Coketown Hands want to live in idle luxury.
We are already enlisted on the workers' side, our natural sympathy
having rejected Gradgrind and his school, Bounderby the 'Bully of
Humility', and the administration of Coketown; while sympathising
with Sissy Jupe, and the two little Gradgrinds. We therefore understand and follow the heavy sarcasm of 'ridiculous idiosyncrasy' and
the rest of the first paragraph.

The second paragraph is one sentence. It tells us only that Stephen
Blackpool lives in Coketown, but it consists of five parallel subordinate clauses, each elaborated into related dependent clauses. The
whole is a grand construction similar to a sustained *anaphora*: for the

introductory words to each clause are similar in meaning although not the same words. It may help for us to see how these five sections of the sentence unfold. The first is the simplest, consisting of one clause ('in the hardest working part of Coketown'). Although simple, we should remember that this clause is only completed at the end of the paragraph. We wait all that time for the answer: *what happened* in the hardest working part of Coketown? The answer is 'lived a certain Stephen Blackpool', 16 lines further on. This, then, is how the five parts of the sentence unfold:

1. (7 words) 1 clause, introduced by 'in the hardest';
2. (23 words) 3 clauses, introduced by 'in the innermost'. Clauses 2 and 3 balanced by nature ('bricked out'), killing airs ('bricked in');
3. (48 words) 8 clauses, introduced by 'at the heart of'. Including repetition of 'courts' and 'streets' in an internal parallelism structure, and a list of 3 participles (shouldering, trampling, pressing);
4. (54 words) 5 clauses, introduced by 'in the last close nook';
5. (42 words) 6 clauses, introduced by 'among the multitude'.

The main clause, together with one small subordinate, 'forty years of age', finish the paragraph. This analysis has shown that Dickens packs more and more into each parallel section of his sentence, until the longest two, parts 3 and 4, seem to be bulging, ready to explode with the details they carry. The paragraph describes the town as crowded, narrow, airless and enclosed: an impression Dickens builds his sentence to reinforce. It is as if each subordinate clause were one of the 'narrow courts upon courts' or among the 'close streets upon streets', overfilled with words that are packed in, and cannot escape.

Looking at the diction of this paragraph, we find quite a high incidence of adjectives and adverbs, as well as nouns and verbs that have descriptive qualities. If we start at the beginning, we find 'hardest working', 'innermost', 'ugly', 'strongly', 'killing', 'narrow', 'close', all within four lines, and soon encounter nouns with two attached adjectives: 'last close nook' and 'great exhausted receiver'. This vein in the diction also confirms our impression of Coketown's crowded narrowness and the feeling of being compressed: 'close' and 'narrow' obviously contribute to this idea, but there are also the images found in this paragraph, which carry a significant proportion of what Dickens wishes to convey to us. As usual, it is helpful to bring complex material into an easily studied form. Here is a list of the images, arranged as literal – figurative:

1. Coketown – an 'ugly citadel' with 'innermost fortifications';
2. Brick walls in Coketown – defences to keep Nature out;
3. Brick walls in Coketown – containment to keep 'killing' air and gas in;
4. Coketown courts and streets – a labyrinth;
5. Coketown courts and streets – personified, in a 'violent hurry';
6. Coketown courts and streets – personified as a family, but trampling each other to death because so crammed in, therefore an 'unnatural' family;
7. Coketown – a 'great exhausted receiver' (possibly a reference to bankruptcy?);
8. Coketown's chimneys – crooked and stunted like the physiques of Coketown inhabitants;
9. What the Coketown 'Hands' should have been, according to 'some people' – (a) only hands (i.e. only the part that works the machine in the factory, without anything else like brain, soul, or even the rest of the body, all of which are unnecessary to their lives); or (b) 'like the lower creatures of the seashore' only hands and stomachs.

Our first observation is that there is a lot of imagery in this paragraph. The literal side starts with Coketown, then moves to parts of Coketown (bricks, streets, courts, chimneys), before transferring to the people in the final (ninth) image. The figurative side begins with four ideas of inanimate but hostile building: fortress, walls (either of a prison or a fortress), and labyrinth. Then, images 5, 6, 7 and 8 build elaborated personification: Coketown is a family, with members trampling each other to death; and its chimneys are personified as stunted and crooked people. Finally, 'lower creatures' are invoked as what Coketown 'Hands' should be. So, our list helps us to see that the literal side moves from the inanimate town to its people; while the figurative side is more complicated: the figurative also moves from inanimate to people, in the form of personification. On the other hand, the metaphors are all about distortions of life: a family, but its members murder each other; people born there, but 'crooked and stunted'; and finally the grim picture of a creature 'only hands', or 'hands and stomach' – and Dickens puts a picture (perhaps) of jellyfish, starfish and shellfish, into our minds. The figurative side of these images, then, takes us via its Gothic 'citadel' and 'labyrinth', into a place where people live unnatural lives and are unnatural to look at. The final image also carries a sharp comment on the industrial economy: their 'hands' are all that society wants from them. The rest of them is really irrelevant, even a nuisance. So, the final image is not only a repulsive picture of what they might be, but also a repulsive picture of the unnatural demands made upon them by industrial work.

Our third paragraph is a straightforward comment on the 'hard life' Stephen has lived, which will soon be explained as his hopeless love for Rachael and his disastrous marriage. Here, with the balanced opposition of roses and thorns, Dickens creates linguistically the 'misadventure or mistake' whereby Stephen has all thorns and no roses. The balance of the proverb thus serves to illustrate how unfair it is to Stephen, and at the same time the social injustice, because 'somebody else had become possessed of his roses' and had given him their thorns to add to his own.

The passage we have studied here, then, contains a fine display of the rhetorical techniques we have become familiar with, as well as a rich vein of imagery and some of the subtle variations in tone that contribute so much to both the general drama of the text, and to the specific dramatic relationship we feel because the author's personality accompanies us so continuously.

Bleak House

The following paragraph comes from Esther's narrative of the journey she takes with Inspector Bucket, in pursuit of Lady Dedlock:

> I could eat nothing, and could not sleep; and I grew so nervous under these delays, and the slow pace at which we travelled, that I had an unreasonable desire upon me to get out and walk. Yielding to my companion's better sense, however, I remained where I was. All this time, kept fresh by a certain enjoyment of the work in which he was engaged, he was up and down at every house we came to; addressing people

whom he had never beheld before, as old acquaintances; running in to warm himself at every fire he saw; talking and drinking and shaking hands, at every bar and tap; friendly with every waggoner, wheelwright, blacksmith, and toll-taker; yet never seeming to lose time, and always mounting to the box again with his watchful, steady face, and his business-like 'Get on, my lad!'

(*BH*, 815)

The first part of this paragraph describes Esther's state of mind. Then, the bulk of it describes Inspector Bucket's behaviour. The opening two phrases tell us of Esther's tense state, and speak to us clearly and directly. Before we pass over such straightforward writing, however, we should notice something else: these two phrases are a *zeugma*, 'I' being the subject of both; and they are in what we could call a 'balancing' relation to each other. They can be analysed as:

- I could (verb, negative)
- I could (negative, verb)

The next two clauses are similarly related, both being governed by her feeling 'so nervous'; while these ideas and sensations in Esther set up the opposition of this and the next sentence, between 'get out and walk' and 'remained where I was'. This provides us with a larger version of 'balance', in the form of a tension between opposites that reflects Esther's nervous state: she is pulled both to get out and to remain in the carriage, simultaneously.

What we are finding, then, is that even at his simplest, Dickens writes with what we can call a sense of 'pattern'. We have found several examples of *anaphora*, *zeugma*, parallelism, lists, antitheses and the whole panoply of rhetorical effects, in our various analyses. Here, however, where we expect nothing elaborate, we are still treated to the patterned brevity of *verb/negative* followed by *negative/verb*. In place of this balance, Dickens might have written, for example, 'I could neither eat nor sleep'. Fine, we might say, both clear and direct; but of course, such a sentence would lack the grammatical inversion that lends what we are calling either 'balance' or 'pattern' to the prose. Let us see what happens when the description turns to Mr. Bucket.

The remainder of the paragraph is a single sentence. Bucket carries out a series of seven activities, each governed by 'All this time ... he was … '. Dickens has constructed a long sentence, which is a kind of structure we are now used to, where clauses separated by semi-colons are strung together in a way similar to *anaphora*, structurally parallel to each other, and in five out of seven cases, introduced by participles. This structure enables Dickens to elaborate his evocation of people or setting, as fully and at as great a length as he wishes. We met another such sentence in the extract from *Hard Times* we have just analysed, and we remarked that the way such sentences are crammed with detail gives them the effect of a sort of bursting fullness. On that occasion we thought the crowded and compressed narrowness of Coketown was conveyed, whereas the sentence we currently consider seems to 'burst' similarly, but this time with the activity and energy of Inspector Bucket.

There is more to notice, however. In order to appreciate the dense quality of Dickens's style, we will look for features in each of the seven subordinate clauses that are allotted to Bucket:

1. Antithesis/balance: Bucket is 'up and down';
2. Antithesis/balance: 'whom he had never beheld before'/'old acquaintances';
3. First 'every';
4. Three participles: 'talking…drinking…shaking';
   Two places: 'bar and tap'; second 'every';
5. Third 'every';
   Four trades: 'waggoner, wheelwright, blacksmith, and toll-taker';
6. And 7. Antithesis/balance: 'never … always';
7. Three adjectives: 'watchful, steady . . . business-like' and a form of *zeugma*: his 'face' and speech ('Get on, my lad!').

This list of features shows that even when we pay attention to what fills the structure of such sentences, there are subordinate structures that Dickens habitually indulges. He creates lists as he writes (see 4 and 5 above); he clearly thinks in terms of oppositions or antitheses; and he uses these habitually also, to construct balanced clauses (see 1, 2, 6 and 7 above); and he naturally spawns extra material, hanging it on his subject or verb in a form similar to *zeugma* or *anaphora* (see 7 above, and also the successive uses of 'every' in 3, 4 and 5). What is more, when it comes to straightforward adjectives, notice that Dickens again fills his writing: just as we found two double adjectives in *Hard Times*, so here there are three adjectives for Bucket at the end of this paragraph.

We have looked at two further passages at the start of this chapter, then, in order to confirm a number of insights into Dickens's style that we have met in previous analyses. In both cases, our study has drawn together several of the single rhetorical features we began to recognise in Chapter 1, and has pointed us towards a complex integration of several such features, or writing that exhibits similar effects and patterns while not quite displaying all the technical features of, say, *zeugma* or *anaphora*. We have learned that, even in those passages that are less overtly 'rhetorical', where Dickens is a storyteller rather than arguing his case, he has a predilection for antithesis, inversion, parallelism, lists and elaboration that patterns the writing throughout. At the same time, we should notice some significant differences between these two passages. Both are full of descriptive detail, but where our *Hard Times* extract contained nine images, the paragraph we have studied from *Bleak House* has none. Vivid, full of life and activity, yes, but literal, not figurative, throughout. We will return to this point in our discussion of **imagery** later in the present chapter.

Irony and sarcasm

In the following extract, Esther reflects upon the character of Harold Skimpole, and his friendship with Mr. Jarndyce:

> ... to find one perfectly undesigning and candid man, among many
> opposites, could not fail to give him [Mr. Jarndyce] pleasure. I should
> be sorry to imply that Mr. Skimpole divined this, and was politic. I
> really never understood him well enough to know. What he was to my
> Guardian, he certainly was to the rest of the world.
>
> (*BH*, 220–221)

This short reflection puts forward several possible truths. First, there are two possible Skimpoles: one is 'perfectly undesigning and candid', the other is 'politic'. Having spotted Mr. Jarndyce's weakness this Skimpole exploits it. Then, there are two possible Esthers.

One Esther suspects that Skimpole is self-interested, taking advantage of his friends' generosity in order to live as a parasite, but the other 'never really understood him well enough' to form such an opinion. The second Esther is the one who began the novel by telling us 'I know I am not clever' (*BH*, 24) and who remains unconfident of her own abilities. Next, there is the author's opinion of Skimpole, which can be judged from the passage of indirect speech that follows Esther's comments, where we hear Skimpole's sophistry as he justifies not paying people for their work. The author also has an opinion about Esther: that she is a great deal cleverer than she thinks, and her humility is an attractive virtue.

Finally, we come to the reader, who has opinions about both Skimpole and Esther. Our opinions are the least definable. We have to be conscious of being modern readers. So, we may find Esther's modesty, and her conviction that she is not clever, too twee and gender-stereotyped for the present day: it is the modesty a Victorian man looked for in a Victorian woman, but it may provoke irritation and impatience in us. What is more, we are likely to find Skimpole inexcusable. We will have noticed that, for a man who knows 'nothing of the value of money' (*BH*, 221), he spends almost all of his time talking about it; and we have already been through the unedifying spectacle of Richard and Esther paying his debts. So, modern readers may well read this passage with a mixture of annoyance and impatience, in the hope that Esther will open her eyes and not continue to be Skimpole's fool. A Victorian reader might, of course, have had a different reaction: Dickens's contemporaries might be more forgiving of Esther's modesty, and read about her with sympathy rather than impatience. On the other hand, they might condemn Skimpole more damningly even than we do.

We have selected these few sentences and formulated the various different viewpoints that are expressed or implied within them. That we can list more than one viewpoint tells us that this extract is ironic, and we have found other examples of irony from Esther's narrative, notably Mrs Woodcourt's visit that we analysed in Chapter 2 above. In this case the irony provokes two views each of Skimpole and Esther; and the effect of this irony is to provoke several further questions for us to meditate. Ultimately, we are led to consider questions about human nature, wisdom and morality. Is it better to be cynical and suspicious, or to expect goodness and trust your fellow beings? If it is better to be optimistic about human nature, at what point should we raise a defensive wall to save ourselves from becoming nothing better than victims? In short, are relations between people inevitably a kind of battle where each of us must fight to defend ourselves? Such questions are potentially also theological: should charity and forgiveness be infinite, or do they reach a reasonable limit?

Our visit to Esther's narrative has led us to some fundamental moral issues. We now turn to an example of irony from *Hard Times*, where Dickens himself is the narrator. Here, the author reflects upon James Harthouse after his departure from Coketown:

> The moral sort of fellows might suppose that Mr. James Harthouse derived some comfortable reflections afterwards, from this prompt retreat, as one of his few actions that made any amends for anything, and as a token to himself that he had escaped the climax of a very bad business. But it was not so, at all. A secret sense of having failed and been ridiculous – a dread of what other fellows who went in for similar sorts of things, would say at his expense if they knew it – so oppressed him, that what was about the very best passage in his life was the one of all others he would not have owned to on any account, and the only one that made him ashamed of himself.
>
> (*HT*, 219)

When looking at irony, we begin by formulating the different points of view that are represented in the text. In this paragraph there are three. First, there is the viewpoint of 'The moral sort of fellows' who expect Harthouse to feel good because he has done the right thing for once. Second, there is Harthouse who feels ashamed because he has failed in his adulterous project, a view which is shared by 'other fellows who went in for similar sorts of things', who would laugh at him if they knew. Third, there is the author's viewpoint, shared with the reader.

The first and second viewpoints, those of 'moral' fellows and of Harthouse, provide us with the irony of the narrative: Dickens indulges this verbal irony as part of his critique of society, thus pointing out the decadence of a fashionable social elite that regards morality as dull, and devotes itself to vice and dishonesty. This irony is neither subtle nor complicated. Dickens makes no secret of his own opinion: that Harthouse's retreat from Coketown is 'one of his few actions that made any amends for anything'. However, there is still one layer of meaning for us to recognise, in the author's patronising tone when he describes the 'moral sort of fellows'. Who are these people? They are optimists; and by implication they are those who expect characters to improve. Perhaps those who expect a story to reach a happy ending? In any event, Dickens paints them as naïve: they do not appreciate the resilience of an immoral society. Harthouse and his kind will resist change, and be ashamed of any good impulses. Society is set, obstinately, against redemption. This third element in the irony is part of a dialogue between author and reader. Dickens tells us not to expect a happy ending, because the real society he describes does not behave like a moral storybook. In fact, we are involved in a discussion of the relation between fiction and reality. Dickens is, as usual, keeping us company and advising us.

Sarcasm is an extreme form of irony: where there is irony, the text suggests or contains more than one meaning, simultaneously, but is not definitive about which meaning is true. Where there is sarcasm, on the other hand, the text's literal meaning is so obviously wrong that there remains only one true meaning: the opposite of that literal meaning. So, for example, when we read Dickens's admission that he thinks English workers work hard, he calls his belief a 'weak idea' and a 'ridiculous idiosyncrasy'. Of course, his opinion of the English worker is true, not 'ridiculous' or a 'weak idea' at all. Those phrases are sarcastic, put there to highlight not the ridiculousness of Dickens's opinion, but, on the contrary, the ridiculousness of the opposite belief. In the context of *Hard Times*, the wrong belief is that held by Bounderby, in the form of his 'golden spoon' idea. Dickens uses sarcasm frequently, and it is a prominent element in that dramatic presence of the author on which we have repeatedly remarked. We will look at examples from each of our texts, beginning with this account of Sissy's youth from Chapter IX of *Hard Times*:

> It is lamentable to think of; but this restraint was the result of no arithmetical process, was self-imposed in defiance of all calculation, and went dead against any table of probabilities that any Actuary would have drawn up from the premises. The girl believed that her father had not deserted her; she lived in the hope that he would come back, and in the faith that he would be made the happier by her remaining where she was.

The wretched ignorance with which Jupe clung to this consolation, rejecting the superior comfort of knowing, on a sound arithmetical basis, that her father was an unnatural vagabond, filled Mr. Gradgrind with pity.

(*HT*, 57)

Dickens writes in a heavily sarcastic mode in this passage. Utilitarianism is mocked in the phrases 'arithmetical process', 'calculation', 'table of probabilities' drawn up by an 'Actuary', and 'sound arithmetical basis', all of which he pretends to advocate, but ridicules. The sarcasm cuts deepest in the judgments: 'It is lamentable to think of', and 'wretched ignorance.' In the meantime, the argument turns out to be between Jupe's belief, hope and faith in her father, on the one hand, and the knowledge that he was 'an unnatural vagabond', on the other hand.

This extract, then, forms a part of Dickens's attack on Utilitarianism, The chapter from which it is drawn continues that attack, as Sissy Jupe gives several examples of how she gives wrong answers in class, that we think are the right answers. The sarcasm points Dickens's polemic, and dragoons the reader into agreement. There is, of course, a serious message about one's outlook upon the world, offering a choice between belief, hope and faith, on the one hand, and on the other hand, an 'arithmetic' that offers nothing beautiful to believe in, only a cynical pessimism. However, it is Dickens's presence, his voice with its withering scorn and bitter sarcasm, that brings him dramatically forward into our company as we read. The vicious phrase 'unnatural vagabond' carries the author's outrage because a child is offered this opinion of her father; and the picture of Sissy's natural belief, hope and faith is entirely sympathetic. We engage with Dickens in this campaign, therefore, because his emotions are engaged on the side of sensitivity and imagination, and against arithmetical calculation. The question of whether we feel browbeaten by Dickens, just as Sissy clearly feels browbeaten by the M'Choakumchilds, remains one for each individual reader to answer.

We have emphasised that there are numerous features of Dickens's writing that bring his personality into a relationship with the reader, and promote the impression that he is with us, and talking to us, continuously. Sarcasm is a frequent element in this authorial personality, and as we have seen, it is regularly called into service against such targets as, for example, Gradgrind's philosophy of 'facts'. Sometimes, however, the writing expresses such outraged and powerful emotion that there is a truly impassioned sarcastic outburst. Arguably, such moments coerce the reader more powerfully than any others. Here is one, from *Bleak House*, recording the death of Jo the crossing sweeper:

> Dead, your Majesty. Dead, my lords and gentlemen. Dead, Right
> Reverends and Wrong Reverends of every order. Dead, men and women,
> born with Heavenly compassion in your hearts. And dying thus around
> us, every day.
>
> (*BH*, 677)

The sarcasm here resides in the respectful address to 'your Majesty', 'my lords' and so on. But this example conveys a level of impassioned utterance beyond the satirical wrongness found in M'Choakumchild's classroom, and we can argue that it is outbursts like this that justify Dickens's habit of keeping company with us for so much of the time as we read.

Imagery

We have remarked on the imagery in several of the passages we have studied. Dickens regularly elaborates his narrative with similes and metaphors, and we have found it enlightening to interpret imagery and draw conclusions from such analysis, as we did, for example, with the paragraph about Coketown at the beginning of this chapter. There are also passages that are literal, where description is elaborated simply with an eye for detail but with no figurative idea – as we found in the extract about Esther and Inspector Bucket. Where Dickens indulges his penchant for the figurative, it is hard to over-estimate the intricacy of his figurative web. Here is a short extract from *Bleak House*, which begins with the simple idea of windows as eyes:

> The place in Lincolnshire has shut its many eyes again, and the house in
> town is awake. In Lincolnshire, the Dedlocks of the past doze in their
> picture-frames, and the low wind murmurs through the long drawing-
> room as if they were breathing pretty regularly. In town, the Dedlocks

of the present rattle in their fire-eyed carriages through the darkness of the night, and the Dedlock Mercuries with ashes (or hair-powder) on their heads, symptomatic of their great humility, loll away the drowsy mornings in the little windows of the hall. The fashionable world – tremendous orb, nearly five miles round – is in full swing, and the solar system works respectfully at its appointed distance.

(*BH*, 678)

With such a richly figurative passage, it is helpful to list the imagery, specifying literal and figurative, as we have done before:

1. The shutters over the windows of Chesney Wold being closed = the house's eyes shutting (i.e. as the house goes to sleep); Possible: the house as Argus (a many-eyed Greek god), suggested by the phrase 'its many eyes'.
2. Lights on and shutters open in the town house = the town house waking;
3. Portraits of Sir Leicester's ancestors hanging in picture frames in Chesney Wold = past Dedlocks dozing;
4. Sound of a low wind = regular breathing of the portraits;
5. The rattle of a carriage = the rattling of the current Dedlocks ('rattle' = slang for trivial conversation);
6. Carriage lanterns = burning eyes of the carriage;
7. Footmen = Mercuries (from Mercury, the Roman god, messenger with winged heels and helmet);
8. Hair powder = ashes, a sign of humility;
9. The fashionable area of West London = a planet with a circumference of five miles;
10. The solar system = a personality who keeps at a respectful distance from the world of fashion.

This is clearly a densely figurative paragraph. Can we see anything more from the list? Yes – there seems to be a group of images that are similar to each other: numbers 1, 2 and 6 compare lit-up houses and carriages at night, to eyes. The lit windows are eyes, therefore looking out. Later this is reversed, as we look in through small windows at Footmen in the hall of the town house. We can link the lit windows/ lanterns image to the ideas of dozing portraits, and a respectful solar system, since all of these image-ideas involve personification. The houses, sleeping and waking; the portraits, breathing regularly; and the solar system, ridiculously respectful of fashion: all of these imbue the setting of Dickens's narrative with conscious life.

Next, there is a possibility that the 'many eyes' of Chesney Wold liken that house to Argus, who was set to watch over the nymph Io – presumably Lady Dedlock. We may object that it is Tulkinghorn rather than the house who acts as a sort of hundred-eyed sentry over the nymph. Nonetheless, the idea of Chesney Wold as a place of many eyes does echo Lady Dedlock's fearful feeling of being watched, as expressed to Esther at their meeting.

Finally, the Mercuries and the absurd vanity of their hair powder being compared to ashes (scattered on the head as a sign of humility, grief and repentance), with the clear implication that they are the opposite of humble; the 'rattle' of trivial chatter and gossip as the carriage rattles; and the ludicrous idea that the solar system keeps its distance from a 'tremendous' five-mile-circumference 'orb': all of these image-ideas contribute to the satire of the fashionable world Dickens initiated in Chapter 2, 'In Fashion'. It was there (on page 20) that Dickens first referred to a 'Mercury in powder', and he has kept to this term for the Dedlocks' footmen, ever since. We have noticed such an extension of imagery before. Dickens no longer bothers with the literal 'footman', substituting the figurative 'Mercury' without explanation. Similarly, we remember how he dropped anything literal, like 'children' or 'pupils', in the opening chapters of *Hard Times*, and quickly began to refer to them by their figurative term, as 'the little pitchers'. In the case of the Mercuries, we have found a figurative idea proposed on page 20, subsequently treated as literal and elaborated some 658 pages later with an additional simile, when their hair powder is compared to ashes worn as a sign of humility.

We can see from this analysis, together with the other instances of imagery we have found during our studies of various extracts, that Dickens's text exhibits two traits. First, it is extremely rich in imagery, and the ideas called forth are varied and changeable moment by moment. Second, Dickens will often cast his writing into such a metaphorical form, that the metaphor becomes the subject of his literal narrative. This effect is difficult to describe, as it seems almost nonsensical. However, when we remember, for example, Dickens's references to 'the mad elephants' in *Hard Times*; the personifica-tion of Tom-all-Alone's as 'Tom' and 'he' (see *BH*, 654–657); or the references to 'that cart of his', the metaphor for Jo's breathing as it becomes 'heavier to draw' (see *BH*, 672, for example), we become aware of the vivid and imaginative world into which Dickens often invites us, by this means. We could describe this technique as 'liter-alising the figurative'.

Symbolism

There is, then, a great deal of imagery in Dickens's writing. How far are we justified in interpreting the many metaphorical ideas? How far do these ideas contribute significance, or add to the meaning of the text? We have already indulged in some interpretations, but in many cases the images seem simply designed to elaborate, or to provide a vivid impression, and so bring the narrative to life. In those cases, the image has temporary effect and importance merely as an idea the reader takes in, in passing; but its significance does not extend any further. Our question about interpretation is a larger and separate issue. Have we found more significant imagery in the passages we have analysed?

We found images that invited interpretation, when we studied the opening passage of each novel. In *Hard Times*, we noticed the sun-beam that shone across the classroom, linking Sissy Jupe and the boy Bitzer. Gradgrind is influenced by this natural accident without realising it, just as, later in the story, nature, in the form of Louisa's attraction to Harthouse and her aversion to her husband, reasserts its power over personal affairs, and shows its power over the Utilitarian 'arithmetic' Gradgrind has taken as his guide. The sunbeam, repre-senting nature, stands for that 'craving' which 'must and would be satisfied aright' because it is part of 'the laws of the Creation' (all from *HT*, 28). The sunbeam, then, can be read as a symbol of nature's power to negate Gradgrind's 'fact'-based philosophy.

When we analysed the opening of *Bleak House*, we commented on the fog that is 'densest' in the Court of Chancery, where the Chancellor sits 'at the very heart of the fog' (*BH*, 12). The fog is described as fill-ing the whole of London, and we know that in Dickens's day such 'pea-soupers' were common, so there is nothing unrealistic about this fog. On the other hand, Dickens leaves us in no doubt that his fog has added meaning: it represents the obfuscation, delays and confusions of the law as practised in the Court of Chancery. In *Bleak House*, then, just as in *Hard Times*, we have remarked that Dickens allocates symbolic meaning to an aspect of the setting. We may also draw conclusions about nature: that a sunbeam comes cleanly to earth, created by nature; while a London fog, which Guppy calls a 'London particular' (*BH*, 37), was created by coal fires and pollution, an unwelcome and unhealthy offshoot of human activity – just like the confusions and delays of the law.

At the opening of each of our texts, then, there are signs that features of the setting are being enhanced with significance, that they carry part of the meaning of the text. Remember that analysing imagery involves defining two sides of a comparison. So, for example, we have analysed a comparison between the steam engines of Coketown and mad elephants, and found that the steam engines are literal (i.e. actually there in the story) and the elephants are figurative (an idea, not literally there). Now, to return to our sunbeam and fog examples: when we analyse these effects as imagery, notice that both sides of the comparison can be considered as 'literal', that is, actually there in the story. We know there is a sunbeam, and there is fog, so these are literal. Is there nature, a 'law of the Creation' ultimately victorious over the 'fact' philosophy, in *Hard Times*? Yes, there is. Nature is there, part of the story, so that is also literal. Is there incomprehensible confusion and exacerbated delay, in the world of the law, in *Bleak House*? Yes, that is also present, part of the real or 'literal' world of the novel. When you find a feature that seems to be significant, and where you can think of both aspects as 'literal', then it is acceptable to call this element in the text 'symbolic'. In this section we will look at some other elements, in each of our novels, that can be thought of as symbols, and can therefore enhance our understanding of the text.

In *Hard Times*, the smoke and smut of Coketown are repeatedly evoked, so that the covering over the town, and its baleful influence over the surrounding area, are like a constant blot in the background. We have noticed this in the overview of Coketown we studied in Chapter 4, and it appears in the background through the windows of Stone Lodge, seen from Gradgrind's study. When Sissy and Rachael go for a walk in the countryside, on the Sunday when they discover Stephen, there is further description of the smoke and industrial dirt associated with the town, as well as a further developed significance to the contrast between nature, and its distortion by industrial workings such as the Old Hell Shaft.

As Coketown cast ashes not only on its own head but on the neighbourhood's too – after the manner of those pious persons who do penance for their own sins by putting other people into sackcloth – it was customary for those who now and then thirsted for a draught of pure air, which is not absolutely the most wicked among the vanities of life, to get a few miles away by the railroad, and then begin their walk, or their lounge in the fields. Sissy and Rachael helped themselves out of the smoke by the usual means, and were put down at a station about midway between the town and Mr. Bounderby's retreat.

Though the green landscape was blotted here and there with heaps of coal, it was green elsewhere, and there were trees to see, and there were larks singing (though it was Sunday), and there were pleasant scents in the air, and all was over-arched by a bright blue sky. In the distance one way, Coketown showed as a black mist; in another distance hills began to rise; in a third, there was a faint change in the light of the horizon where it shone upon the far-off sea. Under their feet, the grass was fresh; beautiful shadows of branches flickered upon it, and speckled it; hedgerows were luxuriant; everything was at peace. Engines at pits' mouths, and lean old horses that had worn the circle of their daily labour into the ground, were alike quiet; wheels had ceased for a short space to turn; and the great wheel of earth seemed to revolve without the shocks and noises of another time.

They walked on across the fields and down the shady lanes, sometimes getting over a fragment of a fence so rotten that it dropped at a touch of the foot, sometimes passing near a wreck of bricks and beams overgrown with grass, marking the site of deserted works. They followed paths and tracks, however slight. Mounds where the grass was rank and high, and where brambles, dock-weed, and such-like vegetation, were confusedly heaped together, they always avoided; for dismal stories were told in that country of the old pits hidden beneath such indications.

(*HT*, 245–246)

There are two mentions of Coketown itself, which both show characteristics the reader has come to expect. We are familiar with the picture of the town producing ash and smoke, and we have met the idea that

Coketown hides itself, or becomes invisible within its own smoke, several times already. For example, Coketown is 'suggestive of itself' although 'not a brick of it could be seen' (*HT*, 105). Here, 'Coketown showed as a black mist'. On this occasion, however, Dickens develops his idea about the town's smoke, comparing the 'ashes' to signs of humility and repentance, and using this idea to criticise those who make sure that other people suffer for the sins they have committed. In this way the town is personified as a character similar to Mr. Bounderby, the 'bully of humility'.

Coketown, then, spreads its ash over the surrounding area. Although Rachael and Sissy are said to travel 'out of the smoke' for their country walk, the landscape still carries significant industrial blots. For two thirds of our middle paragraph the description is mainly positive: despite being 'blotted here and there with heaps of coal', the landscape is green, with trees, larks, pleasant scents and a 'bright blue sky'. Coketown is mentioned, hidden in its smoke: but then we learn of beautiful woodland shadows, and we read 'fresh', 'beautiful', 'luxuriant' and 'everything was at peace'. In this area, then, beautiful nature is in the ascendant, with some blots of coal, and Coketown hiding in the distance. Notice that in two directions the view is clear – towards hills and towards the sea – while only one has the 'black mist'.

The pits do not work on a Sunday, so their wheels are still, enabling Dickens to remind us of nature, that will endure, as 'the great wheel of earth'. This landscape seems to be representative of something larger than Coketown's industry, a nature that will outlast and eventually cover over the workings of humanity. There remain some industrial dangers, even this far away from the town, however. First, we read of a 'wreck' of bricks and beams, overgrown with grass, as the site of deserted works; then Sissy and Rachael carefully avoid 'Mounds where the grass was rank and high, and where brambles, dock-weed, and such-like vegetation, were confusedly heaped together' because these places are the treacherous covering for old pits – such as the Old Hell Shaft into which Stephen has fallen.

Dickens has created, here, a landscape in which each element is significant. There are several examples of wholesome nature, but at the same time there are visual flaws such as piles of coal, and the lean old pit-horses in their endless circles. Then, there is the ambiguity of growth: fresh, beautiful and luxuriant growth, but at the same time, grass growing over the wreck of deserted works, and mounds of fertile growth – grass, brambles, dockweed, and similar vegetation – which have grown over the lethal danger of the worked-out pits. Stephen says of the Old Hell Shaft that 'When it were in work, it killed wi'out need; when 'tis let alone, it kills wi'out need', for he knows that within living memory it has cost 'hundreds and hundreds o' men's lives' (quotes from *HT*, 251). The landscape Dickens depicts in this chapter, then, is almost an allegory for nature versus industry. The passage we have looked at contributes to the critique of an industrial society by describing the 'pious' bosses as those 'who do penance for their own sins by putting other people into sackcloth'; by showing a partly spoiled landscape several miles from the town; and by its description of the dangerous uncapped shafts, left open by those same irresponsible authorities. The governing idea at the start of the passage, we remember, was about the wider spreading of Coketown's smoke and ash. What is spread into the surrounding countryside is not just literal smoke, it is also the danger from hypocritical authorities who ignore petitions and leave everything unsafe. In a sense, we can interpret the Coketown smoke as representing all that is wrong with an industrial society, from the suffering workers to the careless bosses and back again.

Finally, we can apply our test. The smoke of Coketown is the literal side of this proposed comparison. Coketown is an industrial centre based on steam engines stoked by coal, so, yes: the smoke is real and is there, it is literal. What about the careless and unsafe practices of those in charge, and their unwillingness to make any improvements? Are these elements present in the novel? Yes, the wrongness of industrial society is present in *Hard Times*, and is also literal. We can say, therefore, that the Coketown smoke acts as a symbol, part of the significant meaning of the text.

In *Bleak House*, the story of the 'Ghost's Walk', the sound of eerie footsteps along the terrace and Chesney Wold, is told in Chapter VII. There follows a series of descriptions both of the 'curious' noise itself, and of the terrace in different weathers, particularly under rain or darkness. The story is, we must suppose, a superstition. However, what it implies is that a 'calamity' or 'disgrace' will come to the Dedlock family, and their pride will be brought down (*BH*, 104). The sound on the terrace is referred to several times to enhance the sense of tension in the Dedlock household, as the duel between

Lady Dedlock and Mr. Tulkinghorn becomes increasingly desperate and moves towards its crisis. In short, the 'Ghost's Walk' really represents the secret scandal, the falseness and fragility that underlies the apparent prosperity and self-satisfaction of the Dedlocks.

When Esther discovers that she is Lady Dedlock's daughter, she visits Chesney Wold by night, and reaches a new interpretation of the old superstition:

> The way was paved here, like the terrace overhead, and my footsteps from being noiseless made an echoing sound upon the flags. Stopping to look at nothing, but seeing all I did see as I went, I was passing quickly on, and in a few moments should have passed the lighted window, when my echoing footsteps brought it suddenly into my mind that there was a dreadful truth in the legend of the Ghost's Walk, that it was I who was to bring calamity upon the stately house and that my warning feet were haunting it even then. Seized with an augmented terror of myself which turned me cold, I ran from myself and everything, retraced the way by which I had come, and never paused until I had gained the lodge-gate, and the park lay sullen and black behind me.
>
> (*BH*, 540)

Esther is comforted by letters from Ada and from her Guardian, and eventually rejects this idea. Nonetheless, it is true to say that Esther's existence is dangerous to the Dedlocks. In the sense that a calamity and disgrace is stalking the terrace with ominous footsteps, it is rational for Esther to feel that she herself embodies the scandal that is approaching. Certainly, this idea can be traced to other parts of the text also. For example, Guppy becomes set upon his investigative project as a result of recognising the likeness between Esther and her mother, while Esther visits Guppy, hoping to seal off the danger of his revealing anything.

The story of the 'Ghost's Walk' is a vague element in *Bleak House*, being at root a superstition, or an auditory accident. We may ask if it is anything that is literally there, in the book, and we may be puzzled to answer. It is worth remarking how carefully Dickens handles this element, so that our belief does not become over-strained, and so that coincidence further contributes to the effects he achieves. So, for example, when Watt describes the sound, he calls it 'the rain-drip on the stones … and I hear a curious echo – I suppose an echo – which is very like a halting step' (*BH*, 103). He 'supposes' an echo, using the language of a man who finds out how things work, and whose mind works in the scientific manner. Consequently, the sound is 'very like' a step, but it is not actually a step. So, we are convinced that, whatever the beliefs surrounding this phenomenon, it is nonetheless capable of a rational explanation.

Now return to Esther's nocturnal wander to Chesney Wold. The coincidence is prepared by her footsteps making 'an echoing sound', so that the reader is already alerted to previous descriptions of the Ghost's Walk, before her own position suddenly strikes Esther: 'there was a dreadful truth in the legend of the Ghost's Walk, that it was I who was to bring calamity upon the stately house and that my warning feet were haunting it even then'. Manoeuvring Esther into the position where her own feet are sounding the Ghost's Walk upon the terrace of Chesney Wold is a Dickensian masterstroke. As we know, Dickens makes quite shameless use of coincidence; but in this instance it is his ability to place his character perfectly, ready for the prepared moment of realisation about the threat she embodies, that is such a successful confluence between character and plot. At the same time, we can deduce that Dickens employs the 'Ghost's Walk' as a symbol of the Dedlock household's actual fragility, and that this symbol can take in all the dangers that threaten the serenity of Sir Leicester and his house, including, in this instance, Esther, but also Mr. Tulkinghorn on other occasions. We may speculate that the significance spreads to indicate two further insights that are part of Dickens's social critique: first, the weak foundations and vulnerability to scandal of the whole fashionable world; and second, the obsolete political outlook, and waning influence, of the Dedlock class, as shown during the Coodle and Doodle election. The footsteps on the terrace, foretelling the decline of Sir Leicester's kind, and the fragility of fashion in general, is a suitable interpretation of this feature of the text.

We have looked at the smoke from Coketown, a sunbeam and a fog; and we have discussed a superstitious story, a family tradition. These topics have arisen from studying imagery in our two texts, and have led us into the more speculative area called symbolism. I call symbolism more speculative, because it is possible to read significance into almost anything, to see symbolism everywhere. Can you think of a symbolic meaning for Boythorn's bird, or for Bounderby's door knob? Probably a fertile imagination could interpret these details, but at the risk of reading in a meaning Dickens never intended. However, there are some features of these texts that seem to go farther still. These are occasions when the figurative, or the fantastic, seems to dominate the narrative. We have already remarked that Dickens frequently writes in a metaphorical mode, and that we are often plunged into a world where the imagination is as prominent as detailed realism. The following are examples of episodes where Dickens seems to go farther still into a world of imagination.

In *Hard Times*, Stephen Blackpool is pulled from the Old Hell Shaft, and tells Rachael to 'look up yonder', whereupon she 'saw that he was gazing at a star'. Stephen then explains how the star has influenced his mind, so he is now reconciled to his fate. This leads to his 'dyin prayer that aw th' world may on'y coom toogether more, an' get a better unnerstan'in o' one another' (all from *HT*, 252). The star is mentioned again on the next page, when Stephen 'awmust' believes it to be 'the star as guided to Our Saviour's home'; and he is pleased that they carry him away 'in the direction whither the star seemed to him to lead' (all from *HT*, 253). Clearly, Dickens has inserted this star into his narrative in order to highlight a straightforward Christian message: all Stephen's complaints and his sense of anger and injustice are soothed away by the star. It shines into his mind with a message of universal 'unnerstan'in'. There is a little care in the way Dickens writes: Stephen only 'awmust' thinks he sees the Biblical star that guided the three kings, so we are not quite asked to accept a miracle. However, there are touches here that go beyond the natural. First, have you ever followed another person's look and, merely by watching their eyes, been able to identify a star they are looking at? I doubt it. Rachael could not have seen the star, at least not without him identifying it much more precisely than by saying 'look up yonder … Look aboove!' She would probably have seen a hundred stars. Second, the star shone down into the Old Hell Shaft; it 'shined upon me' and 'shined into my mind'. Again, Dickens asks us to stretch our belief. If we think about the reality of Stephen's position, and what we know of the night sky, we will become sceptical. Stephen is far down in the pit, and stars move through the sky as the earth turns, so from where he saw the star, he would only see it for a few minutes at most. Yet, he talks as if the star stopped and shone, directly into the Old Hell Shaft, all night, each night, while he was trapped there. Put simply, the whole idea is most unlikely, but Dickens does not expect us to reject the star, and his final reference to it confirms its supernatural, magic existence: 'The star had shown him where to find the God of the poor; and through humility, and sorrow, and forgiveness, he had gone to his Redeemer's rest' (*HT,* 253).

In this story of Stephen and the star, then, Dickens writes of something that behaves in a magical manner, and yet which we are urged to accept at face value as a part of the real setting of the scene. For these reasons, it is a way of writing that is sometimes called 'magic realism'. It is a way of writing that Dickens occasionally indulges, and often approaches when in his most metaphorical narrative mode. We may question Stephen's forgiving sainthood, since he calls on Gradgrind to clear his name, obviously at the expense of accusing young Tom, but the star's redemptive magic is not only asserted in the final sentence of the chapter, it also extends to its magical behaviour in the sky.

In *Bleak House*, the spontaneous combustion of Krook is the most prominent example of a similar project of 'magic realism'. Dickens goes to considerable trouble to prepare us for the shocking event. The first mention of an unwholesome atmosphere in Krook's house comes on page 469, when Weevle complains that he has been 'stewing and fuming' in his room, and they notice that the candle burns oddly, 'smouldering'. On page 472, Guppy notices his coat sleeve: 'See how the soot's falling. See here, on my arm! See again, on the table here! Confound the stuff, it won't blow off – smears, like black fat!' They mention cooking chops, and a chimney fire, to explain the phenomenon, but as the two young men talk, Guppy was 'still glancing with remarkable aversion at his coat-sleeve'. On page 474 they open the window because there is more of 'this hateful soot' and the room is 'too close'. Then, on pages 475–476, Guppy notices that 'A thick, yellow liquor defiles' his fingers, which is 'offensive' to touch, smell and sight. It is 'A stagnant, sickening oil, with some natural repulsion in it that makes them both shudder'. They are horrified by seeing the stuff running down the brickwork, and Guppy spends the remaining time trying to scrub his hand clean, before Weevle goes down to see Krook. Most of pages 476 to 479 are then taken up by description of the discovery, and the gradual realisation of what has happened to Krook. Clearly, Dickens has prepared this moment elaborately, bringing his reader on board by means of several spaced-out preliminary mentions of soot, of fat, and eventually the disgusting yellow oil. He has prepared us to accept the event by spreading it out as a gradual revelation, naturalistically described. Here again, he writes in a mode that we could call 'magic realism', a mode where the unnatural is described as actually taking place.

Before leaving this example we should note that Dickens defended his account of Krook's spontaneous combustion energetically. When critics declared that it was impossible Dickens pointed out contemporary records claiming that such fires had taken place and been witnessed, seemingly supporting his own sincere belief in the phenomenon (see, for example, the 1853 Preface, page 6, in our edition). Despite his own belief in spontaneous combustion, Dickens evidently realised that he had a difficult job to do to carry his reader's belief with him through this event. Our analysis shows this, by how carefully he prepared the final shock.

We have commented previously on the free use Dickens makes of coincidence, as well as pointing out the free manner in which he develops and pursues certain metaphors, 'literalising' them. The two examples we have given of effects we call 'magic realism', are symptomatic of another observation about the characteristics of Dickens's works: nature is often brought into service, and made to behave in a way that is a convenient adjunct to Dickens's purpose. There is a difference between the 'magic' behaviour of Stephen's star and, say, the natural behaviour of the rainstorm that soaks Mrs. Sparsit when she pursues Louisa, in *Hard Times*; just as Krook's combustion is different from the natural rain that falls on Chesney Wold at various times in *Bleak House*, or from the natural fog of the first chapter. Nevertheless, we can see that Dickens frequently enlists nature and setting as his supporters in adding both drama and appropriate significance to the narrative.

Concluding discussion

In this chapter, we have taken a further look at the texture of the writing in *Hard Times* and *Bleak House*. In doing so we have revisited some of the rhetorical features found in previous analyses, but we have then considered imagery, irony and sarcasm, symbols and 'magic realism' with examples of each. The next chapter attempts to sum up what we have learned in Part 1 of this book. Here, we only wish to emphasise one conclusion about Dickens's style, that is evident whatever the feature we happen to be analysing: Dickens's writing is always hard at work, unceasingly urging us to accompany him, to agree with him, to feel the emotions and reactions he proposes. Everything in his writing pushes, subjects us to the pressure of being with Dickens. So, his style usually works with a ladle rather than just a spoon. Notice, for example, the condensed single-minded intensity with which Rachael and Sissy are presented in *Hard Times*. We are rarely given any rest from the author's shaping and dominating power, whether the method is browbeating sarcasm, vivid significant metaphor, laughter or simply description interwoven with dialogue or narrative. What is the ultimate effect of this continuous engagement with the writer, and this unceasing deployment of linguistic power?

An author who deploys so much personality so prominently runs a risk, of course. He offers us his company and regularly urges us to adopt his opinions: but, what if we do not like him? What if his personality becomes irksome? Or we are critical of his opinions? Individual readers must choose how far Dickens persuades them, and whether there are significant parts of the author's project they reject. You may feel that simply wanting nicer industry and more philanthropy, will never re-structure a capitalist economy or the society it produces. On the other hand, this absence of any solution may be seen not as a fault, but rather as a sign of Dickens's success in showing us a society too riven with corruption, idiocy and injustice, and too complex and overpopulated, to be susceptible of any solution. In the next chapter, we try to set out some of the arguments about Dickens's achievement that remain open, in the form of questions to explore.

Methods of analysis

• Close analysis of extracts uses the same approaches as have previously been demonstrated. However, in this chapter the features of style previously noticed are brought together into a description of Dickens's style as a whole. In particular, we have used lists of:
  – clauses from extended sentences, to highlight features of sentence structure;

- imagery, analysed as literal – figurative, enabling us to see related images or groups of similar ideas, and groups of developing ideas;
- features found in subordinate clauses in an extended sentence, which emphasise the densely 'patterned' style of Dickens's writing.

Making lists is a valuable technique because it presents information in a form that highlights the features or effects we are analysing. We have used several different kinds of lists, but we were constantly impressed by the unremitting level of **'pattern'** in Dickens's style.

- In the latter parts of this chapter, we approached Dickens's use of **irony** and **sarcasm**, as a specific focus for study of his polemical writing, and we looked at the elements of **imagery** that may be called 'symbolic'. In this effort, we examined the text with particular questions in mind, such as:
  - How believable or 'realistic' is this event?
  - How far can this comparison be considered to be literal on both sides?

We found evidence of **symbols** in the Coketown smoke from *Hard Times* and the Ghost's Walk from *Bleak House*. Notice that one stage in this analysis involved defining an abstract element of the text as 'literal': in the case of *Hard Times*, the suffering and injustice – the 'wrongness' of an industrial society; in the case of *Bleak House*, the fragility of the Dedlocks' privilege and fashion. These abstract elements were then said to be 'represented' by the smoke and the Ghost's Walk respectively.

Finally, we found elements of the text where the narrative attempts to carry the reader through unlikely, or what we have called 'magical' episodes. Our examples were Stephen Blackpool's star, from *Hard Times*, and Krook's spontaneous combustion, from *Bleak House*. We suggested that these features could be called **'magic realism'**.

Analysing both **symbolism** and **magic realism** involves reading the text with close attention to the sceptical questions about narrative realism, given above.

Suggested work

1. Taking the list of stylistic features we compiled in the first part of this chapter, select any two pages of either *Hard Times* or *Bleak House* at random, and, using highlighters or underliners and a colour-coding system, identify the features you find in your randomly chosen passage. This will show how Dickens employs multiple techniques, and will reveal the stylistic richness of his text. When you have tackled one text in this way, do the same for the other.

2. In **Bleak House**, study Richard Carstone and Chancery by looking back at the various times he appears in the narrative after he has chosen the law as his profession, and up to his death. From your study of the way Richard's health is described on these occasions, give your own assessment: is the impression that Chancery kills Richard an achievement of '**magic realism**', or not? Therefore, how well does this narrative project succeed?

3. In **Hard Times**, look at the influence of Sissy Jupe, from Louisa's return to Stone Lodge to the end of the novel. What do you think Dickens hoped to achieve with this development of Sissy? Is there a '**magic**' element to her characterisation? Does the project succeed?

6

Summative Discussion and Conclusions to Part One

In this chapter we bring together the outcomes of our studies in Chapters 1 to 5. With regard to **Dickens's techniques**, whether in his manipulation of characters or themes, or in his sentence-by-sentence rhetorical patterns, we have reached some insights that can be summarised:

1. Dickens's writing is always elaborately **patterned**;
2. Dickens is exceptionally present, **keeping his reader company**, and urging us to join him in his **emotions** and to agree with his **opinions**;
3. Dickens usually begins characterisation by depicting a **grotesque**. Some characters later develop psychological or emotional depth;
4. Dickens uses a range of shallow or 'grotesque' background characters to create an illusion of a real population for the world of the text;
5. Dickens's writing is usually rich in **figurative ideas**; often these ideas are **'literalised'** and developed subsequently, giving rise to a narrative mode that depends on metaphor; and
6. Dickens sometimes allocates significance to elements of the narrative, as **symbols**; and occasionally he undertakes a narrative project we could call **'magic realism'**.

Having listed these insights into the author's techniques, we turn to face issues concerning our overall experience of these novels: the themes and content. When we face these issues – for example looking at them as proposing a critique of society, or as representing human nature – then we find that most of the conclusions we have reached are complex, and raise questions rather than laying anything to rest. An example will underline this.

The opening salvos

Dickens's attacks upon Utilitarianism and the Court of Chancery respectively, are such powerfully polemic openings that we asked: how fully does the ensuing novel bear out the campaigning promise of such a start? We reached the conclusion that Dickens continued to work on these themes throughout each novel. So, the rather stilted discussion of philosophy between Gradgrind, Bitzer and Sleary in the penultimate chapter of *Hard Times*, and the death of Richard in *Bleak House*, give evidence that the twin targets of 'Facts' and 'fog' are still in Dickens's sights: that the attacks launched on each novel's opening page, are carried through.

However, we were also slightly dissatisfied by this conclusion. We made two observations about each novel, which at least weakened, if they did not divert us from the initial positive finding. With regard to *Hard Times*, we noticed (1) that the dominant plot of, approximately, the second half of the novel, is the crime and detection story of Tom's theft from the bank; a story that drives events and keeps us turning pages, but which has little relevance to Utilitarianism. Then, we recognised (2) that Dickens develops his critique of industrial society, and depicts the sufferings and injustices imposed upon the working 'Hands', with decreasing reference to Gradgrind's philosophy, and an increasingly direct attack on straightforward greed and the abuse of power. In *Bleak House* we remarked that (1) the dominant and gripping plot at the centre of the novel, is the plot about Lady Dedlock's secret and Esther's parentage. This is a society scandal tragedy, founded on a passionate but doomed romance: a story drawn from the tradition of Gothic fiction. It is this plot that drives our interest through the book, and it has nothing to do with the Court of Chancery. Then we remarked that (2) there is a powerful appeal to our anger and sympathy on behalf of the destitute and abused, in the form of Jo, the brick-makers' wives and the dead baby. This emotional appeal at least competes with, and arguably eclipses, our sympathy for Richard, Miss Flite and Gridley, the victims of Chancery. In both novels, then, we felt that the reader's sympathy is diverted by the appeal of competing themes, and the reader's interest is held by conventional plots, both features which dilute the potency of Dickens's attacks on Utilitarianism and Chancery. Such are the complex conclusions we have attempted to articulate from our studies.

Questions

Instead of attempting to formulate conclusions where each one needs to be elaborated or qualified, we will approximate the state to which our ideas have been brought by our studies so far, by framing a series of questions. Each of these questions should send us back to the text to seek evidence for and against each answer. In each case individual readers may reach their own answers, different from those of other readers. Each of us is likely to reach a complex answer, in any event. We are likely to say that the truth is partly on one side, and partly on the other. One general insight is indicated by this: that Dickens is a writer who provokes a peculiarly personal set of responses.

Here is a list of questions, together with a brief discussion to put each into context.

1. Are the initially stated themes of these two novels developed and sustained?
    We have discussed this question as our example above. We have suggested that the adoption of a central genre-typical plot (crime story; society scandal); and the development of powerful competing themes (wrongness of industrial society; outrage at illiterate destitution) detract from the overall impact of the initial attack, although that theme is also followed through.
2. Is Dickens's characterisation 'realistic' or 'psychological'? How we define 'psychological' will determine our answer here. Esther has her psychology: she underestimates her own abilities, is coy and shy about her love for Allan Woodcourt and covers psychological

discomfort by being busy. Does this amount to a 'psychologically' drawn character? Elsewhere, Louisa Gradgrind is difficult to follow: she seems to be half-psychology and half-development of the Utilitarianism theme. When she is demonstrating Dickens's theory of the irresistible 'law of Creation', Louisa is less convincing. There are acute psychological observations of Richard Carstone: both of his self-deceptions and his obsession.

Many characters experience powerful emotions of shock, horror or emotional pain. Are these 'realistic'? Does a strong emotion make a character 'psychological'?

3. Is the characterisation of angelic women a weakness in the context of Dickens's range of characterisation?

Earlier in our study we suggested that Esther's virtues of humility and housekeeping are qualities that would be admired by a Victorian man in a Victorian woman. We have been critical, as modern readers, of Dickens's angelic women. However, we need to consider how much allowance to make for the contemporary readership. Also, we should recognise that these women carry a significant part of Dickens's overtly Christian message. Therefore, deciding how we respond to these women is also a response to that message.

4. Is Dickens's Christian/individualist philosophy adequate to the task his novels set for it?

This is a very difficult issue to consider, and is one where different readers will reach very different conclusions. Dickens seems to show a high-principled Christianity in action, for example in Rachael's care for Mrs. Blackpool, in Mr. Jarndyce renouncing his right to marry Esther and in Woodcourt's prayer with Jo. Self-sacrifice and forgiveness are the characteristics. However, this high-flown Christianity is not always effective beyond its brief and limited purpose. Notice that Sir Leicester Dedlock's conspicuous forgiveness of his wife does not save her life. We remarked that Sissy wields the power of something we called 'goodness' over Harthouse. She sends him away successfully. On the other hand, he relapses into vice straight away afterwards.

There are also questions about self-sacrifice: do we find that Ada's hiding of her feelings from her husband is too dishonest for our approval? How do we feel about Esther's high-principled rejection of Allan's proposal?

The question here, as with Dickens's social critique, is: what does the author claim for his Christian theme? Do these novels set any particular 'task' for the Christian faith, or is it to be seen merely as a good way of living and behaving, but unlikely to have more than occasional local or domestic benefits?

5. Is there a difficulty in that Dickens proposes only domestic solutions to what are primarily political and economic evils?

We looked at Dickens's critiques of society, in Chapter 4, and we found that there is a preponderance of very powerful and effective anger and outrage at the way things are; but there is a deficit when it comes to analysis or if we look for solutions. We remarked that Dickens would like industrial cities to have more trees, safer and quieter machines and so forth. Similarly, he wants Chancery to deal with its cases expeditiously, without so many lawyers and dusty old files. These prescriptions for reform are vague and optimistic. What comes through strongly, and enlists our outrage alongside that of our companion Dickens, is the apparent social horrors he describes.

The resolution of each novel is worth thinking about when considering this question. In *Hard Times*, remember that Rachael continues working (presumably in Bounderby's mill) and caring for Stephen's alcoholic wife, until she is too old to continue. No change there: and the Gradgrinds live more happily, but in the protective comfort of their wealth and outside town. In *Bleak House*, an idyllic domestic and professional ambit is given to Esther and Allan, in a country area some distance from London. The suggestion that Dickens's novels can only retreat from the world, behind a barrier of privacy and domesticity, when faced by the rampant sores and evils of Victorian society, seems a valid way of describing the resolution offered by these texts.

6. Do these novels propose a society too fractured, complex and corrupted for any coherent interpretation to encompass?

Here we come to a question we have already considered in two of its constituent parts: in relation to the texts' Christianity; and in relation to the analysis of society. Each reader will have to think this one through very carefully for themselves, in order to reach their own accommodation with Dickens. For example, aside from considering the thoughts we have already mentioned in 4 and 5 above, it is also important to acknowledge the crowded population Dickens provides. Look at a world containing the Chadbands, Krook, the Smallweeds, the Bagnets, George and Squod, Vholes, the Snagsbys, the Jellybys and Pardiggles, the brick-makers and their wives, Miss Flite, Mr. Gridley, Conversation Kenge, Jo, Bucket, Guppy and Jobling – and this list is far from complete. Such a world contains a great deal of greed and evil, and a minority of sympathetic people. Furthermore, it is apparent that only those with enough money can hope to control their environment in order to live a reasonable life.

This leads us to a further question, which indicates why readers are so divided about Dickens. It comes as two conditional questions. It is as follows, and we will leave it on the page without further discussion, as it is the crux of our response to *Hard Times* and *Bleak House*.

If you have reached the answer that yes, Dickens does present a fractured, insolubly complex and corrupted society, does this express the author's view, or is it a fatal weakness, an incoherence that represents a failure of Dickens's art?

If, on the other hand, you have decided that Dickens's optimistic Christian message can outweigh the fractures and corruption he also depicts, is this a measure of artistic success, or does it reduce these novels to mere facile moral fables?

PART 2

THE CONTEXT
AND THE CRITICS

7

Charles Dickens's Life and Works

Charles Dickens wrote a vast amount, and lived a full life. This short chapter can do little more than summarise his life and works as briefly as possible, and mention issues relevant to our two texts.

Dickens's childhood

Charles Dickens was born on 7 February 1812, in Portsmouth, where his father John worked in the Navy Pay Office. Charles was the second of six siblings. He had an elder sister, Fanny (born 1810), a younger sister, Laetitia (born 1816), and three younger brothers, Frederick, Alfred and Augustus (born 1820, 1822 and 1827 respectively). The Dickens family moved house five times in the first few years of Charles's life: John's job moved him to London (in 1815) and then to Chatham (1816), where they settled for a five-year spell that Dickens remembered fondly.

At the age of nine, Dickens was sent to a school run by William Giles, an enthusiastic young Baptist minister, and when the family moved to London (1822) Charles remained behind until the end of the term before joining them. Dickens had only one further period of education, at Wellington House Academy, between 1825 and 1827. The school was run by a certain William Jones, described by Dickens as among the 'most ignorant' men who ever existed. From there, the young Dickens left to take employment as a solicitor's clerk. That was the end of his formal education.

Charles Dickens, then, must be regarded as self-educated. William Giles and Mrs. Dickens encouraged his early love of reading, but his schooling was brief and his childhood experiences very chequered. What does seem to have been a persistent part of Dickens's childhood, however, is storytelling and theatricals, with a strong emphasis on live performances. It seems that he brought groups of his friends together, for reading, acting and performing tragedies, comic songs and tales of the marvellous, that he was doing this at the age of 7 or 8 in Chatham, and was still doing it at the age of 16 with his Wellington House schoolmates.

Two further episodes of Dickens's childhood need to be remembered: his father's imprisonment in the Marshalsea Debtors' Prison, and Dickens's employment in Warren's Blacking Warehouse, just south of Covent Garden. Dickens began working at Warren's during February 1824, just after his twelfth birthday; and only a week or two later, his father was arrested for debt and on 20 February entered the Marshalsea Prison where the rest of the family joined him, except for Dickens, who stayed outside in lodgings.

Dickens worked six ten-hour days each week, pasting labels onto pots of blacking, in the factory, and continued at this job for about fourteen months. Towards the end of that time, he and another boy called Bob Fagin worked in Chandos Street, where they worked in front of a window and passers-by would stop to watch them. This public display of menial work was a matter of deep shame to Dickens, seemingly at the time, as well as later in his life: he hid this part of his childhood from public view.

Debtors' prison was a species of enclosed yard with a gate that was locked at night. Dickens's father was detained until he was declared insolvent on 28 May, and consequently discharged from prison. There are several books that describe what the Marshalsea was like at that time. However, for a vivid description there is no need to go further than Dickens's own account, in *Little Dorrit*.

Charles Dickens's childhood consisted of a period of happy play, imagination and fantasy, a short period of good schooling, a period of hard child labour and family disgrace, rounded off with a period of bad schooling. This was a potent mixture. What seems to have resulted is a combination within one young man, which must have been virtually unique: Dickens read voraciously and widely, loved performing, getting up theatricals and exercising his imagination. At the same time, he had picked up a London boy's street wisdom, for he had observed London's street life from the invisible vantage point of a little labouring boy.

Dickens finding his way

Between 1827 and 1833, Dickens worked as a solicitor's clerk, then as a shorthand reporter, first in the court of Doctors' Commons, then in Parliament. He dabbled in reporting other minor events, as a 'penny-a-line' freelance journalist. His earnings during these years were small, and his family's financial situation was still rocky. John Dickens was always improvident: so much so that years later, Dickens more or less forcibly moved his parents to Devon, in the hope that so far from London, his father might stay out of debt.

Dickens was extraordinarily busy during these years. In May 1830 he met one Maria Beadnell, and fell in love. He courted her for three years, but when she returned from a stay in Paris and, on his twenty-first birthday, made it plain that she had lost interest in him, Dickens gave her up.

On most days Dickens spent hours reading in the British Museum. He went to the theatre several times a week; was frequently involved in amateur theatricals; prepared himself for an audition at Covent Garden, hoping for a career as an actor (he fell ill and missed the audition); was often taking down speeches in Parliament until well after midnight (particularly during passage of the first Reform Act, 1832, and the Poor Law Amendment Act, fertile material for *Oliver Twist*); began to write 'sketches' describing curious events and people on London's streets; and pursued Maria Beadnell – all at the same time.

In December 1833, the first of Dickens's 'sketches' to be published appeared anonymously in a small magazine called *The Monthly*, and further sketches appeared subsequently. This was unpaid work, but in the summer of 1834 Dickens finally became a reporter on *The Morning Chronicle* at a salary of five guineas a week. He benefited from a supportive editor, and the *Chronicle* carried more of his London 'sketches', under the pseudonym 'Boz'.

The next three years – to 1836 – continued the enormous invest-ment of energy Dickens had given to his many activities since leaving school. Now, however, he was frantically busy with his work on the *Chronicle*, which involved covering events, elections, accidents and so forth all over Britain; writing more 'sketches by Boz', which were increasingly popular; and a new courtship. An editor of the *Evening Chronicle* was one George Hogarth, and when Dickens met his family, he found the eldest daughter Catherine charming. The fact that she was submissive, and admired Dickens, may have been decisively in her favour in contrast to the coquettish Maria Beadnell. It is probable that Catherine Hogarth represented the comforts of marriage – a housekeeper and sexual satisfaction – without challenging Dickens's superiority. In 1836 they were married, and in the same year Dickens published *Sketches by Boz* as a single volume. This was a great success, and the author immediately started work on a second series. Simultaneously, *The Pickwick Papers* began to appear as a monthly serial, and Dickens negotiated to deliver a novel in November 1837, for a fee of £200. With a different publisher he agreed to write two further novels for £500. At the end of 1836, Dickens was an estab-lished and popular author, had given up his bread-and-butter work on *The Morning Chronicle*, was earning enough to live comfortably, and was a settled married man. In short, both his career and his personal life were fully launched.

As the year 1837 continued, it confirmed Dickens's rise to fame, with continuing episodes of *The Pickwick Papers* and the serialising of *Oliver Twist*. The Dickens family was further established with the birth of a boy, Charles, and their move into a respectable house at 48 Doughty Street. Also in 1837, however, a tragedy occurred in the sudden death of Mary Hogarth, Catherine's seventeen-year-old sister. She had become a close companion of Dickens when staying with them. Dickens was deeply upset by Mary's death, naturally – but he went further, believing her an angel. He was openly convinced that he was more perfectly intimate – even spiritually joined – with Mary, than he was with anybody else. He dreamed of her every night; decided to be buried in the same grave; and took from the corpse's finger a ring that he wore for the rest of his life. How Catherine reacted to these sentimental excesses, we do not know.

Middle years

We have recorded how Dickens became a celebrated author, dominating the popular imagination with his affecting and socially daring fictions. His childhood and rise to wealth and celebrity is the most extraordinary part of his story. We have remarked that, by 1837, he was an established author and family man. We will give only a skeleton account of what we call the 'middle years'. Many biographies overwhelm us with details of his frantic social life and activities, which show that he continued to be phenomenally energetic. He pursued his writings, entertainments, charity work and campaigns for social reform; travelled in Europe and visited America; ran and edited his own periodicals *Household Words* (1850–1859) and *All the Year Round* (1859–1870), after editing *Master Humphrey's Clock* (1840–1841) for Chapman & Hall. He met hundreds of people and participated in countless events. Even the demands of his domestic life ballooned as Catherine underwent ten pregnancies between 1837 and 1852. Nine of the children reached adulthood – a good figure for those days; although Dickens remarked that after his third child, the rest were more-or-less unwanted.

During these 'middle years', however, Dickens's situation remained substantially the same: he was an author, his fame grew, his family grew. He produced theatricals; set up a hostel for reforming prostitutes; tried to live abroad; and took holidays with male friends, away from his crowded home. Dickens comes across as a restless figure, who suffered from contradictory wishes concerning his way of life. He has hardly moved the workmen out of and his large family in to one house, before they take a house at Broadstairs, or they obtain a monstrous coach to carry the household of fourteen people (including, by that time, five children) to Genoa in Italy; or they find another house in London, move the workmen in, and the process starts all over again. It seems that Dickens longed for the settled home he had yearned for in his own childhood; so, he threw himself into creating such homes, one after the other. On the other hand, he had a habit of nomadic restlessness: elsewhere was always more likely to prove satisfying, and the settled contentment of which he dreamed was never where he was. Following Dickens's addresses, let alone his temporary tenancies of seaside houses or country retreats, is a maze of confusing dates and details. However, all such activity, which involved heaving his large family around London, and around Europe, was simply activity, not change. The next major development in Dickens's life came after 20 of these 'middle years', in 1857, when he met Ellen Ternan and separated from Catherine.

Dickens wrote *The Pickwick Papers* to make people laugh; then, he wrote the equally popular *Oliver Twist* to shock, while at the same time powerfully attacking the Poor Law. In 1838 and 1839 *Nicholas Nickleby* was published, again to public acclaim. The schoolmaster, Wackford Squeers, provided high comedy, as did Vincent Crummles and his aged Infant Phenomenon; while poor Smike touched the readers' heart strings. Dickens wrote four novels of boys growing up, the other three being *Martin Chuzzlewit* (monthly, 1843–1844), *David Copperfield* (monthly, 1849 to 1850) and *Great Expectations* (weekly, 1860–1861). In the 1840s Dickens wrote a further three novels (*The Old Curiosity Shop*, *Barnaby Rudge* and *Dombey and Son*). He also published *A Christmas Carol* (1843), the famous story of Scrooge the miser and the Christmas ghosts, and followed this with other 'Christmas books', an annual treat for his readers. His public seems to have had a healthy appetite for tearful melodrama. The grief that greeted the death of Little Nell (*The Old Curiosity Shop*); the pity lavished upon sick Tiny Tim (*A Christmas Carol*); and the public emotion when Paul Dombey died (*Dombey and Son*), all bear witness to a Victorian appetite for weeping. At the same time, the general public took to their hearts a series of comic personalities, following the immensely popular Sam Weller (*Pickwick Papers*) and the Artful Dodger (*Oliver Twist*) with the schoolmaster Squeers, Pecksniff and his daughters (from *Chuzzlewit*), Micawber (from *Copperfield*) and Captain Cuttle (in *Dombey*); and shuddered with fear at the villainous Fagin, Murdstone, Uriah Heep, Carker, the dwarf Quilp, and so on. In short, Dickens played upon the three great chords of his readers' hearts: pity, fun and fear, and there seemed no likelihood that his supply of invention would ever run out.

This said, there were one or two significant weaknesses also on display. The good characters showed a tendency to being colourless, while their selflessness was not always convincing. Both Brownlow and Nancy in *Oliver Twist* have been criticised as characterless and unrealistic respectively. As to the heroines, Dora Spenlow/Copperfield gives us a death scene it is hard to read dry-eyed; we studied Ada's and Rachael's angelic natures in Part 1; Florence Dombey offers little to interest us; and Esther is criticised for overdoing her self-deprecation.

Between January and June 1842, Dickens and Catherine visited North America. They took passage in a steamship, and were ill for most of a rough passage. On their arrival, Dickens was lionised. He found himself welcomed at gala events attended by thousands, and toured New York, Boston, Washington and Richmond before going on a grand sweep ending at Toronto, then back to New York via Montreal and Quebec, before returning to England. Visits to prisons, factories and Congress were arranged for Dickens, who was celebrated in a 'Boz ball' for three thousand excited fans, in New York; met the President; and was fêted wherever he went.

In 1842, however, there was no copyright agreement with the United States, so publishers simply copied books without paying the author. Dickens's works sold in their thousands, but he received nothing. He made speeches campaigning for an international agreement, but all he managed to do was offend the American press. Then, before the end of 1842 Dickens published criticisms of American society in *American Notes*. This left a legacy of bad blood Dickens had to overcome on his second visit to America, in 1867.

In 1844, following disappointing sales of *Barnaby Rudge*, *American Notes*, and *Martin Chuzzlewit*, Dickens quarrelled with his publishers. Eventually, with the help of his lifelong friend and business agent John Forster, these quarrels were resolved, and Dickens went to live in Italy, which was cheaper than London. While in Italy the Dickens's met a couple called De La Rue, and Dickens began giving a course of hypnosis to Mrs De La Rue, to cure her of a nervous complaint. This interest occupied Dickens's attention so thoroughly (he would mesmerise Mrs. De La Rue in her bedroom until four in the morning) that Catherine became jealous: even when they were travelling, Dickens would sit on the box of the coach attempting to hypnotise his patient at a distance.

The family returned to England in the summer of 1845. The autumn and winter were full of activities including amateur theatrical productions; the birth of another boy; discussions with Dickens's philanthropic friend Angela Burdett Coutts, concerning their charitable refuge for street women; and an abortive job as editor of a new *Daily News*. By May 1846 the Dickens's were on their way again, this time to Switzerland, where they settled near Lausanne, intending to stay for a year, but they were in Paris by December, and returned to England in February. The refuge for reforming prostitutes, called 'Urania Cottage' and situated in Shepherd's Bush, opened later in 1847, and Dickens remained active in its management for the next decade.

The Dickens family habitually spent three or four months of the summer away from London, renting a house in Broadstairs (1847, 1850, 1851), the Isle of Wight (1849) or Dover (1852). The summer months of 1853 and 1854 were spent at Boulogne. In November 1851, they had moved their London home to Tavistock House, where Dickens intended to remain for the rest of his life.

In February 1852, the first episode of *Bleak House* appeared. The family now consisted of eight children (Dora, born in 1850, died suddenly in 1851 aged only eight months; Edward, the tenth and last child, was born later in 1852), and Georgina Hogarth, another of Catherine's younger sisters. Georgina or 'Georgy' joined the household in 1842 at the age of 15 to help with the children. She idolised Dickens, quickly became a favourite companion, and she was still single and living with the family at the time of his death. In 1850, Charley, the eldest child, went to Eton. Meanwhile, there had also been two bereavements: Dickens's favourite sibling, his elder sister Fanny, died of tuberculosis in 1848; and his father John died in 1851.

The final episode of *David Copperfield* came out in November 1850, and only a few months later Dickens's mind was already filling with the various strands that would be woven together into his biggest novel: *Bleak House*. In August he wrote an article satirising an imaginary Mrs Bellows, who must 'agitate, agitate, agitate',[1] clearly a prototype for Mrs Jellyby and Mrs Pardiggle; and he followed *The Times's* campaign against Chancery that year. However, the deaths in March and April respectively of his father and his baby daughter, followed quickly by house hunting and the long process of getting the builders into and then out of Tavistock House, made it difficult to start a new novel. After a frustrating delay, Dickens

---

[1] Quoted in Slater, Michael, *Charles Dickens*, New Haven, CT: Yale University Press, 2009, p. 335.

was finally writing the famous opening description of 'Fog every-where' around the beginning of December 1851. On 7 December, he reported that the first number was finished except for one 'short' chapter ('In Fashion').

Bleak House was ignored by the major reviewers, and such com-ments as appeared were disappointing for Dickens. The novel was said to be poorly constructed, and it portrayed a dark world, lacking the humour of his earlier works. On the other hand, it sold well: the public lapped it up. Dickens also had to field some other issues thrown up by *Bleak House*. This was his first attempt at a female first-person narrative: was Esther convincing as a woman? There were those (including Charlotte Brontë) who found her submissive 'busy little housewife' tone irritating and unconvincing.

Next, Dickens was accused of racism in the Borrioboola-Gha satire, and criticised for mistiming his attack on Chancery, a charge publicly levelled by Lord Denman.[2] Then, Lawrence Boythorn and Harold Skimpole were immediately recognised as portraits of Walter Savage Landor[3] and Leigh Hunt[4] respectively. While the Boythorn portrait pleased Landor, Leigh Hunt was offended at his portrayal as the sponger Skimpole. Dickens denied that Skimpole was modelled on Hunt, but the resemblance was such that nobody believed him.

Finally, there was controversy over the death of Krook from Spontaneous Combustion. The philosopher and critic George Henry Lewes took public issue with spontaneous combustion, saying that it was bad science: such things did not happen. According to Lewes, treating the author with patronising amusement, Dickens must have met the phenomenon 'among the curiosities of his reading'.[5] That these niggling criticisms irritated Dickens is evident from the Preface to *Bleak House,* dated August 1853, when he refutes the defence of Chancery offered 'a few months ago'[6] by a judge, reasserts the phe-nomenon of spontaneous combustion against Lewes's criticism, and concludes by boasting the extent of his readership (see *BH*, 5–6).

---

[2] Lord Denman (1779–1854), Lord Chief Justice until 1850.
[3] Walter Savage Landor (1775–1864), English poet and writer.
[4] Leigh Hunt (1784–1859), English critic, poet and essayist.
[5] Quoted in Slater, *Charles Dickens*, 2009, p. 349.
[6] In May 1853, the 'judge' being Sir William Page Wood.

Bleak House was serialised between February 1852 and September 1853, a period embracing Dickens's fortieth and forty-first birthdays. During this time the family passed the summer months in Dover (1852) and Boulogne (1853); Dickens continuously edited *Household Words*; there were amateur theatrical performances in the provinces; his tenth and last child, Edward, was born (April 1852); and he was actively engaged in the management of Urania Cottage. Immediately after finishing this bulkiest of all his novels, coming to the end of 20 months of sustained pressure and work, he took some time off for a jaunt to Switzerland and Italy with his friends Wilkie Collins[7] and Augustus Egg.[8] Returning to England in December, he found the circulation of *Household Words* declining, and was persuaded to undertake a new novel, to be serialised weekly rather than monthly, and to be a quarter the length of *Bleak House*. This became *Hard Times*, and the size and weekly format subjected Dickens to two kinds of constraints to which he was unaccustomed. First, weekly delivery dates allowed little time for the maturing of ideas or for revision; second, the story's brevity did not allow Dickens to indulge his normal more expansive style, exploring character and setting through extended description, direct and indirect speech, with numerous fringe characters and multiple simultaneous stories. This novel, of necessity, would be a more skeletal, spare piece of work.

The final days of 1853 were spent in Birmingham, where Dickens gave public readings from his Christmas stories, for the benefit of the new Birmingham and Midland Institute. Dickens was so exhilarated by the audience's applause and his own performances that the idea of public readings attracted him from that time onwards. Dickens also gave a speech urging a better relationship between workers and owners in the industrial Midlands and north, hoping to improve the worker's lot and the masters' honesty. A long-running strike was taking place in Preston at the time, where the mill masters had locked out their Hands, and families were starving. This national event clearly engaged Dickens's sense of humanity and justice, and he visited Preston at the end of January. The strike contributed much to *Hard Times* (although Dickens resisted identifying the fictitious

---

[7] Wilkie Collins (1824–1889), English novelist.
[8] Augustus Egg (1816–1863), English painter.

Coketown as Preston), just as the campaign in *The Times* had focused his attention on Chancery when his mind was gestating *Bleak House*. During 1854, *Hard Times* was written, serialised and published. The constraints of a much shorter novel and weekly episodes did put a strain on the author. He wanted to add an extra episode at the end, but was persuaded instead to publish a double-length final episode on the final date planned.

The years 1855 and 1856 were also eventful. Perhaps as a sign of his dissatisfaction with Catherine, Dickens met Maria Beadnell again (now Mrs. Winter and a widow). He wrote excited letters to her, perhaps expecting a renewal of his passion, but when they met he was disappointed. She was matronly, plump and not very clever. In 1855, the Dickens family spent most of the summer in Folkestone, then settled in Paris in December. The following April they returned to England, before returning to Boulogne for three months that summer. In March 1856, Dickens bought Gad's Hill Place, a substantial house he remembered from that happy period of his childhood spent in Chatham, Kent.

Another novel, *Little Dorrit*, this time returning to a monthly and full-length format, was serialised between December 1855 and June 1857. Parts of the story were set in the Marshalsea Debtors' Prison. The satire of government institutions so apparent in *Bleak House*'s Chancery and *Hard Times*'s Utilitarian politics, is carried on by the celebrated ministry of state, the Circumlocution Office. These two years are also distinctive for numerous theatrical ventures, and for the increasing number of readings from his own works that Dickens undertook. Dickens's mood was clearly boosted by applause, and he revelled in a personal connection with his mass public. He loved to make them laugh or cry in their thousands, and the charitable tours of 1854 and 1855 were harbingers of the professional tours in Britain and America, on which Dickens would come increasingly to rely during his final decade.

The separation from Catherine

In February 1857 Dickens put on Wilkie Collins's play *The Frozen Deep* at Tavistock House, then in Manchester. Parts that were played by Katey and Mamie Dickens and 'Georgy' in London, were played in Manchester by three professional actresses: Mrs Frances Ternan and her two daughters Maria and Ellen (Nelly). None of the biographies are quite sure what happened – even to whether Dickens was smitten first by Maria, or immediately by Nelly. Whatever the exact details, Dickens clearly fell for Nelly Ternan. During the remainder of 1857 and most of 1858, his life took on an even more elevated level of restlessness: he could not openly live with Nelly, as he fervently desired, and meanwhile, what could be done about Catherine?

Dickens and Ellen Ternan seem to have spent an increasing amount of time together from late 1857 onwards as they gradually found ways to be more together. For example, Dickens paid for Nelly to be employed by the Haymarket Theatre in London. He also helped her sister Fanny to study music in Italy. Straight after *The Frozen Deep*, Dickens and Wilkie Collins suddenly left for a tour of Cumberland, then visited Doncaster for race week, when Dickens knew that the Ternans were working there. Some coy pieces of writing about the narrator's golden-haired 'little reason', or letters in which he fantasises about rescuing the 'Princess I adore' or dying in the attempt, can be strung together to tell us about the progress of the affair, but very little is known even after all the scholarly ferreting that has taken place.

We can find a more connected story when we see how Dickens dealt with Catherine. There had been signs of marital difficulties for some time: Dickens demanded absolute submission from Catherine. He did not expect her to think, and was completely oblivious to any idea of fault in himself. So, for example, in 1853 he commanded her to write to Mrs De La Rue, and accused her of having failed to understand what a wonderful husband she had, when she became jealous (back in 1844). In the same year he asserted that Charley had inherited 'lassitude of character' from his mother. While these arrogant tyrannies were being perpetrated, many of the letters Dickens wrote to Catherine are detailed, intimate and affectionate – but presumably only while she remained submissive.

For a short time in 1857 he characterised the break-up as probably the fault of both sides; but then he reverted to his usual attitude: Catherine was pathetic, lacking the qualities needed to understand an exceptional man like himself. He complained of her constant jealousy, and accused her of being a bad mother:

> ... she has never attached one of them [the children] to herself, never played with them in their infancy, never attracted their confidence as they have grown older, never presented herself before them in the aspect of a mother. I have seen them fall off from her in a natural – not *un*natural – progress of estrangement ...
>
> (From a letter to Angela Burdett Coutts, May 1858)

In a later letter Dickens goes further, telling Miss Coutts that any affection shown between Catherine and the children is only a 'little play', a false act. It is hard to escape the conclusion: the more Dickens wanted Nelly Ternan, the more guilty Catherine became, until she was so guilty that she pretended to love her children!

In his biography *Charles Dickens*, Michael Slater suggests that Dickens progressively wrote Catherine and his marriage out of his life: it was as if what he wrote took on a life of its own, and became a form of truth for the writer. Was Dickens in control when he wrote, or was he a victim of his own persuasion? Slater ends his chapter on this topic by quoting another letter to Miss Coutts, where Dickens says 'That figure is out of my life for evermore (except to darken it) and my desire is, Never to see it again'.[9] Slater's suggestion raises interesting questions about the relationship between Dickens and his fictions; questions perhaps relevant to his public readings, where he experienced a kind of exaltation from his emotionally aroused audience. For it was at about this time, in the spring of 1858, that Dickens embarked upon a new career, giving readings from his works to paying audiences.

The final decade

There were two full-length novels written for weekly serialisation, a prodigious task. These were *A Tale of Two Cities* (serialised in *All the Year Round* during 1859); and *Great Expectations* (serialised in *All the Year Round*, during 1860 and 1861). Both were successful, and there are many who will argue that his best work, with the most powerful unified

---

[9] *Letters*, vol. IX, p. 230.

theme, the most sustained psychological fable, and with the most rigorous avoidance of sentimentality, is *Great Expectations*. Some three years after finishing *Great Expectations*, Dickens returned to monthly serialisation with *Our Mutual Friend* (serialised during 1864 and 1865). There was then another gap before April 1870, when the first monthly episode of a new novel, *The Mystery of Edwin Drood*, appeared. Dickens died before finishing this work.

The volume of Dickens's writing tailed off as the 1860s proceeded. There was no novel for about three years between 1861 and 1864; then another gap of almost six years before the start of *Edwin Drood*. The one major work from the middle, *Our Mutual Friend*, received mixed reviews and disappointing sales. Time has confirmed this as an important novel: the obsessive schoolmaster Bradley Headstone, and the satirical character-group seated around the Veneerings's dinner table, are as good as anything Dickens had done. On the other hand, the plot concerning John Harmon's identity, the Boffins and Bella Wilfer's progress, creaks with awkwardness.

Between 1861 and 1865, Dickens's personal life is little known, because he repeatedly went 'off the map', with frequent covert journeys to France. These were clearly visits to Nelly Ternan, who by this time was surely Dickens's mistress (although there are still some who deny this). The evidence also suggests that Dickens and Nelly had a child together, who died young. Claire Tomalin[10] combs through the evidence of those visits to France about which we know, and suggests dates for the child's birth and death. Two of Dickens's children corroborate this theory: both Katey and Henry stated that there was a child who died in infancy. Tomalin guesses it was born in the winter of 1862–1863 and died in 1865, when Dickens, Nelly and Mrs. Ternan travelled from Dover to London on the ferry-train, and there was an accident at Staplehurst in Kent. A bridge collapsed; Nelly was injured but safely rescued and spirited away before any gossip could start, while Dickens actively helped other trapped passengers.

The remainder of Dickens's final decade tells of intensive reading tours, undertaken despite the author's foot often so swollen he could not walk, or his suffering from chest pains and degenerating health. Dickens and his manager, first Arthur Smith, then, after his death in

---

[10] *Charles Dickens: A Life*, London: Penguin Books, 2012.

1861, George Dolby, would crisscross Britain, giving reading performances in numerous cities in a three-month tour. Often Dickens would perform nightly, with a long railway journey in between. This was gruelling work and Dickens was often exhausted by the schedule. On the other hand, he obtained so much pleasure, and reassurance about his popularity, that he continued undertaking these tours. In April 1869, in Chester and after 74 readings of a lengthy tour, Dickens suffered a stroke and his health finally forced him to cancel the remaining dates. There were a few farewell readings in London, but no more tours.

The one different episode in the eighteen-sixties was Dickens's second visit to the United States. He had had to wait for the American Civil War to end before crossing the Atlantic, but he finally travelled in November 1867 and returned in April 1868. The readings and celebrations of Dickens's visit were all a great success and the tour earned £20,000. However, Dickens's foot was often so bad that Dolby had to help him across stage to his reading desk, and support him offstage at the end. This time, Dickens was complimentary about improvements in the United States, and he became reconciled with his American readers.

Before this visit, Dickens had some hope that Nelly might travel with him. Dolby went in advance to make delicate inquiries of their hosts whether this would be acceptable. The answer was no, so Nelly visited her sister in Italy instead.

By the summer of 1870, Dickens had given his final farewell reading, and was settled at Gad's Hill writing *The Mystery of Edwin Drood*. A close friend, the actor Charles Fechter, had sent a model Swiss chalet as a present. This was erected on the grounds of Gad's Hill, and Dickens was using its peaceful isolation as his study. On Wednesday 8 June Dickens took his breakfast early, went to the chalet to work, returned to the main house for luncheon and then went back to the chalet. In the evening he returned to the house to dine with Georgina. He complained of feeling 'very ill'. During the meal he suffered another stroke and collapsed to the floor. On Thursday 9 June Dickens died, having not recovered consciousness. He was buried in Westminster Abbey, following a small private funeral for close friends and family, but the grave was left open for two further days so that the public could throw flowers upon Dickens's coffin. Crowds continued to come for days, even after the grave had been filled in.

We have mentioned a few of the people who were significant in Dickens's life, but many others have not been named. Dickens was extremely gregarious, living a busy social life. Here is a very selective list of some of his nearest friends.

Of contemporary writers, Dickens knew and published Mrs. Elizabeth Gaskell (1810–1865), including her novels *Cranford* and *North and South*. It seems that Mrs Gaskell was often annoyed by Dickens; in particular she was irritated, when writing *North and South*, to find Dickens's own industrial novel *Hard Times* serialised first. William Makepeace Thackeray (1811–1863), the celebrated author of *Vanity Fair*, was a friend. Dickens and Thackeray admired each other at first, but they quarrelled and did not speak for years. They had begun a reconciliation just before Thackeray's death.

Wilkie Collins (1824–1889) met Dickens in 1851. Both of his most successful novels *The Woman in White* and *The Moonstone* were serialised in Dickens's *All the Year Round*; but Collins became much more than a contributing author. He accompanied Dickens on jaunts to the continent – most notably in 1853 with Augustus Egg; he collaborated with Dickens on plays (they wrote *The Frozen Deep* together) and on the Christmas editions of *All the Year Round*, as well as other projects such as the 'lazy tour' of 1857 which took Dickens and Collins to Doncaster when the Ternans were there. In short, Collins was a close friend and collaborator. His brother Charles married Katey Dickens in 1860, against her father's advice.

Other writers Dickens admired and knew, included Edward Bulwer-Lytton (1803–1873), prolific author and playwright, and Sir Thomas Carlyle (1795–1881), the essayist, and social and political commentator. Dickens also knew George Henry Lewes, the partner of Marian Evans, a.k.a. George Eliot, and he admired Eliot's *Adam Bede* (1859) so much that he offered to serialise her next novel in *All the Year Round*. She refused this offer.

Among Dickens's many friends, some preeminent names have been mentioned, such as Angela Burdett-Coutts, who worked with him running Urania Cottage, a prostitutes' refuge. She also continued to urge a reconciliation with Catherine, for several years. We have also mentioned John Forster, Dickens's closest and most trusted friend of all. Forster helped to manage publishers and contracts, including breaking and renegotiating contracts at Dickens's behest.

He was a constant and dependable adviser and an encouraging critic as well. It was to Forster that Dickens entrusted his 'autobiographical sketch' revealing details about his childhood that were never published in his lifetime (his childhood factory work, and his father's imprisonment for debt, in particular), and Forster was Dickens's authorised biographer.

William Wills (1810–1880) became assistant editor of *Household Words* at its inception in 1850. He was Dickens's journalistic right-hand-man up until he was injured in 1868. Wills was unable to continue working, but had been a vital part of the Dickens 'industry' for nearly two decades.

We have mentioned several members of the Dickens family in passing, but we have not provided a list. Dickens was the second child and had five siblings: two sisters and three brothers. Fanny, who died in 1848, trained at the Royal Academy of Music, and was the closest to Charles. His brother Augustus deserted his wife in 1858, and another brother Frederick was divorced in 1859, provoking some comments about 'the Dickens boys', when the author's marriage foundered at the same time.

Nine of Dickens's children lived to become adults. Dickens wanted the eldest, Charley, to become a businessman, which he did, but without much success. He married against his father's wishes, and had recurrent money troubles and seven children. Mary remained single and at home. Katey became an artist, married Charles Collins who died in 1873, then married another artist, Carlo Perugini, in 1874, apparently a happy union. Walter joined the army in India and died of sickness at the age of 22 (1863). Frank lived to be 42 as a Canadian 'Mountie'. Alfred, and the youngest, Edward, were both on an Australian sheep-station when Dickens died. Sydney became a naval officer and died when he was 25 (1872). Finally, Henry persuaded Dickens to send him to Cambridge rather than stopping his education at 15, which was his father's first idea. He became a successful lawyer and lived a long and prosperous life with his wife and seven children. There were therefore two men – Charley and Henry – and two women – Mamie and Katey – present at their father's funeral. The others were dead or overseas.

Numerous other names could be mentioned here, such as Dickens's first sweetheart Maria Beadnell; the De La Rues; Mr. and

Mrs. Field who hosted Dickens in America; Charles Fechter, actor and donor of the chalet; Mrs. Brown, companion to Miss Coutts; Hablot Browne, pseudonym 'Phiz', Dickens's illustrator; numerous male inhabitants of the London literary scene who shared the entertainment and boisterousness of Dickens's social character; and not forgetting Mrs. Ternan and her three daughters, from 1857 onwards. Perhaps one has to mention Maclise, Macready, Stanfield, and so on, and so on. Reading Dickens's biography is rather like strapping oneself into a roller coaster and holding on tight for a rollicking ride. We leave you to undertake such an entertainment with one of the full-length biographies,[11] where you will meet the many other characters who played larger or smaller parts in Charles Dickens's life.

The influence of his life and the times on Dickens's works

This section is a discussion of how Dickens's life and times can be seen as generating his novels and fuelling his creative energy.

As we have remarked, Dickens's childhood left him peculiarly equipped to become a writer who was also a chronicler of his society. His early habits of reading and make-believe games had turned him into a devotee of the imagination, while his episode of child labour and his father's spell in debtors' prison gave him a perspective on society, that no ordinarily educated young man could have developed. However, his childhood left Dickens with another trait that was to influence his writing life: an unfortunate combination of arrogance about his talent, and need for admiration from others. Dickens seems to have longed to be middle-class, to become a gentleman; and despite his success, he never quite believed that he had arrived. Furthermore, he was forever insecure about money and driven to earn more just to avoid that constant poverty that had bedevilled his father; all this despite his becoming a rich man.

---

[11] You could try Michael Slater's *Charles Dickens,* New Haven, CT: Yale University Press, 2009; Claire Tomalin's *Charles Dickens: A Life,* Viking, 2011; London: Penguin Books, 2012; or Peter Ackroyd's *Dickens,* Vintage, 2002, which are just three of several biographies.

In Dickens's defence it should be said that the English class system resists movement obstinately: you can make a fortune without moving up in social class, in the eyes of the (English) world. So, even if others might forget his origin, Dickens kept the embarrassing parts of his childhood a secret throughout his life. With regard to money, Dickens took on several extra financial commitments in the 1860s: he was looking after the families of dead relatives, paying alimony to Catherine, and funding both the Ternans' and his own homes (he maintained a home in Wellington Street as well as Gad's Hill). The calls on his purse were considerable, but his only complaints were about Catherine's alimony, still resentfully mentioned in his will.

These awkward contradictions in his character gave Dickens a need for regular reassurance and proof that his public loved him. This proof could be found in three ways: first, from the sales figures of his periodicals or his books; second in the form of reviews, the encouragement of his friends, and the general talk about his work; finally, in the form of tears and laughter followed by ecstatic applause at one of his public readings. Increasingly, after the 1850s, public readings apparently brought him the most satisfying form of reassurance. Sales figures were a mixed blessing as each notch of extra popularity had to be sustained – any drop in the figures engendered a terrible anxiety (such as the poor sales achieved by *Our Mutual Friend*, for example).

The suggestion is this: Dickens needed reassurance, so he gave the public what he believed would earn it. Consequently, his novels swing towards melodrama and sentimentality at crucial moments. Further, Dickens's novels adopt the mid-Victorian stereotype of femininity without question. We have seen how Rachael does Stephen's housework by tidying up his wife, in Part I; and we have noted Esther's 'little woman' or 'Dame Trot' housekeeping persona. To these should be added Florence Dombey, Lucie Manette, Bella Wilfer, Caddy Jellyby, Ada Clare/Carstone and numerous others.

This remark levels a serious criticism at Dickens's oeuvre: that where there was the potential for a theme concerning human life or social reality, Dickens chose instead to elicit response on a sentimental level. This is underlined by what happened to the ending of *Great Expectations*. Dickens wrote a rigorous ending, offering no consummation of the romance between Pip and Estella. Such an ending suited the dour themes of money and class, the self-deceiving characterisation of Pip, and the distorted upbringing of Estella, in this dark novel. Unfortunately, Bulwer Lytton begged Dickens to give the romantic pair a happy ending. Claire Tomalin's opinion is that 'amazingly'[12] Dickens complied, and the romantic final chapter is now the actual ending of the book. According to our theory, this not at all 'amazing', – it merely underlines Dickens's vulnerability. For all his brash manners, Dickens was not sure of himself. When there was a choice, an easy popularity ruled over his better instincts.[13]

The social and historical background: Britain

Most of Dickens's novels display themes that call out for **social or political reform**. We are familiar with the critique of Chancery and the law, explored in *Bleak House*; and that of Utilitarian 'political economy',[14] and the evils of an industrial society, in *Hard Times*. The law was already a target when Pickwick was wrongly accused of breach of promise, in *The Pickwick Papers* (1836–1837); then *Oliver Twist* (1837–1839) attacks workhouses and the Poor Law, a theme still present when Betty Higden dies avoiding the workhouse, in *Our Mutual Friend* (1865). Throughout his writing life, Dickens aired his anger at injustice, his pity for the poor and illiterate, and his fury at the hypocrites who presided over such a society. He ridiculed those in charge with biting sarcasm and merciless satire. Dickens was one of several voices calling for reform, and the nineteenth century was the century of reform: parliament legislated to reform the legal profession, provision for the poor, conditions in factories, child labour and to reform the political and electoral systems.

Reform of the British political system had been overdue since the 1780s, when the Gordon Riots (1780) rocked English society, and there were already reform-minded politicians such as Edmund Burke and John Wilkes, calling for liberalisation. However, the double

---

[12] Tomalin, *Charles Dickens*, p. 315.

[13] Although the present ending is defended by some critics, such as Q. D. Leavis and J. Hillis Miller.

[14] John Stuart Mill, the Utilitarian philosopher, published his widely influential *The Principles of Political Economy* in 1848.

foreign shocks of, first, the American War of Independence (1775–1783), and second, the French Revolution (1789), led to a backlash against political progress. The Establishment suppressed calls for reform, using trials for sedition and treason, and giving the excuse that nothing could be done while the war against Napoleon continued. The Battle of Waterloo (1815) brought an end to that war; but there was still an acrimonious debate before the first Reform Act was finally passed, in 1832. This Act abolished the Rotten Boroughs[15] and widened the electorate. However, it was still only one in five adult males who could vote; and several abuses, including the treating and patronage lampooned in the 'National and Domestic' chapter of *Bleak House*, still featured. In summary, then, a society that had waited 50 years was finally granted a measure of partial reform when Dickens was 20; but it was clear that further reforms would be needed: the Second Reform Act, further purging Rotten Boroughs and greatly increasing the electorate, was passed in 1867. Dickens's writing career falls between these two Acts, in the period when parliamentary reform was a constant topic of debate.

Social reform

When Dickens was 22 (1834), the **Poor Law Amendment Act** was passed. Dickens had taken down in shorthand many of the speeches debating this measure, and he was well aware that this legislation would set up an inhumane system that became one of his targets as a writer. Again, as with political reform, numerous small changes occurred over succeeding years, which tinkered with the system (for example when the Poor Law Commission was scrapped in favour of the Poor Law Board, in 1847); but nothing happened to alter the pitiable picture of Oliver Twist's dying mother, or old Betty Higden running away from the workhouse.

The **Factories Act** of 1833 was significant in establishing an inspectorate, and in prescribing the hours children (i.e. those aged 9–13) could work. Further important measures were passed, on hours of

---

[15] 'Rotten boroughs' were those with very few voters, where it was consequently easy corruptly to 'fix' an election.

work permitted, hygiene and safety in factories, in 1844, 1847, 1850 and 1856. The Act of 1847 was a milestone, as it instituted the ten-hour day, and this bill stood as an example of successful factory regulation. We remember Dickens's Coketown mill-owners who complain that they will be 'ruined' by any regulation: written during 1854. In 1855 the owners formed a National Association 'to watch over factory legislation with a view to prevent any increase of the present unfair and injudicious enactments'. This pressure group was particularly against putting safety fences around machinery. In 1856 the safety fences rule was abolished. This detail serves as a reminder that all the reforms of the period, which seem self-evident to us in the twenty-first century, were bitterly fought over in Dickens's day; furthermore, not all the battles were won by reformers: there were steps back as well.

Much of the raw material for **industrial relations** as shown in *Hard Times* clearly came from Dickens's visits to the Midlands and the north during the winter of 1853–1854, and in particular from his visit to Preston, recorded in the article 'On Strike', which appeared in *Household Words*, 11 February 1854. A student of *Hard Times* should read this article. Dickens imagines a conversation on the train, with a Mr. Snapper, a proponent of Political Economy and so a model for Mr. Gradgrind; gives an account of an Union meeting and the dignified bearing of the striking Hands, although a Mr. Gruffshaw is the model for Slackbridge, the union man in *Hard Times*. Over and above these possible direct connections, 'On Strike' also raises three interesting questions. First, it quotes from a placard posted around the town by 'the Committee'. Dickens is rather dismissive: such placards 'were not remarkable for their logic certainly, and did not make the case particularly clear; but, considering that they emanated from, and were addressed to, people who had been out of employment for three-and-twenty consecutive weeks, at least they had little passion in them though they had not much reason'; and he copies one into his article saying: 'Take the worst I could find.' Far from lacking reason or clarity, the text of this placard is eloquent, strongly reasoned and moving. Second, 'On Strike' paints an admiring picture of the striking workers, whose behaviour is moderate and polite throughout; Dickens notes a complete absence of intimidation between the small number of 'blacklegs' still working, and the pickets at the mill-gate; and he shows the fiery Gruffshaw being silenced by the Union meeting chairman. Why, then, does he describe a dominant and effective Slackbridge, and Stephen's being sent to Coventry by the other Hands, in *Hard Times*?

Third, 'On Strike' proposes Dickens's solution, a step that *Hard Times* does not attempt. Dickens finishes 'On Strike' by suggesting that the Preston dispute should be referred to those 'men in England above suspicion, to whom they [Owners and Workers] might refer the matters in dispute, with a perfect confidence above all things in the desire of those men to act justly, and in their sincere attachment to their countrymen of every rank and to their country'.

These men, who are respected by both sides, should arbitrate the dispute, and their judgment would be accepted by both sides. 'On Strike', then, makes a fascinating study in relation to *Hard Times*. You may also wish to read 'Fire and Snow', an article in the 21 January 1854 issue of *Household Words*. This tells of a journey to the industrial Midlands (the 'Black Country') in winter snow, and you may be struck by the jolly people described. It is almost as if the snow changes hardship into a Christmas card for the locals, while Dickens discourses on the cosy slippers and hot drinks provided at the inn.[16]

One of the evils that was a target for particular opprobrium, was **the Court of Chancery**. Dickens was accused of jumping onto the bandwagon with his attack in *Bleak House*, because *The Times* was attacking Chancery at the same time. Considering the sins of Chancery, the complaint about Dickens's timing hardly matters – the Court richly deserved the lambasting it received. As with factory safety, there were several piecemeal reforms, partial repairs to mend the system's worst breakdowns. From the beginning of the century, numerous small measures increased the number of officials who could hear cases, and attacked the system of sinecures that added costs and delayed cases, because lawyers profited from long documents and complicated procedure. Lord Denman criticised Dickens for attacking just as the court was reformed, presumably referring to the Suitors in Chancery Relief Act (1852), which gave court officials salaries, abolished fees and all forms of 'bonus'. Additionally,

---

[16] Dickens's journals *Household Words* and *All the Year Round* are available in full at http://www.djo.org.uk (Dickens Journals Online). You can not only read Dickens's articles there, but also other writers' contributions to the journals he edited.

the Master in Chancery Abolition Act (1852), allowed cases to be heard by judges instead of bounced back-and-forth between judges and Masters. These reforms did increase efficiency, and temporarily reduced the backlog. However, they were not an enduring solution, and further tinkering with the system continued through the 1850s and 60s, before Chancery was finally abolished in the Supreme Court of Judicature Act (1875). Dickens seems to have been right to defend himself in his preface to *Bleak House*. Chancery remained a dust-heap of legal delays, obfuscation, nonsensical procedure and the financial bleeding of all involved, after the Acts of 1852.

Of course, **the legal professions** still have an unappealing reputation; lawyers are still proverbial for high fees and outrageous arguments, and proceedings are over-complicated, slow, and in some respects ridiculous (robes and wigs, for example, have spawned hundreds of jokes). Dickens's attack on the law was not confined to Chancery: Tulkinghorn was a repository for the scandals of a corrupt establishment. *Bleak House* does not quite accuse him of blackmail. Kenge, with his sophistic defence of the legal profession, and Vholes who feeds from his client as a leech fixes on flesh, both carry on a literary tradition stretching back to Chaucer's Man of Law. Sadly, the law still provides numerous examples of absurdity, over-obscure procedures and enormous costs. In this more general sense of the law as an institution, there is nothing that restricts Dickens's target to the 1850s alone.

The provision of **education** expanded during Dickens's working life; but there remained much to be done before basic literacy became widespread. Dickens's active life was bracketed by important legislation in this field. In 1833, Parliament voted regular sums of money to construct schools for poor children. Then, in 1870, the Elementary Education Act set up the board schools and made school attendance compulsory for five- to ten-year-olds. During Dickens's lifetime, therefore, there was gradual expansion of the partly state-funded board schools, of the philanthropic 'ragged schools' for the poor, and liberalisation of the curriculum of grammar schools. We know from the passage in *Bleak House* describing the benighted state of illiteracy in Jo the crossing sweeper's mind,[17] that Dickens's

---

[17] See *Bleak House*, pp. 235–238.

dedication to the cause of literacy was founded on a heartfelt sympathy for the illiterate. Dickens imagined their intellectual darkness vividly.

Dickens also held strong opinions on the kind of education that would most benefit the child. This is a theme to which his novels regularly return. So, in *Bleak House* we have Jo's illiteracy, and Richard who can compose Latin verses and do nothing else.[18] In *Hard Times* the novel opens with an attack on Utilitarians, and ends in debate between the brainwashed Bitzer, a converted Gradgrind and Sleary of the circus. Elsewhere in the novels we meet several so-called educators such as M'Choakumchild, Creakle and Squeers. Perhaps the most effective portraits of education gone wrong are the doomed obsessional, Bradley Headstone, and his self-righteous pupil, Charlie Hexam, from *Our Mutual Friend*. Among these portraits, hypocrisy, sadism, stupidity and a limited intellect, are the faults of teachers excoriated in Dickens's fiction. He favoured educating the sentiments, fancy and imaginations of children, and his best products (such as, for example, Sissy Jupe in Chapter 9 of *Hard Times*) voice the ethics of a loving and forgiving Christianity.[19]

Foreign affairs

So far, we have restricted ourselves to domestic issues, but we must remember that the middle of the nineteenth century was the hey-day of the British Empire, and the power of Queen Victoria, Empress of India, straddled the globe. We cannot undertake any overview of international affairs during Dickens's lifetime. We will have to make do with mentioning three foreign concerns, for their closeness to those years when Dickens was composing *Bleak House* and *Hard Times*.

First, **1848 was the Year of Revolutions in Europe**. Virtually all the countries of the continent suffered from insurrections during that year, some successful, and others brutally put down. The variety and extent of these uprisings, although they were not coordinated, can

---

[18] See *Bleak House*, p. 180.

[19] See *Hard Times*, p. 57, for example, when Sissy's 'To do unto others as I would that they should do unto me' is pronounced 'very bad' by Mr. Gradgrind.

be guessed when Wikipedia tells us of revolutions 'in France, the Netherlands, Germany, Poland, Italy, and the Austrian Empire' and affecting some 50 countries. There seems to have been a combination of causes: royalty and feudal authorities were anathema to both the growing bourgeois-democratic population and the working-class, although these two sections of society did not act together. Marx and Engels published the *Communist Manifesto* in February 1848, but the German Communist League, at whose request it had been written, issued only watered-down demands following the uprising in Berlin. Although little was achieved in the way of progress, the year 1848 was an earthquake that shook the foundations of virtually all European societies. Denmark changed from absolute to constitutional monarchy; France put an end to its royal succession; and serfdom was abolished in several states. Britain was one of very few states to escape the 'Year of Revolutions', although there were rebellious plots, and mass action by the Chartist movement, with a petition presented to parliament in April. One of the critics we mention in Chapter 10 below, sees the events of 1848 as the start of a 'providential discourse' of British complacency, and this in turn as a target of Dickens's social critique in *Bleak House*.[20]

The second 'foreign' issue we mention is the **War in the Crimea**, which began in October 1853 and continued until 1856. Britain and France acted together, joining the Ottoman Empire in a war against Russia, which was regarded as an expansionist threat. The diplomatic situation was far from clear and involved the whole continent, but we are only interested in the campaign of French and British armies besieging Sevastopol, the main Russian port on the Crimea, a peninsula in the Black Sea.

In the late autumn of 1854, there was a battle at Balaclava. During the conflict, the Light Brigade made its famous charge, and the 93rd Highlanders went into history as the 'Thin Red Line'. The action of the Light Brigade, however brave, was an example of stupid military leadership and a waste of life. Furthermore, although the actual battle was won, the camp was rife with disease, and Sevastopol was still in Russian hands. It was during this

---

[20] Morris, Pam, *Dickens's Class Consciousness: A Marginal View*, Basingstoke: Macmillan, 1991. See Chapter 9.

campaign that Florence Nightingale became famous, nursing the sick soldiers. In early 1855 the government fell, ousted largely by war fever, whipped up by the popular press, and the government's handling of the war was portrayed as indecisive. Dickens contributed his article 'Mr. Bull's Somnambulist' that appeared in *Household Words* on 25 November 1854. Dickens imagines the household of 'Mr. Bull' (i.e. John Bull, or England) with a sleepwalking helpless old woman in charge. She is Abigail or 'Aby' Dean (i.e. Lord Aberdeen), a merciless caricature of indecisiveness. The article calls for this hopeless old woman housekeeper to be replaced by one who is 'emphatically – a Man'.

Our third 'foreign' affair is the events that became known as the 'Indian Mutiny'. This series of conflicts erupted in India in 1857, for a variety of reasons. The Indian population nursed a number of grievances concerning both Hindu and Muslim religious traditions: many believed their religion was under attack from the administration. There were also many foolish regulations, such as those regarding inheritance of land. These frictions differed between different localities, but were many, and when taken together make a catalogue of maladministration by the East India Company. When news came of the terrible massacres at Cawnpore in June 1857, where some hundreds of English women and children were hacked to pieces and their remains thrown into a well, Dickens wrote to Miss Burdett Coutts that, given command, he would 'exterminate the race [the people of India] … to blot it out of mankind and raze it off the face of the earth'. Patriotism is one thing, but genocide is quite another! Michael Slater explains Dickens's agitation as images of women being attacked 'were perhaps beginning to resonate in Dickens's mind with his image of Nelly and his fantasies about rescuing her from ogres'. Slater then slips back into the domestic arena: it was 'high time to begin planning the next Christmas number of *Household Words*'.[21] The bathos with which Slater completes his paragraph may be intentional; it implies something typical of Dickens's response to foreign affairs. He was always affected by misery, poverty, slavery, dirt, disease and ignorance when he met these phenomena; and this

---

[21] Slater, *Charles Dickens*, 2011, p. 441.

happened regularly in Britain. Events abroad, however, did not hold his interest: the onrushing demands of his own life naturally reoccupied the central position in Dickens's psyche.

Furthermore, Dickens's reactions to both domestic and foreign issues operated at a particular level. His emotions were quick, his pity and anger both ready, and he was an impressive critic of his society, pitying the powerless oppressed, and hating hypocrites. On the other hand, Dickens was not analytical in the manner of a student of society, and so he did not offer considered solutions to the problems and evils he described. As we have just seen, he offered genocide as the solution to the Indian Mutiny. His solution to the Preston Strike was to find a highly respected man somewhere, who would arbitrate between owners and workers. Imagine the laughter of a true social analyst – Karl Marx, say – at such a suggestion. After all, Dickens's solution appeared six years after the *Communist Manifesto*. Again, we note from 'Mr. Bull's Somnambulist' the caricature of a weak, indecisive leader as an old woman. The solution? Replace her with 'a Man'. Dickens presumably means by this a strong, decisive leader.

One important international event we have not discussed was the **American Civil War**. This took place between 1861 and 1865. One positive result was the abolition of Slavery in the defeated southern states.[22] The war itself was an all-encompassing destruction, the first example of the kind of warfare that would reach its zenith in 1914–1918. This war raged over the whole huge territory of the United States, and left more than 600,000 dead. In 1862, Dickens's contempt for American politics was still so much alive that he could not see 'a pin' difference between the North and the South, and he did not believe that slavery was the issue. Dickens had campaigned against slavery, however, and in the end he was pleased at the victory of the abolitionist North. Aside from his low expectations at the outset, the main effect of the war upon him was to postpone his plans for a second journey across the Atlantic.

---

[22] A student of the Civil Rights movement of the 1960s is entitled to wonder how much difference this made to the life of a southern black, however.

8

The Place of *Hard Times* and *Bleak House* in English Literature

Bleak House and *Hard Times* among Dickens's novels

Dickens wrote fourteen and a half novels, the half being the unfinished *Mystery of Edwin Drood*. He wrote eight before and four and a half after our two texts. The first novel was *The Pickwick Papers* (serialised 1836–1837). This began as a series of loosely connected anecdotes about Mr. Pickwick, but the stories were increasingly extended through several episodes. Dickens was leaning towards full-length narrative. At the same time, with Pickwick and the other club members, and the enormously popular Sam Weller, he was developing his brand of comical characterisation. *Oliver Twist* was serialised from 1837 to 1839, overlapping with *Pickwick*. The pathetic little hero, colourful band of boy-thieves, terrifying villains Fagin and Sykes, and sacrificial heroine Nancy, were all larger than life. Like *Pickwick*, this novel achieved instant popularity, and these two established Dickens's reputation.

The next novel was the first of four that tell of a boy growing up. *Nicholas Nickleby* (1838–1839) is part of this group with *Martin Chuzzlewit* (1843–1844), *David Copperfield* (1849–1850) and *Great Expectations* (1860–1861). Some comparisons between these novels almost tell a story of their own. For example, Nicholas loves his Madeline, and their marriage completes the romantic theme. David Copperfield loves Dora, but she conveniently dies so the hero can discover a more fulfilling love with Agnes. In *Great Expectations*, Pip may be united with Estella after waiting another 11 years. So, in 1838, 1849 and 1860, Dickens expressed three different versions of romance, which make an interesting commentary on his own private life. Other similar 'stories' arise from a comparison of the hero's eventual career with the dominant themes of these three narratives. See, for example, how Nicholas's picaresque travels are loosely connected by the plots of the villainous Ralph, while Pip's social climb explores a dark theme of snobbery, money, justice and class.

Also published before *Bleak House* were *The Old Curiosity Shop* (1840–1841) and *Barnaby Rudge* (February to November 1841), both of which appeared in weekly instalments, and *Dombey and Son* (1846–1848), which came out monthly. The death of little Nell in *The Old Curiosity Shop*, and of little Paul in *Dombey and Son*, gave rise to public displays of grief. These works demonstrated Dickens's growing ability to work with numerous characters and multiple storylines. Dickens began *The Old Curiosity Shop* as a tale told by 'Master Humphrey' of *Master Humphrey's Clock*, following the periodical's plan of publishing stories within a loose frame. After the third chapter, however, Dickens decided to produce a full-length novel, and Master Humphrey is rather summarily made to disappear. By the time of *Dombey and Son*, Dickens planned on a far grander scale. Themes such as the grandfather's gambling addiction, in *The Old Curiosity Shop*, give way to a major critique of finance, snobbery and misogyny, while the grotesque villain Quilp is succeeded by the plausible Carker, who hides his villainy beneath a smooth appearance.

Dombey and Son can thus be considered the first of another group of novels: a group evoking a panoramic picture of society, and developing bitter, critical themes concerning corrupt governance, hypocrisy, suffering and injustice. The next of this kind was to be *Bleak House*, the longest, and in many critics' views, the best of its kind. Belonging to this group were also *Hard Times* (1854), *Little Dorrit* (1855–1857) and *Our Mutual Friend* (1864–1865).

Hard Times needs additional comment, for it was the only novel to be created, as it were, on the spot, and it was designed as a far shorter text than any of the others. So, Dickens's attempt to show several strands of Coketown society from gentry to mill owners to workers, and finally circus performers, was always under constraint from the shorter format. Therefore, the idea that these novels present a 'social panorama' must be subject to a caveat in the case of *Hard Times*: Dickens intended a panorama of Coketown society, but did not succeed in this aim. Nonetheless, with its themes of industrial work and its bitter attack on Political Economy, *Hard Times* clearly belongs within our suggested group.

The list of Dickens's novels is completed by *A Tale of Two Cities* (1859), set in London and Paris during the French Revolution and the Terror; and the half-finished *The Mystery of Edwin Drood*. Notice that the intervals between publication of the novels increased throughout Dickens's career: *Pickwick* and *Oliver Twist* overlapped; *Nickleby* and *Oliver* overlapped. Then, *The Old Curiosity Shop* ended and a week later *Barnaby Rudge* began. There were then gaps of a year or more, such as before *Chuzzlewit*, before *Dombey* and before *Bleak House*. Finally, in the 1860s, there were three blank years before *Our Mutual Friend* and five more blank years before Dickens began *Edwin Drood*. Explanations for these increasing gaps are not hard to find. Dickens quarrelled with publishers, suffered periods of exhaustion and attempted to live abroad; he also edited several journals and produced journalism, stories, and in particular his Christmas editions each year, following the national success of *A Christmas Carol* (1843).

One significant point should be noticed, however: Dickens spent only about two of his last ten years working as a novelist. He suffered with his swollen foot and other ailments, of course, and he spent five months in America. However, the change of occupation is still striking: Dickens became a professional reader and performer in his last decade, and this underlines the gratification Dickens garnered from his audience's applause.

Novels before Dickens

The first novels in English coalesced from various kinds of prose writing, towards the end of the seventeenth century. Stories of exploration, historical allegories such as Sir Philip Sidney's *Arcadia* (1590), or sensational anecdotes such as Aphra Behn's *Orinooko* (1688) were forerunners of the novel form. Fictions began to imitate documentary reporting, and the novel with its illusion of 'realism' was born. Many now think of Daniel Defoe (1659–1731), author of *Robinson Crusoe*, *Moll Flanders* and *Roxana*, as the first writer to synthesise various kinds of prose stories into a recognisable novel. During the eighteenth century, Samuel Richardson told the seduction stories of *Pamela* (1740) and *Clarissa* (1748), followed by *The History of Sir Charles Grandison* (1753). Henry Fielding parodied Richardson in *Shamela* (1741), and followed with his two great novels *Joseph Andrews* (1742) and *Tom Jones* (1749). Laurence Sterne published the nine volumes of *The Life and Opinions of Tristram Shandy, Gentleman* between 1759 and 1767, a novel full of digressions that meanders through the eponymous hero's life (who is not born until Volume 3). *Tristram Shandy's* peculiarities have made it the blueprint for modernist writers in the twentieth century. Both Fielding and Sterne developed a narrator who speaks directly to the reader as if talking. In *Tom Jones*, for example, Fielding introduces the novel as a feast, and the first chapter as a 'bill of fare' or menu, while in *Tristram Shandy*, the first-person narrator becomes a chatty and irritatingly digressive companion. These writers were favourite reading for Dickens, who named his sixth son after Henry Fielding.

In the final decades of the eighteenth century a sensational subgenre of novels gained popularity. So-called 'Gothic' novels were generally set in medieval times, in castles or cloisters filled with intrigue, in Italy and other exotic locations, with imprisoned maidens, wicked noblemen, ghosts and pure-hearted heroes. Typical of the genre was Mrs. Radcliffe's *The Mysteries of Udolpho* (1794). A more disturbing strand of the Gothic, emphasising perversion, is found in Matthew Lewis's *The Monk* (1796). There was a blend of Gothic and realistic romance in the novels of Fanny Burney (e.g. *Evelina*, 1778). Jane Austen parodied the Gothic stereotype in *Northanger Abbey* (1818), while her other novels such as *Pride and Prejudice* (1813) and *Emma* (1815) gave a detailed account of a woman's lot in one sector of society, the minor landed gentry.

Bleak House and Hard Times among their contemporaries

We will discuss two aims that may be attributed to those setting out to write a novel, and one controversy, concerning the author's function. First, a novelist may aim to reflect reality: above all, the descriptions of events, settings and people should be believable. This aim was certainly important to Jane Austen, who compared herself to a painter of miniatures. She described a small sector of society and never attempted to record any class or milieu that was not her own. She never wrote a scene depicting men without a woman present because she did not know how they would behave. Dickens clearly adopted an adaptation of this method as a writer: he was ambitious to portray a social 'panorama', as we have noted. The difference is that Dickens did what Austen could not: if he wished to show a particular setting, Dickens went to look at it for himself. He was known to wander the streets of London at all hours, and we know that he visited Preston, during the strike, to see for himself before writing *Hard Times*.

On the other hand, and arguably in conflict with such 'realism', the novelist may aim to arouse the reader's emotions: pity, fear, grief, elation, shock and laughter are the responses a novelist may seek to inspire. Dickens found the elements of such a project ready to hand: Gothic features and melodramatic settings and events were designed to evoke an emotional public response. Definitions of melodrama all include terms such as 'sentimental', 'extravagant' and 'sensational'. The plot is 'improbable' and more important than characters who are limited to 'the noble hero, the long-suffering heroine, and the hard-hearted villain' who experience 'exaggerated emotions'. These terms such as 'improbable', 'exaggerated', 'sentimental' and 'extravagant', reveal how a writer attracted by melodrama was in conflict with 'realism'. Dickens learned, early in his career, how to inspire the fear of Bill Sykes, pity for little Oliver, both shock and grief at Nancy's fate, and anger at the evils of the Poor Law. These effects succeeded in arousing emotion, but at the same time marked a compromise with 'realism'. Nobody would deny that Oliver is extraordinarily sweet and good; that Fagin and his lair are painted in lurid colours; or that either he or Sykes is a 'hard-hearted villain' in the direct tradition of melodrama and the Gothic. 'Improbable'? 'Sentimental'? These terms describe the compromise Dickens reached between the demands of melodramatic sentiment and those of realism.

Gothic novels continued to be written during Dickens's life. Mary Shelley's *Frankenstein* (1818) came out when Dickens was only six, but Emily Brontë's *Wuthering Heights* and her sister Charlotte's *Jane Eyre* (both 1847) were both published while Dickens was writing *Dombey and Son*. The Brontë sisters each told of improbable events, such as the two dead lovers haunting the moors in *Wuthering Heights,* or the madwoman imprisoned in Rochester's attic, in *Jane Eyre*. Perhaps the pursuit of Lady Dedlock through a blizzard, and the madness of Miss Havisham, are Dickensian instances of similarly 'extravagant' conceptions.

An astute comment on melodrama comes from the film director Sidney Lumet, who observed that 'In a well-written drama, the story comes out of the characters. The characters in a well-written melodrama come out of the story.' With the remarkable exception of Pip in *Great Expectations*, many Dickens characters fail to develop. They react to events, but hardly ever change. For example, in *Bleak House*, Esther meets her mother. This is an emotional scene, and it leads her to visit Mr. Guppy. But, does Esther change? It is very much the same Esther who visits Mr. Guppy, as the Esther who went for a walk and met her mother.

Esther provides a further instance: the love interest with Allan Woodcourt is beset with difficulties, and the two are united only at the end. This is as it should be in a courtship novel. In Jane Austen's *Pride and Prejudice*, Lizzie rejects Darcy's first proposal, just as Esther rejects Allan. However, the two rejections are completely different. Lizzie and Darcy are in the toils of a psychological tangle. Lizzie stokes her anger against him, frightened of being attracted to him, and she boosts her misunderstanding of Darcy and Wickham, while Darcy is still over-confident, depending on his wealth to win Lizzie, rather than his personal qualities. Their troubles, then, are those of character and relationship, and both of them have to develop – have to grow up, change – before they can be united. What is the trouble that interrupts Esther and Allan's romance? There is no psychological or emotional difficulty at all. In other words, the delayed courtship has nothing to do with character. It is purely a matter of plot: Esther is already betrothed to Mr. Jarndyce. Other impediments to their courtship are also matters of plot, not character. Allan has a ridiculous and prejudiced mother; Allan has to go on a long voyage; Allan is 'not rich'.

In this respect *Hard Times* is something of an exception: we have seen in Chapter 2 that both Louisa and Mr. Gradgrind change significantly as a result of their experiences. Mr. Harthouse provokes Louisa to realise things about herself that she had previously suppressed. Louisa's reflections on the mistakes of her upbringing cause a radical re-evaluation of his philosophy in Mr. Gradgrind, and with his altered beliefs come an altered personality and manners.

Dickens's novels, then, can be said to exist in the conflict between 'realism', and using melodrama to arouse the reader's emotions to a sensational pitch. The novels waver between these two dynamic forces. Their best moments achieve an equilibrium, when the melodramatic can take on an aura of naturalness, or (less often) when the natural in character can drive the story. They are at their most suspect when improbable plot devices control the narrative. In *Our Mutual Friend*, for example, John Harmon's identity – even kept secret from his wife on some excuse about testing her loyalty[1] – is never sufficiently justified. Similarly, in *Bleak House*, Mr. Jarndyce's gift of Esther to Allan, with a surprise house thrown in, is an equally unjustifiable device.

One matter of controversy concerned the presence or absence of the author. An author writing in their own voice would break the fragile illusion of reality. On the other hand, there was a long tradition of authors who regularly obtruded an author's personality into their novels – not least, Fielding and Sterne. William Makepeace Thackeray was a successful contemporary of Dickens, whose most

---

[1] Compare this treatment of Bella with the final scene of Shakespeare's *The Taming of the Shrew*. Both are uncomfortable pictures of a demand for absolute female submission.

famous novel, *Vanity Fair* (1847–1848), gives a running commentary on the characters, their faults, and society's shortcomings, from the cynical critic who is the author. As we know, Dickens is often present in his novels, frequently telling us what to think and feel, and we have commented that this sustains an impression that, in reading the novel, we are attending a theatrical performance: what we have called the 'dramatic' flavour of our two texts. Thackeray incorporated himself into his novels in a different fashion. The persona he cultivated was of a friendly old buffer, a bit of a cynic but chatty: in other words, another fictional character. Dickens, by contrast, does not present an ironic personality. The author's character in Dickens is without fault. He has recourse to rhetoric when it is called for, but when he urges us to think and feel like him, he is sincere. Other voices, such as Detective Bucket's or Harold Skimpole's, may be ironic, but the nearest thing to irony in Dickens's voice is generally a bitter sarcasm, as when he exclaims, 'Dead, your Majesty', on Jo's passing (*BH*, 677).

This question of the author's persona is a perennial challenge. Dickens's close collaborator, Wilkie Collins (1824–1889), developed a method whereby the story is told by several narrators who are also characters, each telling the part of the tale they witnessed. He used this method for his crime thrillers *The Woman in White* (1859) and *The Moonstone* (1868). George Eliot[2] wrote passages of moral discussion, taking up points relevant to the narrative, but without obtruding an authorial persona. Thomas Hardy,[3] on the other hand, maintained an objective distance, as if reporting from external observation, creating a pitiless realism he seemed to ascribe to fate itself.

Of other novelists who were more or less Dickens's contemporaries and were also successful, we will mention four. First, the dominant literary figure, Sir Walter Scott, died when Dickens was 20. His historical adventure stories such as *Waverley* (1814), *Rob Roy* (1817) or *Ivanhoe* (1819), must have appealed to his young follower. Second, Anthony Trollope (1815–1882) was a direct contemporary, who established himself with the 'Barsetshire' series of novels, the first of which, *The Warden,* was published in 1855. *The Warden* contains

---

[2] Works include *Adam Bede* (1859), *The Mill on the Floss* (1860) and *Middlemarch* (1871–1872).
[3] Works include *Tess of the D'Urbevilles* (1891) and *Jude the Obscure* (1895).

an attack on Dickens as 'Mr. Popular Sentiment', a novelist whose exaggerations have reformed everything in sight, and whose poor characters are impossibly angelic. Trollope produced over 40 novels, many of which revealed – as did those of Thackeray – a somewhat jaundiced view of human nature, but at the same time a lively sense of humour.

Our third mention goes to Mrs. Elizabeth Gaskell, who wrote of the industrial north, based on her experience as the wife of an Unitarian minister in Manchester. *North and South* (1854) is of particular interest, as Dickens's sudden decision to produce *Hard Times* preempted Mrs Gaskell's novel. She was annoyed, clearly feeling that Dickens was competing against her by getting his work in first. *North and South* is arguably a more sophisticated exploration of society in the industrial north than *Hard Times*. Furthermore, the differences between north and south are explored through character, in the manner Sidney Lumet prescribes for a 'well-written drama', rather than by means of melodrama.

Finally, Edward Bulwer Lytton, some nine years Dickens's senior, was a friend he admired. He was a prolific writer, best known now as the author of *The Last Days of Pompeii* (1834) and for having coined some phrases that have entered the language, such as 'the great unwashed' and 'the almighty dollar'. Bulwer Lytton's novels told of ghosts, mysteries of sinister crime, romance, historical adventure and even science fiction. He was the friend who advised Dickens to give *Great Expectations* a happy ending. There is a Bulwer Lytton Fiction Contest, won by the worst opening sentence for a novel, in imitation of Lytton's:

> It was a dark and stormy night; the rain fell in torrents – except at occasional intervals, when it was checked by a violent gust of wind which swept up the streets (for it is in London that our scene lies), rattling along the housetops, and fiercely agitating the scanty flame of the lamps that struggled against the darkness.
>
> (Edward Bulwer Lytton, *Paul Clifford*, 1830)

We have included Bulwer Lytton in our group of four, to show that Dickens could have poor judgement. Bulwer Lytton was popular in his time, but is hardly ever read in the present day.

Some features of the novel after Dickens

Any systematic survey of the novel since Dickens would be a huge undertaking: our aim here is merely to start some lines of thought that may prove fruitful.

We have referred to Dickens's ambition to present **an overview of society.** Thackeray's *Vanity Fair* held a similar ambition, the title referring to a society founded on 'vanity'. This bears comparison with *Bleak House*'s 'In Fashion' chapter (*BH*, 17–23). However, the idea that the novel format could portray life on a grand canvas, found several subsequent practitioners. The society of an English provincial town, describing several different social levels and occupations, is painted in detail in George Eliot's *Middlemarch* (1871–1872), just two years after the appearance of Tolstoy's huge historical epic *War and Peace* (1869). In Britain, John Galsworthy's *The Forsyte Saga* (1906–1921), a series of novels tracing a single family through generations, and Arnold Bennett's novels about the 'five towns' – the English potteries – display a similar panoramic ambition. In France, Honoré de Balzac (1799–1850) planned to write novels depicting all levels of society, calling his project *La Comédie Humaine* (from 1832). Subsequently, Émile Zola (1840–1902) conceived of his saga of two families, *Les Rougon-Macquart*, as a series of 20 novels. This 'panoramic' strand in the development of the novel marks how prose fiction took over some functions from epic poetry. *War and Peace*, for example, can be compared with the grand scope of Homer's *Iliad*, while the crowded populations of Dickens's works or Balzac's and Zola's projects, are reminiscent of Dante's *Divine Comedy* (1308–1321), William Langland's 'fair field full of folk' in *Piers the Plowman* (1370–1390), or John Bunyan's *The Pilgrim's Progress* (1678). All such collections of people from varied walks of life show a residue of the earlier works' moral themes: the crowd taken together suggests a satisfying range of different sins and virtues.

Of course 'social realism' was never a practical project. No novel, however huge, could embrace the chaos of actual life. A novelist can only impose his own idea of shape, upon nature's raw material. So we come to the death of Krook by spontaneous combustion, in *Bleak House*. We commented that this is an extraordinary event; that Dickens goes to considerable lengths to make it convincing; and we called the event a form of '**magic realism**'. We will mention two later examples of 'magic realism' to show how this feature developed with an increasing interest in psychology and symbolism.

First, in Thomas Hardy's *Tess of the D'Urbevilles*, the heroine spends a winter working in the fields: ' ... strange birds from behind the North Pole began to arrive silently on the upland of Flintcomb-Ash; gaunt spectral creatures with tragical eyes – eyes which had witnessed scenes of cataclysmal horror in inaccessible polar regions of a magnitude such as no human being had ever conceived'. There is, of course, no such place as 'behind the North Pole', nor are there 'cataclysmal' scenes beyond human imagination in 'inaccessible' regions. As Hardy continues, we realise that these birds are a strange manifestation of suffering against the background of a hostile fate, their 'tragical eyes' emblematic of the hopelessness of Tess's heart. These 'magical' birds are just as impossible as Krook's conflagration. Many critics see Krook's death as symbolic of an end to Chancery, brought about by its own corruption. In this view, then, Dickens and Hardy are seen to use 'magic realism' for similar purposes.

A second example is psychological: the murder of Jill Banford by Henry, in D. H. Lawrence's novella *The Fox*. Henry fells a tree, and wills it to fall upon and kill Jill Banford, which it does. Lawrence writes that 'In his heart he had decided her death. A terrible still force seemed in him, and a power that was just his. If he turned even a hair's breadth in the wrong direction, he would lose the power.' Henry's will, the axe-blows, the tree and Jill Banford standing in its way, all make a single magical power, as described by Lawrence, which accomplishes her death. Another novelist from the twentieth century who frequently flirts with or uses magic realism, is William Golding. See, for example, the murder of Piggy in *Lord of the Flies* (1954), or many other examples in works such as *The Spire* (1964) or *The Inheritors* (1955).

Bleak House and *Hard Times* declare themselves, in their opening pages, as **political novels**. For a novel to be so overtly part of a campaign was comparatively new. Novels had attacked social mores before: Jane Austen, for example, provides a full critique of the marriage-market in her segment of society; and Richardson's *Clarissa* is critical of a family's power over a single daughter. The open campaigning oratory of Dickens, however, was something new. Anthony

Trollope, satirising Dickens as 'Mr. Popular Sentiment', noted the new role the novel had taken on. Reforms used to come slowly, after deliberation; now things move faster: 'monthly novels convince, when learned quartos fail to do so. If the world is to be set right, the work will be done by shilling numbers'. Trollope continues: 'Of all such reformers Mr. Sentiment is the most powerful. It is incredible the number of evil practices he has put down: it is to be feared he will soon lack subjects ... .'[4] There have been few followers of this tradition. All published novels are, of course, acts of political consequence, but the vast majority of authors since Dickens's day have been more circumspect in their methods for promoting a political agenda, preferring not to thunder in the author's own outraged voice, as we have found to be Dickens's habit.

Serial publication was a phenomenon of the times, and a brief word about this practice is appropriate here. Readers of Austen's *Northanger Abbey* know that novels were reputedly immoral: young women in particular were encouraged to read sermons, because novels engendered silly romantic daydreams, thus undermining a girl's virtue. This view was itself often ridiculed, but was still widespread in the more pompously 'respectable' sectors of society. So, the novel was thought to be vulgar, and not really part of 'literature'. At the same time, rates of literacy increased rapidly throughout the nineteenth century – and the literate percentage grew particularly during Dickens's working life.

We remember that funding for schools for poor children was voted in 1833 when Dickens was 21, while the first bill to make education compulsory was passed in the year of his death. The publishing industry adapted to the new situation and developed the serial system of 'shilling numbers'. This suited the pockets of the newly literate, who found a complete volume more difficult to afford than 20 cheap 'numbers' spread over more than a year;[5] and it provided novels with excellent publicity, as thousands of readers waited for the next issue discussing the characters and future events. Serial publication still provoked strong public reactions in 1891, when there

---

[4] Trollope, Anthony, *The Warden*, 1855, Chapter 15.
[5] For much the same reason the system of 'Hire Purchase' or 'the Never-Never', for various purchases, became widespread following the Second World War.

was shock at the seduction in Hardy's *Tess of the D'Urbevilles*, or, in 1894–1895, with the shocking unmarried cohabitation of Jude and Sue in *Jude the Obscure*. Dickens was probably more successful than any other writer at developing his reputation into a personality cult. Serial publication and the new mass readership help to explain how Dickens's readings attracted such large audiences, as well as explaining why his novels exploit melodrama and sentimentality so unerringly. Dickens's critics would say serial publication explains why his novels are so vulgar. We can theorize that Dickens's novels are merely fulfilling the prophecy of those pompous 'respectable' people who always disapproved.

Together with the phenomenon of the serialised novel and mass literacy we should also say a word about **the mores of Victorian Domesticity**. Despite his hilarious satires of 'respectable' humbugs (such as Chadband in *Bleak House*, for example, and the Veneerings and their dinner-guests in *Our Mutual Friend*), Dickens played to mid-Victorian prurience and avoided mentioning physical love. Dora Spenlow in *David Copperfield* is a typical Dickens heroine, described as a dazzling halo of spoilt prettiness, but not as a girl. Meanwhile, 'fallen' women such as Emily and Martha, are tearfully evoked, and Dora dies following a miscarriage. However, all is implication of moral horror and gushing sympathy, with a sideswipe at the perfidy of men, but there is no explicit reference to the physical. Dickens also had recourse to coyness, using the Victorian's favourite linguistic device, euphemism. So for example, Bella's and John's embraces in *Our Mutual Friend* are euphemised as her 'disappearing act' within his arms.

D. H. Lawrence remarked that the nineteenth century was 'the century of the dirty little secret',[6] complaining that the Victorians' suppression of the subject of sex made theirs the most dishonest century in British history. Lawrence believed that the twentieth century still lived under an intolerable leftover of prudish denial about sex. Lawrence's views seem to apply to Dickens, and we have considered the issues involved when studying the angelic Rachael and Ada in Chapter 3. However, it would be wrong to accept

---

[6] Lawrence, D. H., 'A Study of Thomas Hardy', in *D. H. Lawrence, Selected Literary Criticism*, Ed. Beal, Anthony, London, 1956, pp. 185–194.

Lawrence's assessment as a general truth about nineteenth-century novels. Readers of George Eliot's *Adam Bede*, with its characterisa-tion of Hetty Sorrel, or of Hardy's *Tess of the D'Urbevilles* and its heroine's seduction, or of her courtship at Talbothays, will real-ise that sensuality and physical passion are powerfully depicted in those texts. Becky Sharp's adulteries in *Vanity Fair* are clearly implied, and although Thackeray does hold back in submission to 'respectable' mores, he was never as prurient as Dickens.

Several of the issues we have discussed in this chapter can coa-lesce to build the impression of Dickens as that unusual creature, the popular artist. In the present day there are still 'literary' nov-els, and the various popular genres: crime thrillers, adventure stories, romance, espionage and so on. There are quality practitioners in all these fields, but Dickens remains preeminent in combining mass popularity, with a sustained reputation as an important writer. Who else occupies such a position? Richardson and Defoe, perhaps, but their 'popularity' does not compare with the Victorian mass reader-ship either in numbers, or in social range. In order to find an artist whose works are still admired, and who reached the ordinary people of England as well as the literate minority, we probably have to go back to Shakespeare, back to a time when the stage entertained both Queen and commoner.

This is a relevant point to make. The history of English Literature is bedevilled by the social dichotomies of Britain's class-ridden society. For most of the centuries concerned, literature was written by and for the educated and privileged few. Even a nonconformist commoner such as Daniel Defoe had to seek and accept patronage from political sponsors. In the present day a snobbism about 'art' remains strong. What, for example, does the popular press say about the annual Turner Prize? In the first three decades of the twentieth century, modernist 'artists' wrote for each other: T. S. Eliot's *The Waste Land* (1922), for example, was like a puzzle of references to classical myth and previous literature, only understandable by those as cultured as Eliot himself. Virginia Woolf and James Joyce experimented with 'stream of consciousness' writing, also puzzling because the reader was expected to follow the character's subconscious associations. So, there remains a divide between writing for 'art' and popular writing. This divide was energetically challenged in the 1950s and 1960s by novelists Alan Sillitoe (*Saturday Night and Sunday Morning*, 1958) and John Braine (*Room at the Top*, 1957), and playwrights such as John Osborne (*Look Back in Anger*, 1956), a group who became known as 'the angry young men', and whose works appealed both to the general population and the literati. Very few works are now able to bridge this divide.

9

A Sample of Critical Views

The scope of this chapter

The literature on Dickens is vast: for the postgraduate student there are bibliographies such as R. C. Churchill's *A Bibliography of Dickensian Criticism 1836–1975* (1975), which can be supplemented from updates in the periodical *Dickens Quarterly*. Our sole aim here is to summarise a few critical views, chosen simply because they differ from each other, in order to stimulate debate. We begin with **Dickens's contemporaries**. Then we report some critics of Dickens from **between then and now**. Finally, we summarise the views of four **recent critics**. This chapter is intended to encourage you to develop your own ideas with confidence, and to read the critics critically.

Dickens's contemporaries

Dickens's novels have always inspired extreme admiration and extreme dislike in more or less equal quantities. Some readers have found themselves admiring and hating Dickens at the same time. When *Bleak House* came out, for example, **Mrs. Oliphant**[1] was offended by the portrait of Chadband, because he was 'a detestable Mr Chadband, an oft-repeated libel upon the preachers of the poor. This is a very vulgar and common piece of slander, quite unworthy

---

[1] Mrs Margaret Oliphant (1828–1897), Scottish novelist and historical writer.

of a true artist'. Despite 'acknowledging to the full how excellently this [Lady Dedlock] portion of *Bleak House* is accomplished', she felt 'obliged to say that we think Esther a failure, and, when she has only herself to talk about, are glad to be done with the complaisant history'. Several others disliked Esther's self-deprecating narrative. **George Brimley** remarked cattily, 'it is impossible to doubt the simplicity of her [Esther's] nature, because she never omits to assert it'.[2] Even **John Forster**, Dickens's friend and biographer, found Esther 'A difficult exercise, full of hazard in any case, not worth success and certainly not successful'[3], while **Charlotte Brontë** expressed another divided opinion: 'I liked the Chancery sections, but when it passes into the autobiographical form … it seems to me too often weak and twaddling.'[4]

George Eliot voiced more serious criticisms of these novels. Writing in *The Westminster Review* in July 1856,[5] she was among several who questioned Dickens's characterisations. While some reviewers felt that 'As a delineator of persons, … [Dickens] stands second only to Shakespeare'[6] George Eliot agreed that he is 'gifted with the utmost power in rendering the external traits of our town population,' but added, 'and if he could give us their psychological character – their conceptions of life and their emotions' he would be a great writer. However, Dickens, she observed, 'scarcely ever passes from the humorous and external to the emotional and tragic, without becoming as transcendent in his unreality as he was a moment before in his artistic truthfulness'. Another reviewer describes this as 'the habit of seizing peculiarities and presenting them instead of characters'.[7] This is a serious charge, as Eliot explains, because 'His frequently false psychology, his preternaturally virtuous poor children and artisans … [have the effect of] encouraging the miserable fallacy that high

---

[2] From 'Dickens's Bleak House', *The Spectator*, 24 September 1853, p. 925.

[3] Forster, John, *The Life of Charles Dickens*, 3 vols., (London 1872, 1873, 1874), page 610.

[4] In a letter to George Smith, 11 March 1852, in *The Letters of Charlotte Brontë Volume III: 1852–1855,* Ed. Margaret Smith, Clarendon Press, Oxford, 2004.

[5] From 'The Natural History of German Life', lxvi, p. 55.

[6] Riggs, C. F., 'Bleak House', *Puttnam's Monthly Magazine*, NY, November 1853, p. 558.

[7] Brimley, George, *The Spectator*, London, 24 September 1853, p. 923.

morality and refined sentiment can grow out of harsh social relations, ignorance, and want; or that the working classes are in a condition to enter at once into a millennial state of *altruism*, wherein everyone is caring for everyone else, and no one for himself'. This is an early attempt to express the oddity and yet realism of Dickens's characters, a preoccupation that persists in Dickens criticism to the present day.

Eliot was also critical of Dickens's attacks on institutions. These were pernicious because 'Mr Dickens's government looks pretty at a distance, but we can tell him how his ideal would look if it were real-ised. It would result in the purest despotism'. George Eliot believed that the law must be cautious, slow and carefully regulated: Dickens's ideal of 'justice freed from the shackles of law' would lead to abuses of arbitrary power. **Lord Denman** was critical of Dickens's attack on Chancery, because the court was already reformed: 'now the reform-ers appear to have gained their end ... now first Mr. Dickens takes an active part in promoting Chancery reform'.

It is clear from these comments that *Bleak House* received a mixed press at the time: Dickens's contemporaries aired doubts that are still debated today. One of these was Esther's irritating humility, another was a sceptical reaction to Dickens's characters, and finally there were objections to the attack on Chancery both because it was too late, and more seriously because it would liberate despotism. At the same time, there were reviews expressing admiration and delight at the style, the characterisation and Dickens's warm-hearted earnestness in the cause of the downtrodden, among whom many selected Jo as a compellingly sympathetic case.

The reception of *Hard Times* was equally controversial and contra-dictory. John Forster who, we have remarked, was Dickens's friend and biographer, made a valiant attempt to defend the novel. One criticism was that the attack on 'fact' was exaggeration because facts are helpful, and society cannot be governed without them. Forster acknowledges that there are those who 'accuse Mr Dickens of attack-ing this good movement and the other, or of opposing the search after statistical and other information by which only real light can be thrown on social questions'.[8] He answers them by referring to

---

[8] Forster, John, from an unsigned review, *The Examiner*, 9 September 1854, pp. 568–9.

Household Words, which is 'a great magazine of facts' and edited by Dickens. Apparently, Dickens knows that 'facts and figures' will not be forgotten 'by the world' so 'he leaves them, when he speaks as a novelist, to take care of themselves'.

Forster meets the objection that *Hard Times* merely argues, like a fable, that to train any man 'properly' we must 'cultivate his fancy, and allow proper scope to his affections', by asserting that the enforcement of this moral is 'not argumentative, because no thesis can be argued in a novel'. Both of these arguments are fallacious: you cannot soothe the angry reader by saying that he will find what is missing from the novel if he looks somewhere else; and it is manifestly untrue to say that 'no thesis can be argued in a novel', let alone in the same breath as 'To enforce this truth has been the object of the story of *Hard Times*', which, surely, contradicts. So, Forster's defence of *Hard Times* is a failure. We could defend the novel much more easily by arguing that the anti-fact passages are satirical exaggeration and successful, and that the book is constructed as a kind of fable, does argue its thesis and is none the worse for that. Forster's reasoning, however, doesn't work.

Thomas Babington Macaulay found *Hard Times* indigestible. It contained, he felt, 'one excessively touching, heart-breaking passage, and the rest sullen socialism'. The 'touching' passage is the scene between Rachael and Stephen as he lies dying, but Macaulay continues: 'The evils which he attacks he caricatures grossly, and with little humour.'[9] This last is the criticism Forster fails to counter. A more even-handed complaint about exaggeration was advanced by **John Ruskin**, who begins by stating that *Hard Times* is 'in several respects, the greatest' of Dickens's novels, and that 'Dickens's caricature, though often gross, is never mistaken'.[10] However, Ruskin requires of Dickens, 'when he takes up a subject of high national importance, such as that which he handled in *Hard Times*, that he would use severer and more accurate analysis'. Ruskin feels that the serious social and economic theme is diminished because, for example,

---

[9] Macaulay, Thomas Babington, *The Life and Letters of Lord Macaulay*, Ed. Trevelyan, G. O. Oxford University Press, Oxford, 1961, p. 614.
[10] From *The Works of John Ruskin*, Ed. Cook E. T. & Wedderburn, Alexander, George Allen, London & NY, 1903–1912, Vol. 17 p. 31.

Bounderby is 'a dramatic monster, instead of a characteristic example of a worldly master', and Stephen is 'a dramatic perfection, instead of a characteristic example of an honest workman'. This is a shame, for Dickens 'is entirely right in his main drift and purpose in every book he has written; and all of them, but especially *Hard Times*, should be studied with close and earnest care by persons interested in social questions'.

Karl Marx appreciated Dickens's provision of 'an accurate picture of the affected, ignorant and tyrannical bourgeoisie',[11] and **Friedrich Engels** agreed, suggesting that Dickens, together with George Sand and Eugène Sue, 'had brought about almost a social revolution in continental literature' by dethroning the kings and princes and elevating the poor, the 'despised class,' to a suitable subject for literature.[12] Such enthusiasm tells us that Dickens's reformist campaigning was appreciated. However, the exaggeration of his characters that was regretted by Ruskin, was castigated by **Anthony Trollope** in his lampoon of Dickens as 'Mr. Popular Sentiment', whose 'good poor people are so very good; his hard rich people so very hard; and the genuinely honest so very honest'.[13] Trollope did write in a more moderate tone elsewhere. He made a virtue of Dickens's popularity, and of the way characters such as Mrs. Gamp, Sam Weller, Inspector Bucket and, of course, Bounderby, have become part of English culture, as have characters from Shakespeare. How can we criticise an author who has been so successful, and who is so loved by the mass of his readers? Trollope asks, writing in *St. Paul's Magazine*, 'It is fatuous to condemn that as deficient in art which has been so full of art as to captivate all men.'

Mrs. Oliphant starts a new strand in *Hard Times* criticism when she complains that the novel lacks the beauties she finds in Dickens's other works. Instead, she finds in *Hard Times* 'The petulant theory of a man in a world of his own making, where he has no fear of being contradicted.' The suggestion is that *Hard Times* lacks the range and variety of the longer novels, and that it is an argument rather than a story, with no room for the comic entertainment to be found in

---

[11] Writing in the *New York Tribune*, 1 August, 1854.

[12] Engels, Friedrich, in *New Moral World*, 1844.

[13] Trollope, Anthony, *The Warden*, 1855, from Chapter 15.

Nicholas Nickleby or *The Pickwick Papers*. Therefore it is unpleasant to read. This is a complaint that has been taken up by later critics as well.

Between then and now

Dickens died in 1870. From then until now, almost every literary figure – author or critic – has aired an opinion of him. As you would expect, the fans and haters are both well represented. **Oscar Wilde** is said to have commented that 'You would need to have a heart of stone to read the death of Little Nell without dissolving into tears – of laughter,' while G. K. Chesterton said 'It is not the death of Little Nell but the life of Little Nell that I object to'[14]; and **Henry James**, rather superciliously called Dickens 'the greatest of superficial novelists'[15].

George Bernard Shaw saw *Bleak House* as the first novel Dickens produced after he discovered the hollowness of the great middle-class pretence:

> ... the discovery of the rottenness of the Court of Chancery was an important instalment of the exposure of the great middle class sham begun in *Dombey and Son*.[16]

Shaw argued the socialist nostrum that property is theft and the property holder a parasite, so the 'rights' Richard Carstone hopes to inherit for himself are really 'wrongs' for everybody else because they maintain the 'spoliation of the industrious by the idle'. Shaw therefore complains that all John Jarndyce's advice to Richard is advanced only to save him from disappointment, not for the much better reason that he has a 'moral obligation to earn his own livelihood by his own exertions'. Dickens also suffers from another

---

[14] In his *Appreciations and Criticisms of the Works of Charles Dickens*, London & NY: Dent & Dutton, 1911.

[15] From his review of *Our Mutual Friend*, in *The Nation* (New York), 21 December 1865.

[16] Shaw, George Bernard, *Shaw on Dickens*, Eds. Laurence, Dan H. & Quinn, Martin, Frederick Ungar, NY, 1985. Quotations are from pp. 20–21.

limitation which commonly follows when somebody has realised that the promise of the middle-class is sham: 'a renewed tenderness towards the upper class' which motivates the 'elaborate portrait of Sir Leicester Dedlock, who, arrogant numbskull as he is, has nothing of Pecksniff or Dombey about him'. Dickens's developing insights into his society and its classes, and his increasing perceptions, meant that 'by this time [when writing *Bleak House*] the deeper and deeper feeling which marked Dickens's advance as a writer had become almost continuous in his books'. Shaw sees an end to the Dickensian tendency to grotesque caricatures and careless laughter. If Mr. Vholes had appeared in an earlier novel such as *Nicholas Nickleby*, he would 'certainly have ended in a horse pond', and while Guppy and Jobling are 'not very mercifully dealt with', they are 'taken quite seriously for all that'.

In his introduction to *Hard Times*,[17] Shaw begins by suggesting a slightly different theory of Dickens's development, saying that 'the first half of the XIX century considered itself the greatest of all the centuries. The second discovered that it was the wickedest of all the centuries'. He likens the changed viewpoint to a religious conversion: ' ... in it [*Hard Times*] we see Dickens with his eyes newly open and his conscience newly stricken by the discovery of the real state of England'. Shaw contrasts *Bleak House*, in which Dickens is still engaged in piecemeal campaigns focussing on 'mere symptoms ... individual delinquencies, local plague-spots', with *Hard Times*, in which 'Coketown is the whole place; and its rich manufacturers are proud of its dirt'. Shaw believes this to be the start of the later Dickens, where 'the occasional indignation' found in the early novels 'has spread and deepened into a passionate revolt against the whole industrial order of the modern world'. Therefore, while earlier novels were written to entertain us, '*Hard Times* was written to make you uncomfortable; and it will make you uncomfortable', but it will 'leave a deeper scar on you, than any two of its forerunners'.

Having thus cried up *Hard Times* as a powerful critique, Shaw turns his fire on what he calls 'one real failure in the book', which is the depiction of the trade union meeting and the activist Slackbridge, who

---

[17] Shaw, op. cit. Quotations on *Hard Times* are from pp. 27–35.

> ... is a mere figment of the middle class imagination. No such man
> would be listened to by a meeting of English factory hands ... even at
> their worst, trade union organisers are not a bit like Slackbridge.

Further, there was a chairman at the meeting, who made no attempt
to preserve the usual order of a public discussion, but allowed
Slackbridge to take over. We remember the effective chairman in 'On
Strike', and wonder why it is so different in *Hard Times*.

This 'failure' of the book is compounded because Dickens 'expressly
says ... that the workers were wrong to organise themselves in trade
unions': Stephen Blackpool's statement that it is 'they as is put ower
me, and ower aw the rest of us' shows that Dickens believed it was
the responsibility of the upper class to find a solution to the ills of
industry. Shaw, then, believes that *Hard Times* is a passionate attack
upon a whole society that is not merely incidentally, but structurally
wrong. At the same time he recognises that Dickens does not understand industry, and offers only a rather feudal answer to its problems.

G. K. Chesterton[18] distinguishes the novels that came before
Bleak House as picaresque: their heroes travel from place to place,
so that the plots of those stories are rather 'rambling'. *Bleak House* is
different: it is 'no longer a string of incidents; it is a cycle of incidents.
It returns upon itself; it has a recurrent melody and poetic justice'
because 'the whole story comes back to Bleak House'. Developing
his point, Chesterton praises the beginning of the novel, which gives
us 'the feeling that the author sees the conclusion and the whole.
The beginning is alpha and omega ... He means that all the characters and all the events shall be read through the smoky colours of
that sinister and unnatural vapour'. In fact, *Bleak House* has 'artistic
unity' because characters such as Miss Flite and Krook are symbolic
of Chancery; Chancery is responsible for the death of Jo: 'almost
everything is calculated to assert and reassert the savage morality of
Dickens's protest ... The fog of the first chapter never lifts'.

Two further features of *Bleak House* impress Chesterton. First,
he regards the characterisation of Richard Carstone as a triumph of

---

[18] Chesterton, G. K., *Appreciations and Criticisms of the Works of Charles Dickens*,
London & NY: Dent & Dutton, 1911. All quotations are taken from Chapter 15
('Bleak House') and Chapter 17 ('Hard Times').

psychological realism, and as the only example of true tragedy in Dickens. Second, he finds the figure of Caddy Jellyby an admirable piece of work:

> Every touch in her is true, from her first bewildering outbursts of hating people because she likes them, down to the sudden quietude and good sense which announces that she has slipped into her natural place as a woman … Miss Caddy Jellyby is by far the greatest, the most human, and the most really dignified of all the heroines of Dickens.

Chesterton does have criticisms, however. He finds the early scenes with Skimpole delightful, but complains that by the end of the book Dickens has involved his character in 'mere low villainy'; and he comments that it is one of Dickens's weaknesses, that his characters become 'coarser and clumsier' when they take part in 'the practical events of a story'. Other than Skimpole, and with the exception of Chadband and Turveydrop, Chesterton opines that the characters are more 'delicately' and 'faintly' drawn than in earlier novels.

Hard Times, Chesterton tells us, is 'the highest and hardest' of those 'angles of [Dickens's] absolute opinion' that 'stood up out of the confusion of his general kindness, just as sharp and splintered peaks stand up' from a forest. In this novel, more than anywhere else, we meet the 'sternness' of Dickens. We meet the 'expression of a righteous indignation which cannot condescend to humour', so that when we take Dickens's hand in *Hard Times*, it is startlingly cold, and we realise that we have 'touched his gauntlet of steel'. However, we cannot assess *Hard Times* without discussing the politics of its time. Chesterton felt that politics had been 'getting into a hopeless tangle' for a hundred years. He traces the origin of Dickens's English liberalism to the American and French Revolutions, but suggests that the English forgot two of the three central pillars of revolution: 'if they had more and more liberty it did not matter whether they had any equality or any fraternity'. Herbert Spencer, Bentham and Mill all lost their direction, while Dickens kept his head: in *Hard Times* 'he specially champions equality. In all his books he champions fraternity':

> In an England gone mad about a minor theory he reasserted the original idea – the idea that no one in the State must be too weak to influence the State.

Chesterton finishes by re-emphasising that *Hard Times* is different from the other novels: it is 'bitter', 'hard' and 'harsh'. Previous satirical characters such as Nupkins, or Bumble, are treated to 'half affectionate derision' and 'his very abuse was benignant', whereas Gradgrind and Bounderby are described with 'a degree of grimness and sombre hatred' that is very different. *Hard Times* is 'perhaps the only place where Dickens, in defending happiness, for a moment forgets to be happy'.

Aldous Huxley[19] records a less sympathetic view of Dickens, suggesting that the creator of so many 'old infants' – examples are the Cheeryble brothers, Tim Linkwater – 'and so many other gruesome old Peter Pans, was obviously a little abnormal in his emotional reactions. There was something rather wrong with a man who could take this lachrymose and tremulous pleasure in adult infantility'.

Huxley believes, then, that there is an emotional peculiarity in Dickens that he insists is 'pathological'. He then continues in an even more damaging vein, this time turning his attention towards an element in Dickens's works that has often been criticised: those passages often traduced as sentimental melodrama. Huxley's contention is that 'whenever in his writing he [Dickens] becomes emotional, he ceases instantly to use his intelligence'. This shutting down of his brain, according to Huxley, comes as a function of Dickens's desire to 'overflow' as his 'overflowing' heart 'drowns his head and dims his eyes'. When 'Mentally drowned and blinded by the sticky overflowings of his heart, Dickens was incapable, when moved, of recreating, in terms of art, the reality which had moved him.'

Virginia Woolf explains her reaction to Dickens in an essay she calls 'Phases of Fiction',[20] and she introduces the 'romantic' by turning from Scott, Stevenson and Mrs. Radcliffe to Dickens, whereupon, 'We enter at once into the spirit of exaggeration.' By this, she means that the characters have 'eccentricity and vigour', they are larger than life, and are repetitive in their words and actions: 'This perpetual repetition has, of course, an enormous power to drive these characters

---

[19] From *Vulgarity in Literature: Digressions from a Theme*, London: Chatto & Windus, 1930.
[20] In *Granite and Rainbow: Essays*, NY: Harcourt, Brace and Company, 1958, pp. 93–148.

home, to stabilize them [Mrs. Jellyby, Mr. Vholes, Mr. Turveydrop];
all serve as stationary points in the flow and confusion of the narrative.' Their exaggerated appearance shows Dickens's eye for character:
'an eye gluttonous, restless, insatiable, creating more than it can use'.
Woolf clearly believes that Dickens's characters represent something
excessive, and describes her impression of *Bleak House*: 'Human faces,
scowling, grinning, malignant, benevolent, are projected at us from
every corner. Everything is unmitigated and extreme' (quotations are
from pages 11 to 12).

This is not all, however, for in Woolf's view there is one more natural character who threatens to distract us from the gargantuan world
inhabited by the rest. This is Inspector Bucket, whose 'character is no
longer fixed and part of the design; it is in itself of interest. Its movements and changes compel us to watch it'. The detective is a mistake
in the novel's structure because Dickens has:

> sharpened our curiosity and made us dissatisfied with the limitations and
> even with the exuberance of his genius. The scene becomes too elastic,
> too voluminous, too cloud-like in its contours. The very abundance of
> it tires us, as well as the impossibility of holding it all together. We are
> always straying down bypaths and into alleys where we lose our way and
> cannot remember where we were going.
>
> (*VW*, 13)

Dickens felt indignant at the injustices of society, but 'he lacked sen-
sitiveness privately, so that his attempts at intimacy failed'. His characters 'do not inter-lock' and are often out of touch with each other.
Often, 'when they talk to each other they are vapid in the extreme or
sentimental beyond belief'. Since he created Bucket, Woolf argues,
Dickens has inadvertently given us a taste for something more 'in
proportion to the figure of a normal man', so that we now want 'this
intensification, this reduction' – something that Dickens cannot provide. According to Woolf, we will find this elusive quality in Jane
Austen.

We can now come to **George Orwell**, whose essay 'Charles
Dickens' was published in 1940.[21] Orwell sets himself the task of

---

[21] From *Inside the Whale and Other Essays*, London: Gollancz, 1940.

defining the kind of novelist Dickens was, and notes that there is an 'utter lack of any constructive suggestion anywhere in his work. He attacks the law, parliamentary government, the educational system and so forth, without ever clearly suggesting what he would put in their places'. This is because Dickens's criticisms of society are all 'moral' and not political. He does not want to change the system, nor does he believe that it would be better if changed. Instead, 'His whole "message" is one that at first glance looks like an enormous platitude: If men would behave decently the world would be decent.' Orwell then argues that this is not a platitude, but, on the contrary, a valuable message. It is for this reason, for example, that there is a series of good, rich men in Dickens's novels: John Jarndyce and Gradgrind after his conversion, being two examples.

Orwell spends some time pointing out that Dickens has no revolutionary agenda. So, for example, he does not complain about child labour. Instead, he complains that a delicate nature like that of Copperfield (Dickens himself, of course) should have to 'sink' into the company of the 'rough boys' with whom he worked. The revolutionary mobs in *Barnaby Rudge* and *A Tale of Two Cities* are described as subhuman lunatics, not forward-looking democrats, and the trade union in *Hard Times* is 'not much better than a racket, something that happens because employers are not sufficiently paternal'. Finally, when it comes to education, Dickens attacks almost every type of school then in existence. Orwell remarks, 'It seems that in every attack Dickens makes upon society he is always pointing to a change of spirit rather than a change of structure. It is hopeless to try and pin him down to any definite remedy, still more to any political doctrine. His approach is always along the moral plane.' This is what Orwell means by a 'moral' revolutionary, one who focuses on human nature because there is no point in changing society if human nature remains in its present wicked and foolish state. So Dickens's attitude is 'not such a platitude as it sounds'.

Orwell then turns to Dickens's lower-middle-class origin, which imposes some limitations on his outlook – particularly underpinning the idea that most of the institutions of government, whether Parliament or the Circumlocution Office, are unnecessary and do no useful work. His origin also gives him some advantages, however: together with his lack of interest in world affairs, he lacks the English habit of despising foreigners. So, he never describes a battle: 'in any case he would not regard a battlefield as a place where anything worth settling could be settled' and Orwell comments that 'It is one up to the lower-middle-class, puritan mentality.' There are many examples of descriptions that convey a feeling of repulsion and contempt for the poorest classes and slum dwellers, and some disgust and fear of sinking into poverty.

Turning to Dickens's style, Orwell notices what he calls the Dickens 'touch', by which he means that everything is piled up, 'detail on detail, embroidery on embroidery', so the novel ultimately gives a 'rococo' impression. Sometimes, such embroidery leads Dickens astray and his elaborations strike a false note. This does not matter, as 'He is all fragments, all details – rotten architecture, but wonderful gargoyles – and never better than when he is building up some character who will later on be forced to act inconsistently.' To explain this last remark, Orwell acknowledges that 'Generally he is accused of doing just the opposite. His characters are supposed to be mere 'types', each crudely representing some single trait.' On the contrary, Orwell sees characters who ought to have been purely static, such as Micawber, Squeers, Wegg and Skimpole, 'finally involved in "plots" where they are out of place and where they behave quite incredibly'. This, in Orwell's opinion, is because Dickens was a caricaturist, but thought he was not, and so he was constantly putting static characters into action.

Orwell's conclusion emphasises Dickens's sense of outrage and his championing of the underdog as special qualities even in the absence of any social agenda. When imagining Dickens, what Orwell sees 'is the face of a man who is always fighting against something, but who fights in the open and is not frightened, the face of a man who is *generously angry* – in other words, of a nineteenth-century liberal, a free intelligence, a type hated with equal hatred by all the smelly little orthodoxies which are now contending for our souls'.

In 1948 the influential critic **F. R. Leavis** published his study *The Great Tradition*, declaring that there are four 'great' novelists in English: Jane Austen, George Eliot, Joseph Conrad and Henry James. The novelists before Austen were leading up to her, and the three since Austen, favoured by his approval, were continuing in her 'tradition'. This 'great' tradition seems to mean that everything about the 'great' novel has one purpose: 'the end is a total significance of a profoundly serious kind'.[22] Leavis finds most Dickens's novels lacking in this, for although Dickens was 'a great genius ... permanently among the classics', nevertheless, 'The adult mind doesn't as a rule find in Dickens a challenge to an unusual and sustained seriousness.' We note the Leavisite idea of 'sustained seriousness' again. He finds such a quality in only one work – *Hard Times* – which he praises. *Hard Times* has 'a perfection that is one with the sustained and complete seriousness for which among his productions it is unique'. This is partly because it is much shorter than Dickens's other novels, and consequently 'leaves no room for the usual repetitive overdoing and loose inclusiveness' found in his works. More generously, Leavis supposes also that Dickens was not tempted to expand in his usual manner, because 'he was too urgently possessed by his themes; the themes were too rich, too tightly knit in their variety and too commanding'.

Most of Leavis's remaining remarks concern Gradgrind and Bounderby, and the theme of Utilitarianism which he finds to be successful, satisfyingly countered by the opposition of Sleary's Horse-Riding. Finally, Leavis turns to his 'great' novelists and acknowledges that there is clear evidence of Dickensian influence in some of George Eliot's 'less felicitous characterization', in Henry James's Princess Casamassima and in D. H. Lawrence's *The Lost Girl*. Despite approving of *Hard Times*, Leavis allows his concept of 'seriousness' the last word, for even if the works of these other writers evince 'a clear relation to the Dickensian', they are nonetheless 'incomparably more mature, and belong to a total serious significance'.

Philip Larkin wanted to say something about 'the whole Dickens method'.[23] What he said shows a sharp insight: 'it strikes me as being less ebullient, creative, vital, than hectic, nervy, panic-stricken'. He pursues this idea further, suggesting that Dickens had a desperate rather than abundant imagination: 'This jerking of your attention, with queer names, queer characters, aggressive rhythms, piling on adjectives – seems to me to betray basic insecurity in his relation with

[22] Leavis, F. R., *The Great Tradition*, London & NY: Faber and Faber, 1948, p. 19. All quotations are from pages 19 to 21.
[23] *Philip Larkin: Letters to Monica*, Ed. Thwaite, Anthony, Faber & Faber, London, 2011.

the reader.' Larkin's remark comes from a private letter. However, he does seem to identify an aspect of Dickens we mentioned in Chapter 8: his need for reassurance, the brittle lack of confidence that could look like arrogance and his increasing need for shared emotion, for applause from the audience at his readings.

Recent critics

We now summarise a portion of the arguments put forward recently by four professional critics. We make no claim that these four are representative – that would be an impossible aim. They have been chosen only because they are different. Reading their arguments should encourage you to develop your ideas – whether similar to theirs or very different – with the confidence that your responses can be equally valid. We summarise not merely their conclusions, but also their arguments, so you can judge their reasoning as well as their opinions.

The first in our sample is *Dickens's Villains: Melodrama, Character, Popular Culture*, by **Juliet John**.[24] She begins by explaining what led her to write this study: 'Many notable critics have dismissed Dickens's villains as "melodramatic" or "stagey", while at the same time praising Dickens's complex understanding of deviant psychology' (*JJ*, 1). John's book was 'born' in response to this 'false logic'. Critics have approached Dickens from within the tradition of intellectual elitism, but such an approach is not appropriate. John, on the contrary, believes that Dickens had a purpose:

> Dickens's writings attempt to collapse the artificial opposition between 'high' and 'popular' culture … The privileging of the mind above emotion underpins, for Dickens, the misguided intellectual elitism which, far from improving the lot of the workers, compounds their cultural alienation.
>
> (*JJ*, 3)

---

[24] John, Juliet, *Dickens's Villains: Melodrama, Character, Popular Culture*, Oxford & NY: Oxford University Press, 2001. Page numbers will appear in brackets preceded by *JJ*, thus: (*JJ*, 15).

Melodrama avoids 'interiority' and concentrates on 'ostension'; and Dickens uses 'melodramatic aesthetics … as a point of ideological principle – the principle of cultural inclusivity'. Critics have brought inappropriate assumptions to Dickens, from the elitism of the Romantic tradition instead of approaching him with the popular culture conceptions appropriate to melodrama. So they read Dickens 'in terms of cultural assumptions to which he was opposed' (*JJ*, 16).

Villains originated in allegory in a Christian context, so they are types, not psychological individuals. This would seem to make them ideal for melodrama. However, John argues that in any work, the villains are definable as such 'because of the threat they pose to the value system' of the genre. So, villains in melodrama threaten the dominant melodramatic aesthetic. This means that they are often the most intelligent characters in the story, 'threatening its general elevation of emotion over intellect' (*JJ*, 11); they are individualists, and they may be role-players, dandies, intellectuals or Romantics. So, villains can often sabotage 'the attempt dramatically to marginalise the psyche' which was at the heart of 'Dickens's populist, anti-intellectual project' (*JJ*, 11). Having explained her reasons for not including Quilp or Pecksniff in her survey of villains (they belong in carnival rather than melodrama), and having taken into account the objection that novel reading is essentially a private and interiorised activity (Dickens's 'theatrical' novels work against this tendency), John concludes her introduction by saying:

> Dickens's novels in fact present a self-consciously idealized and problematized version of reality in which, most importantly, the mind is marginalised.
>
> (*JJ*, 20)

George Henry Lewes commented on Dickensian characters' 'brainlessness', but since then critics have been 'slow to investigate the political purposes informing Dickens's externalized aesthetics' (*JJ*, 20).

In her chapter, 'Dickens and Dandyism', John quotes the passage on 'Dandyism', from Chapter 12 of *Bleak House* (see *BH*, 172–173), noting that Dickens has a broad concept of Dandyism: he applies the term to any fashion that is unjustifiable, so there can be a Dandyism of religion, for example, as well as Dandies who wear the latest clothes. She then turns to a discussion of Skimpole, who 'personifies the artistic and moral issues surrounding the elevation of beauty over ethics in *Bleak House*' (*JJ*, 157). There is a philosophy implicit in the broader concept of Dandyism that Dickens calls the 'more mischievous' kind, which is that expressed by Skimpole, who elevates art over life. He therefore has no emotional connection with others. While the fashionable Lady Dedlock is 'distorted by the effort of repressing passion … Harold Skimpole is portrayed as free from such struggles. This apparent absence of interior struggle functions as a sign of his monstrosity' (*JJ*, 159).

With art elevated above life, what happens is that the brain takes the place of the heart, and John brings forward examples of Skimpole's words and actions from *Bleak House* to show that his philosophy is irresponsible, ignores the human in favour of art, and is potentially fascist (see, for example, Skimpole's remarks about slaves, *BH*, 273). Skimpole speaks of himself in the third person, and we can conceive this habit either as that of an actor being separate from his role, or as an aesthete's 'view of himself as a work of art' (*JJ*, 161). To bring this discussion of Skimpole as a representative of Dandyism back to the main thesis of her book, John points out that it was his intellectualism, his dogma that placed the intellectual and elitist culture above the needs of others, that led Dickens to develop this Dandy as villainous:

> In his use of the intellect to advocate the elevation of art over life, or the divorce of art from its social consequences, Skimpole personifies the kind of art that was anathema to Dickens. He is significant because of his aesthetic philosophy, an ethos which Baudelaire, Wilde, and, before them, Dickens realized was dangerous.
>
> (*JJ*, 161)

Skimpole's character helps in 'demonstrating the link between aestheticism and immorality' (*JJ*, 162) which John suggests contributes to Dickens's hostility to the demands of 'high' or elitist culture.

In *Bleak House,* Dickens investigates what, in Thomas Carlyle's 1836 novel *Sartor Resartus,*[25] are called the 'Dandiacal' and 'Drudge' sectors of society. When Skimpole evicts Jo, this is symbolic of 'the

---

[25] John presumably refers to *Sartor Resartus* as Dickens is known to have read and admired it.

division of England into the privileged and the neglected, or 'the dandies and the drudges', and is ironic also as Skimpole has no more money than Jo: it is his 'cultural capital' that gives him access to 'elite circles' (*JJ*, 166). *Bleak House* constantly juxtaposes slums and dire poverty against wealth and ease, and there is little communication between these two worlds. Dickens makes clear that the Dandies:

> ... are not mysterious, anomalous monsters; rather, they are monstrous products of their time. The implication of Dickens's critique of a polarized, unequal society is obviously to reinforce the desirability of the idea of cultural inclusivity to which dandyism is an affront ... And just as Victorian dandies were products of their social environment, Dickens's dandies can never be divorced from their novelistic environment.
>
> (*JJ*, 167)

Writing in 2012, **Valerie Purton**[26] identifies her critical project as a close fellow of Juliet John's. Both of these critics seek a 'fuller, fairer reading of Dickens' (*VP*, 160): John on account of melodrama, and Purton from examining the sentimental tradition. John, she says, argues that Dickens avoided 'interiority' by adopting a 'theatrical aesthetic' in service of his 'anti-intellectualism'. Purton goes on to define her own direction: 'This chimes in with the argument of the present work that Dickens uses the sentimentalist tradition to disable thinking in his readers, in order to prompt in them the healthy overflow of tears.' Purton is not convinced that Dickens was always anti-elitist. However, 'what is public and populist (sentimentalism or melodrama) needs to be recognised as having a cultural, if not an aesthetic, value equal to that of the individual and private (the Romantic)' (all from *VP*,156).

In *Bleak House,* we find Dickens developing Goldsmithian characters in Esther, Jarndyce and, most of all, in Harold Skimpole. Purton compares the bailiff scenes between *Bleak House* and Goldsmith's *The Good-Natured Man*, in which Dickens acted in 1847. In Skimpole, Dickens 'showed himself capable not only of Goldsmith's undermining of hypocrisy, but of a true satirist's ferocity' (*VP*, 59). Skimpole is

---

[26] Purton, Valerie, *Dickens and the Sentimental Tradition: Fielding, Richardson, Sterne, Goldsmith, Sheridan, Lamb,* London & NY: Anthem Press, 2012. Page numbers will appear in brackets preceded by *VP*, thus, (*VP*, 15).

the 'false sentimentalist' in the scene with Coavins, while the whole
action is refracted through the 'sentimental heroine' narration by
Esther: 'In both scenes, hypocrisy is certainly attacked but sentimental values, through Esther's and Honeywood's charity, are finally
reinforced' (*VP*, 61). This shows that, by the time of *Bleak House*,
Dickens has developed a 'sentimentalist rhetoric' complex enough to
attack the hypocrisies of his day, and Purton suggests that this is an
inheritance from Goldsmith's play.

    Bleak House has a 'sentimental heroine' as one of its narrators.
However, both narratives explore 'the web of connections which
make up English society and which is the novel's real focus of attention'. When Esther constructs Ada as the 'sentimental heroine' with
obvious reference to her childhood companion, her beloved doll, this
is astute psychology on Dickens's part: 'a characterisation rather than
an uncritical presentation of the sentimental vision' (*VP*, 140). As
we examine *Bleak House*, we find that there is a wide-ranging critique of sentimental values. 'Self-denial' is exemplified by Esther, and
found to be of limited value, while a healthy selfishness leads to the
happy ending. Benevolence is also found wanting in the character of
Jarndyce, due to his mistaken support of Skimpole, his inability to
deal with Chancery, and his general passivity: 'the Good-Natured
Man is not adequate in the world of this novel'. Richard Carstone is
the frank and honest young hero, but 'frankness, openness, generosity are not enough'. Woodcourt comes out on top, but he 'hardly
qualifies as the sentimental hero'. Purton therefore argues that the
happy ending is not so much an 'endorsement' of sentimentalism, as
a 'demystification' (all from *VP*, 141), where various versions of the
sentimental have been found wanting.

    Skimpole is the sentimental hypocrite, the Joseph Surface[27] of
Bleak House. His selfishness is

> ... textually exposed in the juxtaposition of his cruelty to Jo and his
> singing of a blatantly sentimental ballad about a peasant boy, a song, he
> says, which "always made him cry". Thus Dickens critiques the senti-
> mental tears he elsewhere works so successfully to elicit. It is a powerfully

---

[27] Joseph Surface is the hypocrite who professes 'sentiments' to cover his selfish
ends, in Richard Brinsley Sheridan's play *The School for Scandal* (1777).

self-reflexive even deconstructive moment, part of the complexity of Dickens's sentimentalist strategy in this novel.

(*VP*, 141)

Purton then turns to Jo's death, because it is 'the key moment ... in which the resources of sentimentalism are exploited to the full'. Jo's double is Skimpole, the false child set against the real but denied child. The labouring cart metaphor shows 'Dickens's dazzling linguistic shifts between the physical and the metaphorical'. Whether we are religious or not,

> Jo is in death literally given, by Woodcourt, the empowerment of words, allowed for the first time to share the linguistic inheritance of the rest of society. The security of the sentimental tradition, steeped as it is in drama and theatricality, is the enabling factor in that terrifying ending, as the expected sentimental narrator ... turns to snarl at the audience ... "Dead, your majesty ... etc.".

(*VP*, 142)

Purton finds *Hard Times* a less successful novel. Dickens had used the hard/soft opposition, a sentimentalist structure, with Dombey and Florence in *Dombey and Son*, and attempted the same thing with Gradgrind and Sissy. 'The novel's focus is weakened, however, by the accompanying industrial plot of the confrontation' between Bounderby and Stephen. That plot is an 'artistic failure', and virtually all of the characters and relationships in *Hard Times* are, according to Purton, wrong. Bounderby is from the 'sentimental hypocrite' plot, but Stephen and Rachael are from the 'sentimental selfishness' plot, so the two sides do not work together. The pairing of Gradgrind and Sissy is diluted by the presence of Louisa, which 'weakens the sentimental catharsis' (all from *VP*, 143).

There is discussion of Herbert Spencer's *Principles of Psychology* which insists on the necessity of merging the cognitive (head) and affective (heart), and it is suggested that Dickens's writing is at its greatest when he combines what an early critic, H. P. Sucksmith, called the 'rhetoric of sympathy' with 'the rhetoric of irony'. Sucksmith thought that this healthy combination of intellect and emotion was the project and success of *Hard Times*. Purton disagrees: 'but *Hard Times* as a reading experience is a dramatisation of a desperate opposition, not a co-operation, ending with the triumph of Sissy's world-view over Gradgrind's'. Another feature of *Hard Times* that distinguishes it from the sentimental tradition is that 'it ends, untypically, with failure – the failure of Louisa to achieve full womanhood' (*VP*, 144).

Valerie Purton appends a concluding chapter, which commentates the sentimental tradition, suggests that the twentieth century was not a congenial time for it, but that there may be the beginnings of a resurgence of the sentimental now that the twenty-first century is under way, because there are signs 'that, in the twenty-first century, the physical and the spiritual are once more being linked' (*VP*, 158). Sentimental tears 'are not to be dismissed as unintelligent simply because they do not involve the intellect: perhaps when we cry in a crowd or when reading Dickens we are losing our identity but experiencing the ecstasy of being purely, merely, irrationally, human' (*VP*, 159). To lose one's self in an emotion shared with the crowd is a sentimental phenomenon Purton seems to recommend. Many, on the contrary, will find unthinking mob emotion a disturbing and potentially frightening idea.

In Juliet John and Valerie Purton, we have sampled two critics who are most concerned with the type or genre to which Dickens's writing belongs, and who are both – whether on behalf of melodrama or the sentimental – constructing their 'fuller, fairer' readings within the contentious area of the novels' aesthetics. We now turn to a different approach. Our third critic in this section, **Pam Morris**,[28] considers *Bleak House* in the context of the social and political background, beginning with the effect she ascribes to the events of 1848:

> The cluster of threatening events in 1848 – cholera, revolutions in Europe, and Chartism at home – and their seemingly miraculous dispersal without dire consequences gave rise, in England at the turn of the decade, to a hegemonic discourse upon the ways of Divine Providence. It was a discourse characterised by congratulatory complacency. Great Britain, it seemed evident, was under a special dispensation.
>
> (*PM*, 81)

---

[28] Morris, Pam, *Dickens's Class Consciousness: A Marginal View*, Basingstoke: Macmillan, 1991. This summary draws upon Chapter 4: '*Bleak House*: Alienated Readers', pages 81 to 98. Page numbers will appear in brackets preceded by *PM* thus, (*PM*, 15).

Morris explains this 'discourse' in greater detail, drawing on material from *Methodist Magazine*, the *Christian Observer*, and other evidence from the time showing a belief that God was on Britain's side. To quarrel with the establishment status quo of wealth and influence, the '"eternal settlement", was to quarrel with the will of God' (*PM*, 82). Since God organised everything, this conviction of divinely ordained goodness extended to prosperity also: if you were prosperous, you could assume that this was a reward for your goodness. The poor, who were not 'materially able to exhibit 'godly' signs', were 'interpellated into a damning system of meaning' (*PM*, 83), in which their misfortunes were interpreted as being their wickedness: 'Righteous art Thou O Lord, and just art Thy judgments,' wrote the *Methodist Magazine*, commenting on the death of a drunken man in a house fire, presumably because he was a sinful victim of God's righteous justice. However, 'Despite the surface complacency engendered by this discourse on Providential settlement, there were points of fracture and contradiction which became the focus of nagging social anxiety' (*PM*, 84). By the time Dickens came to write *Bleak House*, there was increasing anxiety about the fabric of society, which was seen to be threatened: 'The interconnected malaise of poverty, prostitution, disease, illegitimacy, and juvenile crime was undoubtedly the 'Tough Subject' of the early 1850s' (*PM*, 85).

Morris then turns to *Bleak House* itself. Her thesis is that the novel 'is centrally concerned with the ideological subjection of subjects and positions itself dialogically in the midst of the conflicts articulated within Providential discourse'. The divided narrative between the omniscient third-person voice, and the restricted view of Esther, contributes to the enacting of such a dialogue, where the all-knowing external narrator is a 'parodic representation of a Providential viewpoint' (both from *PM*, 86). As the reader connects the pieces of meaning, it becomes clear that all the evils that happen are due to human, not providential, causation.

> Law is represented in the text as at the centre of this proliferating system of misreading, subsuming all other structures of mystification. This is wholly appropriate, since law is the ultimate foundation and guarantor of the existing providential dispensation of property, privilege, and power ... In *Bleak House*, the imposition of a sense of guilt and

illegitimacy – in the widest sense of having no right to exist – is unveiled
as the mechanism of submission, constructing subjects who 'willingly'
subject themselves to subjection.

(*PM*, 87)

Morris looks at the way Mr. Snagsby becomes entangled in the plotting and power games of Tulkinghorn and Bucket, and comments on
how he becomes mystified and confused, and convinced of his own
guilt. It is so with the other victimised characters: 'All are marked by a
sense of powerlessness, fatalism, and guilt' (*PM*, 90).

Turning to consider Esther and her narrative, Morris points out
how her origins are paired with Jo's, even before these two are connected by disease. Esther, like the other victims, does not know how
or why she is stigmatised with guilt. However, she becomes 'more
than willing to pay the price of admission into social community'
(*PM*, 92) and resolves to 'try as hard as ever I could, to repair the
fault I had been born with' (*BH*, 27). Esther's narrative is compared
to 'confessional' writing that was much indulged by young women
writing in the *Methodist Magazine* at that date. Several critics have
noticed the inner boastfulness of Esther's humility, and Morris is
another: like the autobiographical writers in *Methodist Magazine*,
Esther's narrative discourse:

> ... exploits the licence offered by the confessional form to covertly
> catalogue moral virtue while proclaiming humility. Her retrospectively
> organised personal history culminating in the happy domestic ending,
> constructs a causal moral plot in which her original virtue is recognised
> and rewarded at last, and Esther assigned her proper place at the very
> centre of that little adoring company of the elect at Bleak House.
>
> (*PM*, 93)

Submission, self-denial and industry are the 'admission price of social
acceptance and love'. So, Esther, having obeyed her godmother's
strictures, eventually achieves her reward. However, we cannot read
only Esther's narrative in *Bleak House*, for it is set against the external,
third-person narrative, which provides a more cynical and ironic set
of social connections which work against any 'providential' complacency conveyed by Esther. Morris now discusses Jo, almost as if he is

Esther's *alter ego*: 'Unlike Esther, though, there is no fairy-tale element of transformation in Jo's story ... The representation of Jo, read in conjunction with the characterisation of Esther, unveils the means by which such inexplicable submissiveness in the poor was maintained' (*PM*, 95). The slum where he lives is described with allusions to the infernal, but it is a hell made by human agency (in fact, Chancery). The name 'all-Alone' emphasises Jo's illegitimate condition, and his 'loss of all social connection'. Furthermore, his illiteracy cuts him off, as 'None of its [society's] structuring systems of signs conveys any meaning or offers any position to him at all' (both from *PM*, 96). Jo is sustained by the compassion of other orphans: Guster pats him on the shoulder; Charley Neckett cares for him, followed by Esther, and finally he is in the care of Phil Squod.

As Jo becomes connected to other people, he begins to show some subjectivity, a dawning consciousness of himself. However, like the child Esther, this is 'self-perception founded upon such an extreme of difference that inevitably with it there comes a sense of lack and shame' (*PM*, 97). Morris points out that the very poor can only read their distance from all objects of desire, as a measure of their unworth. Jo's conception of his own history is in the form of self-blame, and he therefore seeks 'to justify his existence by reparation':

> Having discovered at last the power of signifying systems, Jo is eager to pay the admission fee for a place within social discourse. Like Esther he is ready and willing to confess. He commissions Mr. Snagsby to 'write out, wery large so that anyone could see it anywheres, as that I was wery truly hearty sorry that I done it'. The chapter is entitled 'Jo's Will', and this is his bequest. It is the only thing society does not begrudge the poor: a willed and willing moral guilt.
>
> (*PM*, 98)

Morris more or less sums up her analysis in her final sentence, supporting her contention that in *Bleak House* Dickens has provided a critique of society's means of controlling the disconnected, the victims and the poor. This critique analyses society's means of maintaining the status quo to the benefit of the controlling class: Jo 'catches its [society's] most pernicious infection. It is the infection of shame, imposed with the inequality of class, and ensuring the willing subjection of the poor in perpetuity' (*PM*, 98).

Our fourth and final critic in this section, **Stephen J. Spector,**[29] begins by asking why Stephen Blackpool and Rachael, the Coketown workers in *Hard Times*, are so boring and represent such a failure on Dickens's part, as characterisations of the working class. Spector quotes George Eliot and George Bernard Shaw, but these comments still beg the question: why did Dickens feel confident that he could bring to life a class about which he knew nothing? In answer, Spector writes: 'In this essay I will argue that Dickens's confidence, and ultimately his failure, rests upon his implicit faith in the power of language, and more specifically upon epistemological assumptions embedded in the rhetoric of realism' (*SS*, 230).

A realistic text is one that 'intends to tell the truth', and whether praising the accuracy of *Hard Times* or criticising its portrayal of a northern industrial society, readers typically assess it as convincing or otherwise. In other words, it is treated as a 'realistic' text. Rhetorical analysis has identified *metonymy* as the basic trope in realism: 'Broadly speaking, *metonymy* is a figure in which one entity is identified by another with which it is contiguous; to cite the standard example, a king is called the crown because he wears one … To identify an invisible quality – character – by a visible exterior is realism's fundamental *metonymy*' (*SS*, 231). Dickens and other realistic writers have made the assumption that *metonymy* can also work the other way: you can discover the character by observing the exterior. So, Dickens embarked on *Hard Times* in the confidence that he could observe and therefore realistically characterise industrial workers.

Near to the beginning of *Hard Times* comes the 'Keynote' description of Coketown, which is a powerful and successful passage because Dickens transforms the scene through the use of figurative language, introducing the metaphors of serpents, mad melancholy elephants, and the red and black 'painted face of a savage' within the context that the town is a transformation of nature, with its clay turned to brick, its purple river and its black canal. In this passage the people are no more than parts in the working, machine-like town. Like

---

[29] Spector, Stephen J, 'Monsters of Metonymy: *Hard Times* and Knowing the Working Class', in *Modern Critical Views: Charles Dickens*, Ed. Bloom, Harold, Chelsea House Publishers, NY and Philadelphia, 1987, pp. 229–244.

the streets, they are 'equally like one another' and their behaviour is 'same ... same ... same ... same'. Spector comments:

> This reading, which imagines industrialisation as a cataclysm for the workers, promises to be a disaster for the novelist subscribing to Victorian ideas about character; without differentiation and individuation the Dickensian novel cannot exist. Thus *Hard Times* must ultimately repudiate its keynote.
>
> (*SS*, 233)

Stephen, Rachael, Slackbridge and the Hands are not, of course, 'equally like one another', so the keynote fails and this infects other aspects of the novel. Louisa realises that she is totally ignorant of the workers, about half way through the novel. In the second half, the workers disappear, except for the brief scene of Stephen's death.

Spector then brings in the article 'On Strike', which Dickens wrote for *Household Words* just after he began writing *Hard Times*, and which gives an account of his visit to Preston in January 1854, to observe the long-running strike there. When he answers his fellow passenger, who he calls 'Mr. Snapper', for his rigid opinions about the strike, Dickens the reporter uses heavily qualifying language so that his answer conveys deep uncertainty. Dickens's statement, 'in all its calculated *class*iness, inaugurates a distance between Dickens and the workers that will not be easily overcome' (*SS*, 234). Sure enough, when he spends time in Preston, the emphasis is on Dickens's expectations of the working people. After such a long-running dispute, he expects to find an angry and dangerous mob, and he is surprised at the restrained and courteous behaviour he witnesses. He repeatedly expresses relief that he is treated so politely by the strikers and other workers.

In 'On Strike', Dickens is astonished by a contrast between 'the deliberate collected manner of these men proceeding about their business, and the clash and hurry of the engines among which their lives are passed'. Spector points out why he is so surprised:

> What he knows comes from a 'reading' of the new industrial scene that is based on the familiar assumption of realism, that men must be like their environment: the workers should be like the most striking and

visible aspect of their lives, the machines. Thus the expectation that the
workers will be a violent, unthinking mob is based explicitly on their
contiguity with the violent, unthinking machines.

(*SS*, 236)

Throughout his career, beginning when he wrote *Sketches by Boz* and
created characters out of external bits and pieces, minutely observed,
Dickens had relied on *metonymy* for characterisation. Now, suddenly,
'The premise that 'to look' or 'to see' is 'to know' does not stand up,
and as a consequence the figure loses its reliability' (*SS*, 237).

Of course there are numerous *metonymies* of character: we need
only think of Gradgrind's squareness (forefinger, wall-like forehead
and square house), the appearance of Slackbridge that reveals his
malignance, or the filth of Mrs. Blackpool. However, when Dickens
came to reprise his keynote, at the start of Chapter 11, it is noticeable that the description of Stephen and his fellows at their looms
contrasts them 'quiet, watchful, and steady' against the 'crashing,
smashing, tearing' machines. Dickens even apostrophises the reader
with a piece of meditation: put any work of God (the working men)
next to any work of man (the machines), and the work of God will
come out with dignity from the comparison. As for the workers,
Dickens admits that 'there is an unfathomable mystery in the mean-
est of them, for ever'. Spector seemingly credits Dickens with having
sensed the failure of *metonymy* to guide him towards a realistic characterisation of the working class. Nonetheless, 'Dickens's intention in
Hard Times is to move beyond a surface reading of the workers and
to reveal them in their particular, complex reality' (*SS*, 238). That he
fails in this endeavour should not lead us to undervalue his awareness
of the 'gap' between himself and his subject.

'Mystery' and 'muddle', figures of illegibility, are repeatedly
invoked in *Hard Times*, as is the maze or labyrinth, at the same time
as the Coketown 'Hands' are described as unknowable, an instance
of correspondence between the workers and their environment.
In this there is a form of *metonymy*, but Spector points out that it is 'a
metonymy that signals its own limitations' (*SS*, 239).

Next, Spector initiates a comparison between *Hard Times* and
Engels's *The Condition of the Working Class*. Returning to Dickens's
workers 'all equally like one another', a metonymic figure which equates

machine-like work with an automaton worker, he sees Engels going even further. In Engels's description, workers all belong to one of two kinds. Either their repetitive, automatic labour reduces them to a sub-human level where they live like animals, or, their obstinate rebellion against such labour turns them aggressive and angry. When Engels observed the miners' strike of 1844, he was – like Dickens ten years later – astonished at the rational self-control of the striking miners. So far from their behaviour reflecting the subhuman filth and vio-lence of their place of work, on the contrary, their behaviour was that of 'moderation, rationality, self-control' – all middle-class virtues Engels hardly thought to witness during such a bitter dispute. Engels's reactions, like those of Dickens, show a crude reliance on *metonymy* as a means of decoding observation, of 'seeing' to know. However, Dickens differs in that, implicitly, he recognises his mistake:

> The lifelessness of Dickens's industrial workers in *Hard Times* …
> paradoxically may be taken as a sign of his humaneness. Instead of
> allowing them to develop into savages or grotesque robots, he lets them
> fade into the colourless anonymity of moral personifications while
> quietly relinquishing the project of presenting the truth about them.
> He permits his initial expectation that the new industrial world would
> be peopled by a mob of interchangeable, mass-produced characters to be
> shown a delusion, revealing in the process that he had been mistaken in
> assuming a necessary connection between Coketown and its inhabitants.
> Because it dramatises its own futility, *Hard Times* displays an unusual
> intellectual and moral honesty.
>
> (*SS*, 244)

This shows how Spector, who is clearly of the opinion that the indus-trial theme of *Hard Times*, and the characters of both Stephen and Rachael, all fail, manages to find an unexpected positive quality – honesty in failure – with which to credit Dickens.

Further varieties

Dickens has been regularly attacked by his detractors, accused of being melodramatic and sentimental. Our first two critics, Juliet John and Valerie Purton, defend Dickens by agreeing with his attackers, but at the same time arguing that melodrama and sentimentality belong to respectable aesthetic traditions. Yes, Dickens is melodramatic; or, yes, he is sentimental, but these are strengths, not grounds for lowering our estimate of his contribution to the canon of English Literature. John goes further, and introduces us to a Dickens who campaigned against intellectualism on the grounds of cultural inclusion: he was a champion of popular culture. Purton goes further still in her final chapter, suggesting that a bright new era of mass sentimentality may be about to dawn.

Our third critic, Pam Morris, takes an entirely different approach. She takes the 'Providential discourse' of the mid-nineteenth century – the conviction that God and Providence favoured the English – as her starting point. With convincing reference to *Bleak House*, Morris analyses the means society employs to maintain the status quo and to oppress the disconnected poor, as these are demonstrated through characters such as Mr. Snagsby and Jo the crossing sweeper. This analysis reveals a thorough social theme in *Bleak House*, but raises the very interesting question: does the novel demonstrate the means of social control because it innocently describes the society of its time? Or, does Dickens consciously critique society's oppressive techniques?

Finally, we met Stephen J. Spector, whose starting point is completely different again. As he develops his argument, his interest in the social structure – this time related to *Hard Times* and the industrial north – might suggest he is on a similar tack to Pam Morris. He begins, however, with the rhetorical figure: *metonymy*; and it is from this feature of Dickens's language, generalised into a metonymic habit of mind, that Spector's argument stems. Spector brings other contemporary documents into his analysis, citing Engels's description of the working class, and Dickens's own report of his visit to Preston, 'On Strike'. Spector believes Dickens was conscious of his failure to describe the workers, and sees the author acknowledging his own limitation. So, our four critics approach Dickens from different starting points, and, except for Pam Morris, who leaves open the question of Dickens's intentions, all seem obliged to deal with adverse criticisms of the novelist.

You will quickly find more varieties of approach: each new critic you read will introduce another angle. **Barbara Hardy**, in her *Dickens* *and Creativity,*[30] builds a part of her argument by considering various narrators in Dickens's novels, one of whom is Esther Summerson. She describes the contrasting narrators of *Bleak House,* suggesting that the Godlike overview of the one, and the first-person subjectivity of the other, represent two extremes of narrative voice. Then, the omniscient narrator's 'social indignation is Dickens's but the narrator's lack of gender, history and personal identity anticipate T. S. Eliot's ideal of impersonality just as the bifocal narrative anticipates Joyce' (Hardy, op. cit., p. 54). Later in her study Hardy focuses on what she calls 'crises of imagination' and analyses two deathbed scenes, that of Jo from *Bleak House,* and that of Mrs. Gradgrind from *Hard Times.* She finds that in both of these scenes 'Dickens is open to the charge of softening deathbed distress and idealising the capacity for deathbed vision, but the scene of Mrs. Gradgrind's dying and seeing, like Jo's, is unsentimental because its psychology is so profound, coherent and particular' (Hardy, op. cit., pp.105–106). We have read elsewhere (George Eliot) that Dickens's characters have no psychology, and (Valerie Purton) that Jo's death is the paradigm of sentimentality. Hardy is on a different tack, and she follows these investigations by looking at what she calls 'Creative conversations', among which she analyses Louisa's two crucial dialogues with her father, and Sissy Jupe's victory over the verbal ironist James Harthouse.[31]

Another completely different approach is taken by **Hilary M. Schor** in her *Dickens and the Daughter of the House.*[32] The title of this book should immediately remind us that Esther's life is largely shaped by her being the daughter of Lady Dedlock, while Louisa Gradgrind is ruinously damaged by being the daughter of her father's 'house'. However, Schor takes as her starting point the memoir written by Mrs. Kate Perugini – Dickens's eldest daughter – after her father's death. In this memoir Mrs. Perugini regrets that she did not show loyalty to her mother, but on the contrary she abandoned her, following her father's wishes. Schor reads Perugini's text sceptically, seeing it as a 'story' from the daughter of a novelist. She then goes

---

[30] London & NY: Continuum Literary Studies, 2008.
[31] Hardy, op. cit., Chapter 10: 'Creative Conversation in *Hard Times, Great Expectations* and *Our Mutual Friend*', pp. 127–132.
[32] Cambridge: Cambridge University Press, 1999.

on to consider various kinds of 'property' and 'inheritance' both in comparison to what these daughters (Esther and Louisa) inherit, whether it be emotional, psychological, or in the form of a story or a text (Lady Dedlock's document that Esther must burn, for example; Louisa's lack of stories); and in comparison to the laws and conventions regarding female inheritance, and the position of daughters, at the time when these novels were written:

> Within the story Esther is telling, the story figured psychically as the story of the dead mother and the dead child, there is a different story of inheritance: one we can follow only through the fragments, torn documents, the story of resemblance written on the wandering 'face' of the female plot. Where it leads is not only a different version of *Bleak House*, but a different version of property altogether: the daughter's quest for her maternal legacy.
>
> (Schor, op. cit., p. 112)

It is clear from such an extract that Schor is ready to interpret both intellectually and metaphorically, drawing together threads of her ideas and weaving them into a complex reading of the text. So in the above sample, she cites the 'story' of dead mother and daughter, which refers to the fact that both Esther and Lady Dedlock were told that the other died in childbirth. In her chapter called 'The Social Inheritance of Adultery', Schor discusses Edith Dombey and Louisa Gradgrind, and ends by imagining Louisa who 'sits silent and alone by the cold hearth fire ... unable herself to wander, to adulterate, to rejoin the plots of marriage and childbirth' (Schor, op. cit., p. 83). Schor presents some startling insights in her commentaries: but we must be careful. Louisa sits by the fire, yes (*HT*, 273); but the fire is lit. Where Schor's 'cold' hearth comes from, I do not know.

Alexander Welsh[33] takes our two novels together because 'the two are the first of six completed novels of Dickens's later career, the period most celebrated by academic critics' (Welsh, op. cit., xiii). In coining the title *Dickens Redressed*, Welsh's idea is that Esther is a sort of 'cross-dressed' David Copperfield; and that Dickens 'redressed his protagonist's childhood, compensated for it, restored the abandoned

---

[33] *Dickens Redressed: The Art of* Bleak House *and* Hard Times, New Haven & London: Yale University Press, 2000.

self to love and success in life' (ibid., xiv). Dickens's novels are typically of 'egocentric design' because every detail is mediated through the 'desires and fears and satisfactions' of the protagonist. Esther's narrative increasingly subdues, but does not silence, the other narrator, whose main function is to satirise: and, 'The very premise of his satire is the interconnection of the human inhabitants of London, great and small' (ibid., xv).

Welsh sees *Hard Times* as 'redressing' *Bleak House*. Here there is no central ego. The most sympathetic character is again a woman, Louisa, but is seen from the outside. The language sometimes 'grates', as if Dickens were 'too impatient' (Welsh, xvi), and the careful counterpoint of the *Bleak House* narrators is no more. Perhaps Dickens took on 'a more intractable social question than any he had approached thus far' (ibid., xvi), in the conflicts of the new industrial order. Meanwhile, Welsh thinks it possible that Bounderby is a satirical self-portrait, and is inclined 'to think of the novel itself as a kind of circus' and to see *Hard Times* as constantly tipping towards 'clowning'. For example, names such as M'Choakumchild are comedy, and the schoolroom scene is more ridiculous than horrific. In these ways, Welsh distinguishes these two novels as Dickens 'redressing' his novelist's art. *David Copperfield* was finished in 1850, and Dickens lost his father at the beginning of 1851. In the context of these events both professional and personal, *Bleak House* and *Hard Times* mark the start of the later period, and a 'redressing'.

Having summarised four recent critics, we have now mentioned three more. The one truth that is apparent from all of them is that there is an unlimited supply of different approaches to the study of Dickens's novels. You can set out from any angle of approach. You can follow any number of different interests, whether you are most fascinated by genre, structure or technique: by language and style, by social commentary, by character and psychology, or by the cultural and social context. Each and any of a multitude of angles can yield exciting insights, and may open the reader's eyes to new views of the text. It is hoped that this chapter, although quite unable to present anything in the nature of a survey, will have stimulated independent thought, suggested a variety of approaches, and encouraged you to pursue your own angles and your own interests with confidence.

Further Reading

Your first job is to study the text. There is no substitute for the work of detailed analysis. Once you are familiar with the text itself, you may wish to read around and about it. This brief chapter is only intended to set you off: there are hundreds of relevant essays, articles and books and we can only mention a few. Most good editions and critical works have suggestions for further reading or bibliographies of their own. Once you have begun to read beyond your text, you can use these and a good library to follow up your particular interests. This chapter is divided into *Works by Charles Dickens*; *Reading around the text*, which lists some works by other writers, which are contextually relevant either by date, content or genre; *Biography*, which lists some of the many accounts of Dickens's life; and *Criticism*, which gives a selection of suggested titles that will introduce you to the varieties of opinion among professional critics.

Works by Charles Dickens

Dickens wrote fourteen and a half novels, and if you want to read just one more Dickens novel, choose *Great Expectations* (1860–1861), regarded by many as his best work. In this book we have focused on *Bleak House* (1852–1853) and *Hard Times* (1854). None of Dickens's other novels is similar to *Hard Times*. It is much shorter than any other, and is the only book by Dickens set in the industrial north. We have suggested that *Bleak House* belongs with *Dombey*

and Son (1846–1848) and *Our Mutual Friend* (1864–1865) as all
three novels present a panoramic view of society. *David Copperfield*
(1849–1850), *Great Expectations* (1860–1861), *Nicholas Nickleby*
(1838–1839) and *Martin Chuzzlewit* (1843–1844), all tell the story
of a boy's life from childhood to adulthood. Aside from *Bleak House*,
in which Esther tells half of the story, Dickens wrote two further
novels where the protagonist is a young girl: *The Old Curiosity Shop*
(1840–1841) and *Little Dorrit* (1855–1857). The other novels are *The
Pickwick Papers* (1836–1837), *Oliver Twist* (1837–1839), *Barnaby
Rudge* (1841) and *A Tale of Two Cities* (1859). These last two are
historical, the former set during the Gordon Riots of 1780, the latter
in London and Paris during the French Revolution and subsequent
Reign of Terror (1789–1793). Finally, a Dickens enthusiast may look
at the earliest published work, which made the author's reputation,
and read *Sketches by Boz* (1836), as well as the unfinished mystery he
was writing when he died, *The Mystery of Edwin Drood* (1870).

Dickens also wrote numerous short stories, and was a prolific journalist. A good example from his short stories is 'The Signalman', a
ghost story from the 1866 Christmas edition of *All the Year Round*.
In the 1840s, Dickens also wrote special Christmas novellas, the best
known of which is *A Christmas Carol* (1843) with its miserly Scrooge
and the sick child, Tiny Tim. This was followed by *The Chimes* (1844),
The Cricket on the Hearth (1845) and two more. The three named
here were often on Dickens's programme at his public readings, as
they fit well into an abridged form. The whole of *Household Words*
and *All the Year Round* are available online at www.djo.org.uk. We
already said that anyone studying *Hard Times* should read the article
'On Strike' from *Household Words*, 11 February 1854. You may also
want to browse through Dickens's other articles. There are political
satires about the family of Mr. Bull (John Bull and family = the
British Government), or attacks on the law, institutions, hypocrisies
and humbug, and you will quickly gain a feeling for Dickens's life as
a working journalist.

For his own children, Dickens wrote *A Child's History of England*
(1851–1853) and *The Life of Our Lord* (published in 1934). *The
Selected Letters of Charles Dickens*, edited by Jenny Hartley (Oxford
University Press, Oxford, 2012) is more approachable than the huge
Pilgrim Edition *The Letters of Charles Dickens,* edited by Madeline

House, Graham Storey, and Kathleen Tillotson (12 volumes, Clarendon Press, Oxford, 1965–2002).

You can read almost all of Dickens's writings online, free, from such websites as Project Gutenberg (www.gutenberg.org) or the Dickens's journals website mentioned above. In this way you can dip into a variety of texts, and quickly become familiar with a range of his works.

Reading around the text

This section suggests some novels to consider when 'reading around' Dickens. Among Dickens's predecessors you may try Henry Fielding's *Tom Jones* (1749), one of Dickens's favourite novels: he named his eighth child Henry Fielding. To gain an idea of the Gothic melodramatic tradition that was so influential at the beginning of the nineteenth century, look at Mary Shelley's *Frankenstein* (1818). In Dickens's final years, the first novels written by George Eliot appeared. Try *The Mill on the Floss* (1860): the characterisation of Maggie Tulliver may seem surprisingly modern, in contrast to that of Esther Summerson in *Bleak House*.

Having mentioned predecessors and a successor, the next suggestion is to sample Dickens's contemporaries. One novel uncomfortably close to *Hard Times* in date and theme is Mrs. Elizabeth Gaskell's *North and South* (1854–1855). A wide-ranging work portraying a 'panorama' such as we find in *Bleak House*, is William Makepeace Thackeray's *Vanity Fair* (1847–1848). Thackeray's image for the social world as a 'vanity fair' is reminiscent of the 'In Fashion' strand in *Bleak House*, although many readers think that Thackeray's analysis is more cynical, and therefore more rigorous, than Dickens's. Next, Emily Brontë's *Wuthering Heights* and Charlotte Brontë's *Jane Eyre* (both 1847) have elements of the Gothic, and passionate fables. Finally, Wilkie Collins (1824–1889) was a close friend of Dickens. They collaborated on the melodrama *The Frozen Deep,* in which Dickens acted the tragic role of Wardour, and on several of the Christmas numbers of *Household Words*. Collins wrote successful novels of crime and mystery, and developed a technique in which different narrators tell those parts of the story in which they were most involved, rather as Esther tells her parts of *Bleak House*. Try Collins's *The Woman in*

White (1859–1860). There are others we could mention, of course. Both Thackeray and Wilkie Collins wrote numerous other works, and Anthony Trollope (1815–1882) published his first Barsetshire novel, *The Warden* (1855) the year after the publication of *Hard Times*.

Biography

There are many biographies of Dickens. The first was the life written by his close friend and official biographer, John Forster. It was to Forster that Dickens entrusted the *Autobiographical Sketch*, which revealed his childhood hardships – working in a factory while his family was in the Marshalsea Debtors' Prison. Forster was true to his friend, and published the *Life of Charles Dickens* in three volumes between 1872 and 1874. There is an abridged, illustrated edition available, edited by Dr. Holly Furneaux and published by Sterling Signature, NY, 2011; the full original text can be read on project Gutenberg (www.gutenberg.org).

We will mention just three for you to choose from, of the many other biographies of Dickens that are available. *Charles Dickens: A Life*, by Claire Tomalin (London, NY et al.: Penguin Books, 2011) is readable, and has some useful lists of families and other people, and maps of Dickens's homes in London and Kent, at the beginning. Michael Slater's *Charles Dickens* (New Haven and London: Yale University Press, 2011) is also well written, detailed and reliable. Neither of these shirks the awkward questions about Dickens's behaviour to his wife Catherine. Peter Ackroyd's massive *Dickens* (first US edition, NY: Harpercollins, 1991), can still be obtained, but the abridged edition (London: Vintage, 2002), gives us another clear narrative of Dickens's life. Any of these biographies will provide the background information you need.

Criticism

We mentioned some critical works from between Dickens's death and recent years, in our 'Sample of Criticism' chapter, and these make a reliable foundation for your reading of recent critical views.

George Bernard Shaw's *Shaw on Dickens* (edited by Dan H. Laurence and Martin Quinn, Frederick Ungar, NY, 1985); G. K. Chesterton's *Appreciations and Criticisms of the Works of Charles Dickens* (London & NY: Dent & Dutton, 1911); and George Orwell's essay '**Charles Dickens**' in *Inside the Whale and Other Essays* (London: Gollancz, 1940), were all influential studies in their time. We also mentioned some negative reactions to Dickens, found in works by George Eliot, Virginia Woolf and Aldous Huxley, as well as in F. R. Leavis's *The Great Tradition* (London & NY: Faber and Faber, 1948). If you are interested in the Leavisites' controversies, F. R. Leavis and Q. D. Leavis revised their view of Dickens, devoting a whole critical work to him: *Dickens the Novelist* (London & NY: Penguin Books, 1970). In view of our discussion of the theatrical effects Dickens achieves, you may also be interested in Robert Garis's *The Dickens Theatre: A Reassessment of the Novels* (Oxford: Oxford University Press, 1965).

The four more recent critical works we summarised in Chapter 10 are, first, Juliet John's *Dickens's Villains: Melodrama, Character, Popular Culture* (Oxford & NY: Oxford University Press, 2001); second, Valerie Purton's *Dickens and the Sentimental Tradition: Fielding, Richardson, Sterne, Goldsmith, Sheridan, Lamb* (London & NY: Anthem Press, 2012); third, Pam Morris's *Dickens's Class Consciousness: A Marginal View* (Basingstoke: Macmillan, 1991); and finally, Stephen J. Spector's '**Monsters of Metonymy: *Hard Times* and Knowing the Working Class**', in *Modern Critical Views: Charles Dickens*, edited by Harold Bloom (Chelsea House Publishers, NY and Philadelphia, 1987), pp. 229–244.

Modern critics take a wide variety of approaches to Dickens. We mentioned Barbara Hardy's *Dickens and Creativity* (London & NY: Continuum Literary Studies, 2008); Hilary M. Schor's *Dickens and the Daughter of the House* (Cambridge: Cambridge University Press, 1999), and Alexander Welsh's *Dickens Redressed: The Art of* Bleak House *and* Hard Times (New Haven & London: Yale University Press, 2000). To these could be added Catherine Waters's *Dickens and the Politics of the Family* (Cambridge: Cambridge University Press, 1997), Philip Collins's *Dickens and Crime* (Basingstoke & NY: Macmillan, 1995), John R. Reed's *Dickens's Hyperrealism* (Ohio: Ohio State University Press, 2010) and Michaela Mahlberg's *Corpus Stylistics and Dickens's Fiction* (Oxford & NY: Routledge, 2012). With the exception of Alexander Welsh's *Dickens Redressed* and Stephen J. Spector's article, which concentrate on *Bleak House* and *Hard Times*, all of those mentioned so far are full-length works which discuss several or all of Dickens's novels. Use the index or the contents page to find their analysis of the novel(s) you are studying, then read that part of the work, followed by the concluding chapter. Anthologies of critical essays and articles are a good way to sample the critics. You can then go on to read the full-length books written by those critics whose ideas and approaches you find stimulating. Stephen J. Spector's article that we summarised, appears in *Modern Critical Views: Charles Dickens*, edited by Harold Bloom (Chelsea House Publishers, NY & Philadelphia, 1987). Also compiled and edited by Harold Bloom is *Charles Dickens's Bleak House* in *Bloom's Modern Critical Interpretations* (Chelsea House, NY and Philadelphia, 1987). There are also *The Cambridge Companion to Charles Dickens*, edited by John O. Jordan (Cambridge University Press, Cambridge, 2001) and *Charles Dickens: Bleak House (New Casebook)*, edited by Jeremy Tambling (Palgrave Macmillan, Basingstoke and NY, 1998); and *David Copperfield and Hard Times: Charles Dickens (New Casebook)*, edited by John Peck (Palgrave Macmillan, Basingstoke and NY, 1995).

This chapter is intended to act as a bridge towards further study. Numerous articles, essays and books on Dickens are published each year. Most of the books mentioned here also contain bibliographies, or a list of works referred to, so each one can help you to follow up your interests in the critical literature. Finally, remember that your own responses and ideas are as valid as those of any critic; test them first of all against the text you are studying, then look at the critics as a way of further refining your own response to Dickens.

Index